# Lecture Notes
# in Business Information Processing 376

More information about this series at http://www.springer.com/series/7911

Adam Przybyłek ·
Miguel Ehécatl Morales-Trujillo (Eds.)

# Advances in Agile and User-Centred Software Engineering

Third International Conference
on Lean and Agile Software Development, LASD 2019
and 7th Conference
on Multimedia, Interaction, Design and Innovation, MIDI 2019
Leipzig, Germany, September 1–4, 2019
Revised Selected Papers

 Springer

*Editors*
Adam Przybyłek 🆔
Gdańsk University of Technology
Gdansk, Poland

Miguel Ehécatl Morales-Trujillo 🆔
University of Canterbury
Christchurch, New Zealand

ISSN 1865-1348 ISSN 1865-1356 (electronic)
Lecture Notes in Business Information Processing
ISBN 978-3-030-37533-1 ISBN 978-3-030-37534-8 (eBook)
https://doi.org/10.1007/978-3-030-37534-8

This Springer imprint is published by the registered company Springer Nature Switzerland AG
The registered company address is: Gewerbestrasse 11, 6330 Cham, Switzerland

# Preface

While agile as well as user-centred software development has already become mainstream in industry and a strong community has crystallized around the new way of thinking, making the transition to the new mindset is still challenging for many companies. Hence, there is a need for providing a platform for spreading best practices and stories of successful transitions. The LASD (Lean and Agile Software Development) and MIDI (Multimedia, Interaction, Design and Innovation) conference series have become prominent forums where practitioners, researchers, and academics meet to share and discuss their concerns, experiences, research findings, and trends.

This year, both LASD and MIDI took place under the umbrella of the 14th Federated Conference on Computer Science and Information Systems (FedCSIS 2019) in Leipzig, Germany, during September 1–4, 2019. In total, we received 36 submissions, out of which 9 were accepted as full papers and 3 as short papers. The accepted papers were presented to a well-focused audience, thus the discussion provided the authors with new ideas and directions for further research.

After the events, authors of 8 selected papers were invited to submit revised and extended versions of their work to this post-conference monograph. Topics discussed in this volume range from recent evolutions in the field (such as scaling agile, balancing agile and plan-driven methods, agile methods for safety-critical systems), through agile adoption and trends, to human issues (such as elements of the agile mindset, empowering agile teams with collaborative games, and gamification).

We would like to express our gratitude to everyone who made LASD 2019 and MIDI 2019 successful. First of all, we thank all the authors for their contributions, the many attendees for creating fruitful discussion, as well as the members of the Program Committees for taking the time and effort to provide insightful remarks. We acknowledge the chairs of MIDI 2019, i.e. Krzysztof Marasek, Andrzej Romanowski, and Marcin Sikorski, for their collaboration. We are also deeply grateful to the chairs of the FedCSIS conference series, namely Maria Ganzha, Leszek Maciaszek, and Marcin Paprzycki, for their help with the organization of our events. Moreover, we are indebted to Karolina Walaszek for LaTeX typesetting assistance. Finally, we would like to thank the team at Springer (especially Alfred Hofmann, Ralf Gerstner, and Christine Reiss) for making this volume possible.

We hope that you find this monograph useful for your professional and academic activities, and we wish you a stimulating read. We also cordially invite you to visit our conference websites at https://www.fedcsis.org/2020/lasd and https://midi.pja.edu.pl, and to join us for the upcoming editions.

November 2019
Adam Przybyłek<br>Miguel Ehécatl Morales-Trujillo

| | |
|---|---|
| Fernando Marques Figueira Filho | Universidade Federal do Rio Grande do Norte, Brazil |
| Gabriel Alberto García-Mireles | Universidad de Sonora, Mexico |
| Javad Ghofrani | HTW Dresden University of Applied Sciences, Germany |
| Krzysztof Goczyła | Gdańsk University of Technology, Poland |
| Sangharatna Godboley | NIT Rourkela, India |
| Javier Gonzalez Huerta | Blekinge Institute of Technology, Sweden |
| Janusz Górski | Gdańsk University of Technology, Poland |
| Peggy Gregory | University of Central Lancashire, UK |
| Ridewaan Hanslo | Council for Scientific and Industrial Research, South Africa |
| Sebastian Heil | Chemnitz University of Technology, Germany |
| Uwe Hohenstein | Siemens AG, Germany |
| Philipp Hohl | ZF Friedrichshafen AG, Germany |
| Marko Ikonen | Projektivarikko Oy, Finland |
| Andrea Janes | Free University of Bolzano, Italy |
| Janne Järvinen | F-Secure Corporation, Finland |
| Aleksander Jarzębowicz | Gdańsk University of Technology, Poland |
| Miloš Jovanović | University of Novi Sad, Serbia |
| George Kakarontzas | Aristotle University of Thessaloniki, Greece |
| Kalinka Kaloyanova | Sofia University, Bulgaria |
| Benjamin Kanagwa | Makerere University, Uganda |
| Georgia Kapitsaki | University of Cyprus, Cyprus |
| Matěj Karolyi | Masaryk University, Czech Republic |
| Aleksandra Karpus | Gdańsk University of Technology, Poland |
| Mohamad Kassab | Innopolis University, Russia |
| Marija Katić | School of Computing, UK |
| Wiem Khlif | University of Sfax, Tunisia |
| Jens Knodel | Fraunhofer IESE, Germany |
| Martin Kropp | University of Applied Sciences and Arts Northwestern Switzerland, Switzerland |
| Pasi Kuvaja | University of Oulu, Finland |
| Maarit Laanti | Nitor, Finland |
| Timo O. A. Lehtinen | Aalto University, Finland |
| Valentina Lenarduzzi | Tampere University, Finland |
| Grischa Liebel | University of Gothenburg, Sweden |
| Ivan Luković | University of Novi Sad, Serbia |
| Ilaria Lunesu | Università degli Studi di Cagliari, Italy |
| Viljan Mahnič | University of Ljubljana, Slovenia |
| George Mangalaraj | Western Illinois University, USA |
| Bartosz Marcinkowski | University of Gdańsk, Poland |
| Manuel Mazzara | Innopolis University, Russia |

# Organization

## LASD 2019

**Event Chair**

Adam Przybyłek                Gdańsk University of Technology, Poland

**Program Committee**

Muhammad Ovais Ahmad          University of Oulu, Finland
Ibrahim Akman                 Atilim University, Turkey
Sikandar Ali                  China University of Petroleum, China
Fernando Almeida              University of Porto and INESC TEC, Portugal
Mohammad Alshayeb             King Fahd University of Petroleum and Minerals,
                                Saudi Arabia
Samuil Angelov                Fontys University of Applied Sciences,
                                The Netherlands
Irena Bach-Dąbrowska          WSB Gdańsk, Poland
Alessandra Bagnato            SOFTEAM R&D Department, France
Alvine Boaye Belle            École de Technologie Supérieure, Canada
Nourchene Benayed             Higher Colleges of Technology, UAE
Mario Bernhart                Vienna University of Technology, Austria
Vikram Bhadauria              Texas A&M International University, USA
Nik Nailah Binti Abdullah     Monash University Malaysia, Malaysia
Miklós Biró                   Software Competence Center Hagenberg and Johannes
                                Kepler University Linz, Austria
Jan Olaf Blech                RMIT University, Australia
Markus Borg                   SICS Swedish ICT AB, Sweden
Adam Brzeski                  Gdańsk University of Technology, Poland
Alena Buchalcevova            University of Economics, Czech Republic
Jim Buchan                    Auckland University of Technology, New Zealand
Luigi Buglione                Engineering Ingegneria Informatica SpA, Italy
Alexandros Chatzigeorgiou     University of Macedonia, Greece
Daniela Cruzes                SINTEF ICT, Norway
Wiktor Bohdan Daszczuk        Warsaw University of Technology, Poland
Igor Dejanović                University of Novi Sad, Serbia
Anna Derezinska               Warsaw University of Technology, Poland
Philipp Diebold               Fraunhofer IESE, Germany
Arpita Dutta                  NIT Rourkela, India
Maria Jose Escalona           Universidad de Sevilla, Spain
Imane Essebaa                 Hassan II University of Casablanca, Morocco
Fabian Fagerholm              University of Helsinki, Finland

| | |
|---|---|
| Antoni-Lluís Mesquida Calafat | University of the Balearic Islands, Spain |
| Jakub Miler | Gdańsk University of Technology, Poland |
| Gloria Miller | Skema Business School, Germany |
| Sanjay Misra | Covenant University, Nigeria |
| Durga Prasad Mohapatra | NIT Rourkela, India |
| Miguel Ehécatl Morales-Trujillo | University of Canterbury, New Zealand |
| Richard Mordinyi | Vienna University of Technology, Austria |
| Jürgen Münch | Reutlingen University, Germany |
| Mirna Muñoz | Centro de Investigación en Matemáticas, Mexico |
| Karolina Muszyńska | University of Szczecin, Poland |
| Anh Nguyen-Duc | University College of Southeast Norway, Norway |
| Arne Noyer | University of Osnabrueck and Willert Software Tools GmbH, Germany |
| Hanna Oktaba | National Autonomous University of Mexico, Mexico |
| Marco Ortu | University of Cagliari, Italy |
| Tosin Daniel Oyetoyan | SINTEF Digital, Norway |
| Necmettin Özkan | Kuveyt Turk Participation Bank, Turkey |
| Subhrakanta Panda | Birla Institute of Technology and Science, India |
| Rui Humberto R. Pereira | Instituto Politecnico do Porto - ISCAP, Portugal |
| Aneta Poniszewska-Maranda | Łódź University of Technology, Poland |
| Alexander Poth | Volkswagen AG, Germany |
| Michał Przybyłek | University of Warsaw, Poland |
| Raman Ramsin | Sharif University of Technology, Iran |
| Sonja Ristić | University of Novi Sad, Serbia |
| Bruno Rossi | Masaryk University, Czech Republic |
| Zdenek Rybola | FIT CTU in Prague, Czech Republic |
| Dina Salah | Sadat Academy, Egypt |
| Mattia Salnitri | University of Trento, Italy |
| Eva-Maria Schön | University of Seville, Spain |
| Jorge Sedeno | University of Seville, Spain |
| Mali Senapathi | Auckland University of Technology, New Zealand |
| Marcin Sikorski | Polish-Japanese Academy of Information Technology, Poland |
| Michał Śmiałek | Politechnika Warszawska, Poland |
| Michel Soares | Federal University of Sergipe, Brazil |
| Álvaro Soria | ISISTAN Research Institute, Argentina |
| Maria Spichkova | RMIT University, Australia |
| Olga Springer | Gdańsk University of Technology, Poland |
| Tor Stålhane | Norwegian University of Science and Technology, Norway |
| Christoph Johann Stettina | Leiden University, The Netherlands |
| Davide Taibi | Free University of Bolzano, Italy |

| Ayca Tarhan | Hacettepe University Computer Engineering Department, Turkey |
| Jörg Thomaschewski | University of Applied Sciences Emden/Leer, Germany |
| Carlos Torrecilla Salinas | University of Seville, Spain |
| Michael Unterkalmsteiner | Blekinge Institute of Technology, Sweden |
| Andrzej Wardziński | Gdańsk University of Technology, Poland |
| Jan Werewka | AGH University of Science and Technology, Poland |
| Dominique Winter | University of Applied Sciences Emden/Leer, Germany |
| Michał Wróbel | Gdańsk University of Technology, Poland |
| Murat Yilmaz | Çankaya University, Turkey |
| Nacer Eddine Zarour | University Constantine 2, Algeria |
| Katarzyna Łukasiewicz | Gdańsk University of Technology, Poland |

## Additional Reviewers

| Paweł Markowski | Polish-Japanese Academy of Information Technology, Poland |

## MIDI 2019

### Event Chairs

| Krzysztof Marasek | Polish-Japanese Academy of Information Technology, Poland |
| Andrzej Romanowski | Łódź University of Technology, Poland |
| Marcin Sikorski | Gdańsk University of Technology, Poland |

### Program Committee

| Cezary Biele | Information Processing Institute, Poland |
| Peter Forbrig | University of Rostock, Germany |
| Sissel Guttormsen | University of Bern, Switzerland |
| Danijel Koržinek | Polish-Japanese Academy of Information Technology, Poland |
| Agata Kołakowska | Gdańsk University of Technology, Poland |
| Agnieszka Landowska | Gdańsk University of Technology, Poland |
| Masood Masoodian | Aalto University, Finland |
| Jakub Miler | Gdańsk University of Technology, Poland |
| Mohammad Obaid | Uppsala University, Sweden |
| Ewa Satalecka | Polish-Japanese Academy of Information Technology, Poland |
| Pavel Slavik | Czech Technical University, Czech Republic |
| Krzysztof Szklanny | Polish-Japanese Academy of Information Technology, Poland |
| Marcin Wichrowski | Polish-Japanese Academy of Information Technology, Poland |

| | |
|---|---|
| Alicja Wieczorkowska | Polish-Japanese Academy of Information Technology, Poland |
| Marco Winkler | Université Nice Sophia Antipolis, France |
| Adam Wojciechowski | Łódź University of Technology, Poland |
| Krzysztof Wołk | Polish-Japanese Academy of Information Technology, Poland |
| Juergen Ziegler | University of Duisburg-Essen, Germany |

# Contents

Scaling Agile – A Large Enterprise View on Delivering and Ensuring
Sustainable Transitions . . . . . . . . . . . . . . . . . . . . . . . . . . . . . . . . . . . . . .   1
   *Alexander Poth, Mario Kottke, and Andreas Riel*

Release Planning in a Hybrid Project Environment . . . . . . . . . . . . . . . . . . .   19
   *Kristina Marner, Sven Theobald, and Stefan Wagner*

Identification of the Agile Mindset and Its Comparison to the Competencies
of Selected Agile Roles . . . . . . . . . . . . . . . . . . . . . . . . . . . . . . . . . . . . . . .   41
   *Jakub Miler and Paulina Gaida*

Adapting Agile Practices to Security Context – Practitioners' Perspective. . . .   63
   *Katarzyna Łukasiewicz and Sara Cygańska*

Quantitative Analysis of the Scrum Framework. . . . . . . . . . . . . . . . . . . . . . .   82
   *Ridewaan Hanslo, Anwar Vahed, and Ernest Mnkandla*

Scientific Collaboration, Citation and Topic Analysis of International
Conference on Agile Software Development Papers. . . . . . . . . . . . . . . . . . .   108
   *Muhammad Ovais Ahmad and Päivi Raulamo-Jurvanen*

Playing the Sprint Retrospective: A Replication Study . . . . . . . . . . . . . . . .   133
   *Yen Ying Ng, Jędrzej Skrodzki, and Maciej Wawryk*

Comparison User Engagement of Gamified and Non-gamified
Augmented Reality Assembly Training . . . . . . . . . . . . . . . . . . . . . . . . . . .   142
   *Diep Nguyen and Gerrit Meixner*

**Author Index** . . . . . . . . . . . . . . . . . . . . . . . . . . . . . . . . . . . . . . . . . . . . .   153

# Scaling Agile – A Large Enterprise View on Delivering and Ensuring Sustainable Transitions

Alexander Poth[1](✉) ⓘ, Mario Kottke[1], and Andreas Riel[2]

[1] Volkswagen AG, Berliner Ring 2, 38436 Wolfsburg, Germany
{alexander.poth,mario.kottke}@volkswagen.de
[2] Grenoble Alps University, G-SCOP Laboratory, 38031 Grenoble, France
andreas.riel@grenoble-inp.fr

**Abstract.** Established large enterprises have to address their existing culture and their huge amounts of people during an agile transition. An approach based on coaching supported by a toolkit has been established at Volkswagen Group IT in order to facilitate and scale agile transitions through systematic coaching of agile practices and the agile mindset. Agility has been rendered sustainable thanks to an inter-organizational facilitation network that leverages team-independent and decentralized sharing and improvement of know-how and experience. Furthermore, a measurement framework allows determining agile maturity of teams during the transition and beyond for an enterprise grade governance. The transition approach captures the organizational context of the team during the transition. The capturing is mapped to current opportunities for the transition to derive suitable actions and to coach adequate approaches and relevant methods. The holistic approach ensures a high quality and sustainability for scaling agile in an enterprise.

**Keywords:** Agile transition · Scaling agile · Agile governance

## 1 Introduction

In agile corporate settings, the objective of each team is to run their products and businesses autonomously. To do this, the teams have to be empowered to deliver their businesses in a reliable and safe way. The objective of an enterprise is to align people – and teams of people – to contribute to the enterprise business vision and goals. To balance this individualization of the teams, large enterprises have to find ways of developing the teams' autonomy yet ensuring their alignment with the enterprise's business goals. The purpose of the presented approach is to support scaling agile in such enterprise environments. Each established enterprise has their own culture, i.e., their ways of handling people and operations. Consequently, transition initiatives affecting teams have to actively the cultural change processes towards an agile mindset while at the same time preserving relevant parts of the established culture. Existing frameworks are not sufficiently practicable because they fail to take into account systematically the current organizational culture and setting both on global and individual team levels.

© Springer Nature Switzerland AG 2020
A. Przybyłek and M. E. Morales-Trujillo (Eds.): LASD 2019/MIDI 2019, LNBIP 376, pp. 1–18, 2020.
https://doi.org/10.1007/978-3-030-37534-8_1

Furthermore, a big challenge is to scale agile to all the different people and teams with a limited amount of coaches for facilitating the transition. The main objective from a corporate management's point of view is to achieve the agile transition of the teams with a minimum of coaching efforts. Therefore, the focus is on highly effective coaching aiming at empowering teams to go ahead on their own after a short time of highly targeted support. The context of the presented work is the coaching of several diverse organizational units of the Volkswagen AG. Agile coaches from Volkswagen Group IT have the mission to facilitate the agile transition of these units, which all departed from very different agile maturity levels.

## 2   Research Question and Methodology

The presented novel approach is based on hypotheses derived from research questions, and has been validated using innovative metrics.

### 2.1   Research Question

The research question focuses on how an effective, efficient and sustainable agile transformation can be achieved by efficient usage of resources (like the facilitating by coaches) in large corporate organizations characterized by a huge number of heterogeneous domains and an established enterprise culture.

Thereby, the effectivity shall be defined as the change of team maturity between the start and the end of the coaching phase from an agile transition perspective. Sustainability is indicated by the change of team maturity after a longer period of absence of coaches. The efficiency can be derived from a trend of the amount of projects a coach can facilitate per year.

### 2.2   Hypotheses

To find a holistic answer to the complex research question, the following hypotheses were made:

H1: Coaching with a structured toolkit supports a minimum effectivity of the agile transition.

H2: Coaching and toolkit are like a flywheel approach, because the coaches learn working with the toolkit, and the lessons learned from the coaches help improve the toolkit. Both lead to a higher effectivity of the agile transformation.

H3: A holistic toolkit that includes a maturity measurement and a self-service offer facilitates the continuous improvement of teams without coaching assistance.

H4: The generalization of the teams' agile transformation success is supported by mapping the teams' mindsets to a generic model.

To be able to validate each of these hypotheses, the following quantitative indicators were used:

HI1: The ramp-up time of new coaches diminishes with the enhancement of the toolkit.

HI2: The alignment between the coaches' demand and know-how about the artefacts provided by the toolkit increases over time.

HI3: The transition process governance structure facilitates knowledge management and feedback of teams and aligns the toolkit with the organizational culture.

HI4: The mapping of the team's maturity to the spiral dynamic model indicates a continuous maturity growth over time.

## 3   Related Work

For an agile transition, different aspects are relevant for a holistic approach. In large enterprises, the change management aspect is important to start moving people to new horizons. In case of an agile transition, the lean and agile frameworks with their methods and tools are relevant inputs, which need a selection about best fit to the enterprise culture etc. Furthermore, on an enterprise level, a governance is needed to ensure systematic development and enhancement of all the teams. Therefore, agile maturity measurement approaches have to be evaluated to identify those methods and artifacts that are most appropriate for each particular team.

### 3.1   Change Management

Change management is a structured way from a status-quo to a desired status of an organization [1]. Often an action research approach is used to systematically enhance an organization [2]. In case of a successful change process, the aspects in scope and focus move over time [3]. Change management has to handle the resistance to change adequately [4]. This leads to the demand that any organization has to develop a change capability [5] with management support as a necessary condition [6]. Existing work is more oriented on non-agile organizations [7, 8]. However, some work address the differences of agile and non-agile organizations [9]. Furthermore, selected methods and tools support systematic change progress [10]. Change management also addresses automation in agile environments to reduce time to market [11].

### 3.2   Lean and Agile Frameworks

To start the transition process, Scrum or Kanban, as well as some artifacts like DoD are often used to realize the basic quality demands [12]. Many lean and agile frameworks exist like Safe [13], Less [14] and others. However, none of the established models handles (process) governance systematically, which is why specific approaches have to be defined and established [15]. Some of the aspects are addressed in [16]. Furthermore, enterprise aspects like quality assurance have to be added [17] to address specific regulations [18].

### 3.3    Agile Maturity Measurement

Maturity models for processes like CMMI or SPICE have been applied for many years. These models are useful in complex process-driven development environments with for example a large external supply chain. Some similar process-driven models have been derived for agile environments [19, 20] and compared in [21, 22]. Agile organizations are more team-focused and therefore necessitate maturity models that go beyond processes [23] and provide more team- and organization-oriented criteria and indicators [24]. These leads to a wide set of measurement aspects [25]. For more team- driven development with an end-to-end responsibility for their outcomes the high process orientation can be an inadequate overhead. Finally, also in agile organizations measures focus on effectivity and efficiency [26]. Value and velocity have key importance [27], and quality is focused on defect measures [28].

## 4    Targeted Transition Process

Delivering deterministic quality of transitions is based on a delivery process. The process has to be designed to scale to support an enterprise scaling of agile. To ensure scaling agile, the process has to be based on approaches, methods and tools fitting to the enterprise culture and the maturity of the (product or service) teams.

The implementation of the transition process can be supported or better facilitated by a coach, but also accomplished in a self-service approach in case of mature teams. The coach has to identify the starting point of the team with respect to their agile mindset and maturity. Based on the initial analysis, the coach co-develops with the team an approach to achieving the desired team maturity, as well as the specific desired outcomes of the transition. The coach supports the team to the point that the team is capable to run the transition themselves. To realize the self-service transition early, the coach provides the team with a toolkit aligned with the enterprise culture. The toolkit has to be applicable to teams with different agile maturity levels. It has to be adequate for the specific company culture and reflect the state of the art of lean and agile habits, approaches, methods and tools.

### 4.1    Requirements to the Toolkit

For an agile toolkit to provide adequate support in the agile transition process, the requirements derived from the above objectives are as follows:

- The toolkit shall contain best practice and state of the art artifacts.
- These artifacts shall comprise approaches, methods and tools to facilitate an agile transition.
- The toolkit shall be like a "menu" allowing choosing adequate artifacts.
- The toolkit shall offer at least one artifact to support a transition team demand.
- The toolkit shall be structured by attributes to find adequate artefacts for the specific demand.
- The structure and the artifacts shall be set up to be applicable as a self-service.

– The toolkit shall have a life-cycle for aligning it with future demands and enhancing it based on lessons learned which could thereby be concentrated in the toolkit.
– The life-cycle of the artifacts in the toolkit shall allow substituting "old" artefacts by newer ones or artefacts fitting better to the company culture.

Based on these requirements, it becomes evident that not all possible artifacts have to be evaluated and integrated in the toolkit. The artifacts are essentially based on a first-fit approach based on the demand by the teams and the organization.

## 4.2  Governance of the Process and Its Self-service Toolkit

In an enterprise environment, standardization is often controlled by a governance instance. Figure 1 from [29] shows the governance's role and interdependencies. The governance guides the team transition with the toolkit and collects their feedbacks to enhance the toolkit over time. However, also the governance has to check the teams outcomes like products or services for compliance derivations and handle their risks adequately. This risk-handling can lead to e.g. an internal regulation action applied to the toolkit to avoid systematic risks or failures.

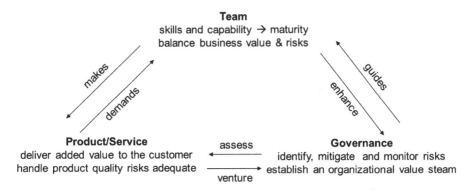

**Fig. 1.** Relationships between the team and its governance and product/service.

To ensure that the transition process and its toolkit fits to the organization, a central instance is responsible for the maintenance of the transition toolkit. The objectives of these central governance are:

– to ensure that the toolkit contains artefacts aligned with the enterprise culture (the current and the desired development direction of the culture in the future);
– to maintain the feedback and lessons learned procedure;
– to check the effectiveness of the toolkit in the transition teams, and
– to initiate changes to the toolkit and its artifacts if needed (also includes to fit new external regulations etc.).

The governance instance has to be open for innovations and enhancement of the toolkit and its artifacts, but also enforce fast changes to the toolkit if needed e.g. to fit new regulations. A further aspect is to offer a space for the company to develop their own artifacts for specific demands that are not covered by the results of a (public) search for approaches, methods or tools.

### 4.3 Generic Approach for Agile Transitions in Enterprises

The identified requirements for the toolkit and its governance process lead to a generic approach to using the toolkit. Figure 2 [29] shows the approach, which is built on initiating an agile transition within a systematic facilitation phase. The latter starts with a readiness check to determine the current state of the team and its transition objectives. A more or less intensive coaching phase helps the team to get the capabilities needed to become an autonomous team. The autonomy readiness is given by the capability check at the end of the coaching phase. The governance randomly selects teams and checks their continuous transition to autonomy using project reviews during the life cycle of the team or their organization.

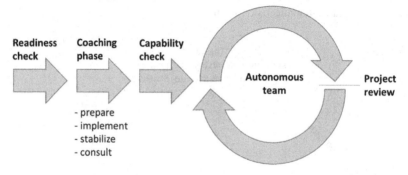

**Fig. 2.** A generic process to establish autonomous teams with an agile transition.

This generic process offers systematic opportunities to collect feedbacks during the coaching phase and the project reviews from the governance perspective.

## 5   Transition Kit Development

To develop the transition kit, the grounded theory [30] approach shall be used. As the approach comes from sociology, it fits to the context with the team maturity and enterprise culture as an important part of the setting of the agile transition. Grounded theory uses as artifacts codes, concepts, categories and theory to derive the insights. Codes are key points in the data gathered in the field. Concepts are the groupings of similar codes. Categories are the derived patterns or insights from the concepts as a basis for the theory.

The data is based on the selected artifacts that have been evaluated for the integration into the transition kit. The first step is to identify relevant artifacts. This is done by scouting with a first fit approach artifacts. The scouting of publicly available artefacts (public data) shall be aligned with the toolkit requirements identified in Sect. 4.1 for the selection. All of these pre-defined codes are positive indicators for a particular artifact to fit into the transition kit. In a second step, the selected artifacts shall be evaluated in the target enterprise during a transition with experienced coaches to check how the pre-selection of artifacts fits to the culture and the real team settings. The objective is to eliminate codes that are indicators or evidences for a mismatch. Mismatch indicators are e.g. negative side-effects like silo-thinking of the team or leverage of individual power instead of team creativity. These negative indicators during artifact application depend on the environment which is driven by the team's maturity and the enterprise culture. The codes are used for deriving concepts like for which team maturity level the artifact is useful to avoid the mismatch indicators. In case of mismatch in all concepts, the artifact shall not be selected for the transition kit, instead other alternatives shall be looked up and evaluated. The remaining artifacts are grouped in categories like approaches for agile working, methods to identify require-ments and deliverables or tools to structure requirements. The categories have to support the life cycle of the team's products and service in different team maturity levels. The final setting of the transition kit is the grounded theory in the enterprise setting which fits to the current teams and the enterprise culture. Furthermore, depending on the enterprise specific concepts can be identified and grouped in order to support their agile transition from their specific product settings.

## 5.1  Structure of the Transition Kit

The structure of the transition kit with its methods and tools for self-service is based on two categories which are used to classify the different artifacts to address the team maturity and their product or service complexity. For measuring team maturity, the spiral dynamics model [24] is used. Product or service complexity is mapped to the Stacey matrix [31].

*Spiral Dynamics Model.* The spiral dynamic model is used because it offers for an easy explanation of the maturity levels (color) aspects like the people structure, their motives and the characteristics of the teams. This helps teams to identify the current pain points in their current structure and habits to grow, cf. Table 1 from [29].

*Stacey Matrix.* The Stacey matrix distinguishes four different categories: trivial, complicated, complex and chaotic. These categories are applicable to technical and social or organizational structures. This helps teams to map their products and services.

## 5.2  Outcomes of the Systematic Evaluation and Data Gathering

The outcome of the toolkit's application to the Volkswagen AG Group IT is shown in Table 2 from [29]. The first column lists the toolkit's artifacts as methods and tools resulting from the grounded theory derivation process. The second column represents the team maturity rating according to the spiral dynamics model. The third column shows the Stacey matrix mapping. It is certainly possible to apply methods/tools in other settings of the spiral dynamics or Stacey mapping, however in the specific enterprise setting this is not recommended.

**Table 1.** Spiral dynamics model with its mappings for teams to see strengths and potentials.

| Level-name | Structure | Motives | Characteristics |
|---|---|---|---|
| Beige | Loose bands | Survival | Archaic, instinctive, basic, automatic |
| Purple | Tribes | Magic, Safety | Animistic, Tribalistic, Magical, Mystical |
| Red | Empires | Power, Dominance | Egocentric, Explorative, Impulsive, Rebellious |
| Blue | Pyramidal | Order, right & wrong | Absolutistic, Obedient, Purposeful, Authoritarian |
| Orange | Delegative | Autonomy, achievement | Materialistic, Strategic, Ambitious, Individualistic |
| Green | Egalitarian | Approval, Equality, Community | Relativistic, Personalistic, Sensitive, Pluralistic |
| Yellow | Interactive | Adaptability, Integration | Systemic, Conceptual, Ecological, Flexible |
| Tortoise | Global | Compassion, Harmony | Holistic, Global |

**Table 2.** Example for a specific company's transition tool kit derived with grounded theory.

| Method/tool | Spiral dynamic model team maturity | Stacey mapping of product/service context |
|---|---|---|
| Retrospective | Purple or higher | All |
| Design Thinking | Blue or higher | All |
| Minimum Viable Product (MVP) | Orange or higher | Complex & complicated |
| Simple Lovable and Complete (SLC) | Blue or higher | Complex & complicated |
| Business Model Canvas (BMC) | Purple or higher | Complex & complicated |
| Product Vision Board (PVB) | Purple or higher | Complex & complicated |
| INVEST | Purple or higher | Complex & complicated |
| Definition of Ready (DoR) | Blue or higher | All |
| Definition of Done (DoD) | Blue or higher | All |
| Levels of Done (LoD) | Blue or higher | Complex & complicated |
| Product Quality Risk (PQR) | Ref or higher | Complex & complicated |
| Scrum | Purple or higher | Complex & complicated |
| Extreme Programming | Green or higher | Complex & complicated |
| KANBAN | Beige or higher | Complex & complicated |
| SAFe | Red or higher | Complex & complicated |
| LeSS | Blue or higher | Complex & complicated |
| Nexus | Orange or higher | Complex & complicated |
| Scrum@Scale | Orange or higher | Complex & complicated |

# 6  Agile Maturity Measurement

To support the teams to reach the desired objective of the agile transition departing from their current situations, the approaches, methods and tools recommended by the toolkit have to fit to the teams' specific maturity levels. A team develops maturity over time. This is driven by group dynamics [32] as well as the demands of their product or service life cycle. Furthermore, the enterprise culture develops at the same time, and impacts the entire organization as well as the individual teams [33]. The transition kit addresses culture with the governance approach, which triggers in/out-decisions of artifacts to support the enterprise culture development. The specific team maturity is addressed by the spiral dynamics model, which is mapped to each artifact of the transition kit.

The key concept is that each team can be evaluated by a coach considered external to the team, or alternatively by self-evaluation. In any case, evaluations are based on the spiral dynamic model. This is a chance for each team to reflect their progress in team maturity. The team maturity is important for the agile transition because the agile working mindset is team oriented. This helps teams to use adequate approaches, methods and tools that render their daily business more effective.

During the coaching phase, the coach as team facilitator makes the initial evaluation of the current state of the team's maturity to select with the team artifacts adequate for their agile transition. The coach also prepares the team for carrying out this capability check themselves in a self-service approach. Furthermore, during the team-external project review, any team has the option to get an evaluation as a kind of feedback about their current team maturity state in the context of the presented and applied agile approaches, methods and tools during the review.

# 7  Case Study

The case study is taken from the Volkswagen AG Group IT. The Group IT offers a wide range of IT services to the brands and is responsible for group wide IT services of the Volkswagen AG. The Group IT implementation of the presented holistic agile transition kit is based on an instantiation of the agile transition process applying the kit. The established transition governance uses the measurements for making progress transparent. Furthermore, the continuous improvement and enhancement is established in conjunction with the governance and representatives of agile transitions, which ensures addressing the real teams context and keeps the relevance of the kit's "content".

## 7.1  Instantiation of the Transition Process

The transition process has initially been established with the coaches of the Agile Center of Excellence (ACE). The coaching team has been growing moderately over time and offers coaching packages to support transitions [26]. In order to scale better, the ACE established a 2-year trainee program for Coaches and Scrum Professionals (CSP). The CSPs come from different business areas and coach transitions in a "localized fashion". Figure 3 shows the numeric growth of the ACE and CSP coaches over time. The CSPs are independent, however can use offers of the ACE like the Agile Community or Coach Guide to stay up to date. The ACE implemented the process from Fig. 3 and established a governance together with the quality team of the Group IT [16].

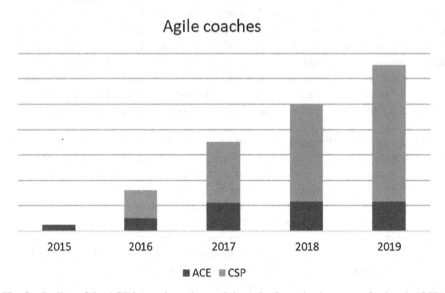

**Fig. 3.** Scaling of the ACE internal coaches and the trained coaches/scrum professionals (CSP).

Over time, the ACE collected data from its coaching activities. Figure 4 shows the proportions of conducted readiness and maturity checks over time. It shows that not all readiness checks led to a coaching. Sometimes the team were not ready, sometimes the ACE had to prioritize the transitions. In the last years, the ACE focused on transitions of bigger programs and organizational units instead of individual teams, which is the reason explaining that the amount of maturity checks did not grow fast (each coaching program with more teams is count as one and is often handled by two coaches). The project reviews established later on address the sustainability aspect to ensure that the long-term effects have been reached, as well as to ensure that the "self-service" transitions (often supported by the CSP) are well aligned with the Group IT framework. The project review checks different aspects like value delivery, delivery speed or defects as quality delivery indicator of the product or service, as well as a set of process and team aspects. The project reviews are also used for field analysis and for triggering organizational improvement actions [29].

**Validation Measures.** The instantiation of the transition process supports HI1: coaches get productive fast also in programs by the systematic process that guides teams and coaches during the structures checks at the beginning and the end. This gives all involved people – including the coaches as facilitators – focus and supports an effective artifact selection to address the identified potentials. With each application, the coaches learn more about the artifacts of the transition kit and can integrate their experience in future toolkit versions to continuously improve and enhance it. This supports HI2. The

## ACE team/program facilitations

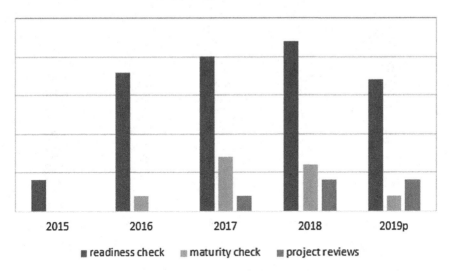

**Fig. 4.** Scaling over time (with 2019 partly) of the 3 types of checks/reviews.

standardized transition process is used by the governance to address enhancements about strategic (like culture aspects) and compliance (like new legal requirements) demands, which supports HI3. The process design itself with the "check-points" at the beginning and the end of the coaching, as well as the randomized project review gives measuring points for the team maturity to address HI4.

### 7.2  Instantiation of the Transition Kit

The instantiation of the transition kit with "content" was done by a first-fit approach. The focus for the initial version of the kit was to use state of the art "artefacts" which are proven in use. This approach reduces the acceptance risk in the initial evaluation phase and ensures a fast start with real life teams. Over time, experience and feedbacks of the performed transitions extended the "content" for a better fit. The program aspects are currently the biggest drivers for changes on the transition kit. The usage of the spiral dynamics model and the Stacey matrix support to find the right options of the transition kits offers. Figure 5 shows a sample of the maturity check evaluation mapped to the Scrum values. The teams got a high understanding and adoption of agile and Scrum values in their coaching phase with the application of the transition kit.

**Validation Measures.** The instantiation of the transition kit supports HI1 by giving coaches an approach of making a relevant pre-selection of the wide set of available methods and tools for application to a team having specific maturity and complexity levels. By using the transition kit, with each instantiation of the artifacts in real team transitions, the coaches will learn details about the selected approaches, methods and tools in the specific team context. This alignment with the transition kit based on

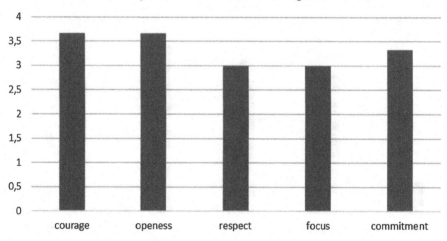

**Fig. 5.** Average values on a range of 0 to 5 (best) of team maturity indicators from a sample.

lessons learned and application experience supports HI2. HI3 is supported by the feedback of the coaches through their lessons learned and experiences made. The coaches' and teams' feedbacks are used by the kit's governance to improve and enhance the kit for future use. The team maturity filter makes transparent what kind of approaches, methods and tools are recommended based on the team's current maturity. This kind of making facts evident against the spiral dynamics model and other teams leads to growing team objectives, which supports HI4 in a "competition" approach. Reaching out for higher maturity levels will also lead to getting the chance for experimenting with new methods and tools. Team externals can observe the speed of the team's progress.

### 7.3    Instantiation of the Measurement Framework

The measurement frame is established over time as the organization obtained the maturity to collect (Fig. 4) and handle the data (Fig. 5). The interpretation of Fig. 5 in the measurement context is that a 3 or higher score shows a clear indicator for orange or higher team structures. The team leaves the red and blue mindset of the Taylorism hierarchy's. In a last step, the data is correlated between the teams, and trends are visualized. Figure 6 shows a sample of different transitions and their average change to focus on the agile values. The first value set is as expected: shifting to deliver software. The second got a small push into planning which is motivated by the fact that at their starting point, teams are often too enthusiastic on change handling and they learn to be aligned with other teams in the release process as a kind of maturity. We can observe a similar behavior with the customer interaction and contracting: the pendulum deflection from one to the other end is initially often not based on the right momentum in less mature teams.

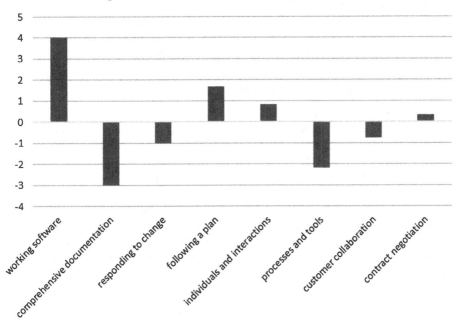

**Fig. 6.** Average change of agile value indicators on a range from −5 to 5 (more) from a sample.

**Validation Measures.** The readiness check measures the team maturity for agile at the beginning of the coaching and helps the coach to focus and deliver a fast ramp-up. The constant focus to the transitions progress and the creation of team autonomy readiness is measured at the end in the maturity check in the form of a final report of the coaching. The focus reduces "waste" in lean thinking and thereby directly supports HI1. The governance reviews the three types of team checks to ensure overall growing maturity of the teams and initiates action in case of unacceptable derivations or missing culture alignment. This supports HI3. HI4 is addressed inherently by applying the transition kit and helps the teams to make the growing performance transparent.

### 7.4 Reflection of the Presented Transition Kit and Governance Approach

We challenged the transition kit with the participants of two international conferences, each uniting more than a hundred representatives from industry and academia: the 3rd *Lean and Agile Software Development* Conference, as well as the 26th EuroSPI conference in its *Experiences with Lean and Agile* track. Both expert groups (more than 40 experts) identified that domain specific demands are not addressed. Examples are domain specific requirements for finance or safety regulations. Such specific requirements or aspects have to be added to ensure that the relevant domain specific outcomes are realized. In both conferences, the expert groups did not identify any issues linked with the generic transition kit approach itself. This implies that it should be easy to apply the transition kit concept in other enterprises after adaptation to the specific domains and strategic cultural objectives. The experts came from all over the world, including countries like Japan, Brazil, Turkey, Denmark and Spain. The experts' domain know-how was widely spread to fields such as finance, insurance, semi-conductors/sensor, medical, defense, automotive, and software consulting.

### 7.5 Experiences and Lessons Learned

The instantiation of the transition kit with the standardized process and measurement framework as a holistic approach has clearly shown its effectivity in helping teams getting their autonomy. The amount of teams grows, as does the throughput of coaches. Figure 7 shows the trend of the efficiency of the ACE's systematic facilitation approach with the transition kit. The team transitions grow faster than the size of the ACE, cf. Figs. 3 and 4. The chart shows the teams that reached the maturity to go ahead autonomously with their transition. A big scaling factor is that for two years, the ACE has been an accepted transition partner also in non-IT business areas for big programs (including several hundreds of people) and their teams. This also led to the introduction of a new Key Performance Indicator (KPI): the average number of teams per transition coaching.

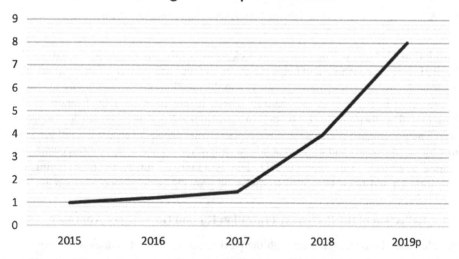

**Fig. 7.** Scaling of the transition performance indicator: number of teams per transition.

The sustainability of transitions is measured with the project review, which can be correlated to the readiness check of the team to show the global growing of team maturity.

The experience is that it is difficult to measure effectivity and efficiency in complex social environments, since only indicators can be measured. The overall system has many unknown parameters that influence the effectivity and sustainability of the transitions.

A lesson learned is that it takes a lot of time (even years for huge enterprises) to establish an entire Deming cycle for a systematic and holistic check of agile transitions on an enterprise level. The main issue was the establishment of the sustainability monitoring via a governance approach. Furthermore, a lesson learned is that the transition of teams is never really finished, and the coaches have to act as initial facilitators to give the teams the maturity for acting in mastery and autonomy on their individual agile journey.

# 8 Conclusion and Outlook

The conclusion summarizes the presented holistic transition approach including its key contributions and the result evaluation. Finally, the limitations are discussed and future enhancements are identified.

## 8.1 Key Contributions

The key contribution to scaling agile transitions in large enterprise is that sustainability is reached by combining a generic transition process with a life cycle view of the transition, a transition toolkit that is adaptable to the specific team's demands, as well as a team maturity approach to challenge and support the team's agile mindset.

All together is delivered as a self-service approach, as well as with an offer for coaching support. To ensure scalability, the coaching support is designed as a limited support with focus on helping teams to reach a high level of autonomy fast. To ensure sustainability of the transitions and keep the three key components up to date, a systematic governance is established.

A key conclusion for establishing a governance in agile environments is that from the outset, a focus has to be directed on teams and products *more than* on processes. Moderation and facilitation are *more* essential *than* defining and controlling. Checks shall be used as enhancement triggers *more than* as deviation measures.

## 8.2 Evaluation of Results

The key results are the life cycle view of the team transition during their agile journey with a team-external enterprise governance view. The presented indicators about effectivity and efficiency show that the approach works as expected. However, the indicators only focus on specific aspects that are covered by the indicator design. In a complex enterprise environment, however, it is difficult to define indicators and measures proofing complex social, organizational and technical influencing factors.

## 8.3 Limitations and Future Research and Development

One limitation of the holistic approach is that the transition process as well as the kit have to be aligned with the enterprise. There is no "one size fits all" out-of-the-box approach. Furthermore, the evaluation results are limited because an agile transition and the sustainability of a team depends on much more factors than can be monitored with a practical measure set. Often, external effects like the re-organization of the business unit can destroy teams and their transition process in a small amount of time.

In the future, a more systematic team maturity model can help to better map social and agile aspects together. Furthermore, agile transitions can be linked better to non-product and service delivery aspects like finance processes to give mature teams more degrees of freedom to act faster and more market-driven.

# References

1. Hornstein, H.A.: Using a change management approach to implement IT programs. Ivey Bus. J. Online **72**(1) (2008)
2. Wendel, L.F., Cecil, B.: Organization Development: Behavioral Science Interventions for Organization Improvement, p. 18. Prentice-Hall, Englewood Cliffs (1973). ISBN 978-0-13-641662-3. OCLC 314258
3. Kerber, K., Buono, A.: Rethinking organizational change: reframing the challenge of change management. Organ. Dev. J. **23**, 23–38 (2005)
4. Pieterse, J.H., Caniëls, M.C.J., Homan, T.: Professional discourses and resistance to change. J. Organ. Change Manag. **25**(6), 798–818 (2012)
5. Heckmann, N., Steger, T., Dowling, M.: Organizational capacity for change, change experience, and change project performance. J. Bus. Res. (2015). https://doi.org/10.1016/j.jbusres.2015.07.012
6. Holten, A., Brenner, S.: Leadership style and the process of organizational change. Leadersh. Organ. Dev. J. **36**(1), 2–16 (2015). https://doi.org/10.1108/LODJ-11-2012-0155
7. Mento, A., Jones, R., Dirndorfer, W.: A change management process: grounded in both theory and practice. J. Change Manag. **3**(1), 45–59 (2002). https://doi.org/10.1080/714042520
8. Pettigrew, A.M., et al. (eds.): Innovative Forms of Organizing, pp. 72–94. Sage, London (2003)
9. Poth, A., Sasabe, S., Mas, A., Mesquida, A.: Lean and agile software process improvement in traditional and agile environments. J. Softw.: Evol. Process. (2018). https://doi.org/10.1002/smr.1986. 31. e1986
10. Mas, A., Poth, A., Sasabe, S.: SPI with retrospectives: a case study. In: Larrucea, X., Santamaria, I., O'Connor, R.V., Messnarz, R. (eds.) EuroSPI 2018. CCIS, vol. 896, pp. 456–466. Springer, Cham (2018). https://doi.org/10.1007/978-3-319-97925-0_39
11. Kösling, M., Poth, A.: Agile development offers the chance to establish automated quality procedures. In: Stolfa, J., Stolfa, S., O'Connor, R.V., Messnarz, R. (eds.) EuroSPI 2017. CCIS, vol. 748, pp. 495–503. Springer, Cham (2017). https://doi.org/10.1007/978-3-319-64218-5_40
12. Davis, N.: Driving quality improvement and reducing technical debt with the definition of done. In: Agile Conference, Nashville, TN, pp. 164–168 (2013). https://doi.org/10.1109/agile.2013.21
13. https://www.scaledagileframework.com/
14. https://less.works/less/framework/index.html
15. Stojanov, I., Turetken, O., Trienekens, J.J.M.: A maturity model for scaling agile development. In: 2015 41st Euromicro Conference on Software Engineering and Advanced Applications, Funchal, pp. 446–453 (2015). https://doi.org/10.1109/seaa.2015.29

16. Poth, A., Kottke, M.: How to assure agile method and process alignment in an organization? In: Larrucea, X., Santamaria, I., O'Connor, R.V., Messnarz, R. (eds.) EuroSPI 2018. CCIS, vol. 896, pp. 421–425. Springer, Cham (2018). https://doi.org/10.1007/978-3-319-97925-0_35

17. Poth, A., Heimann, C.: How to innovate software quality assurance and testing in large enterprises? In: Larrucea, X., Santamaria, I., O'Connor, R.V., Messnarz, R. (eds.) EuroSPI 2018. CCIS, vol. 896, pp. 437–442. Springer, Cham (2018). https://doi.org/10.1007/978-3-319-97925-0_37

18. Poth, A., Wolf, F.: Agile procedures of an automotive OEM – views from different business areas. In: Stolfa, J., Stolfa, S., O'Connor, R.V., Messnarz, R. (eds.) EuroSPI 2017. CCIS, vol. 748, pp. 513–522. Springer, Cham (2017). https://doi.org/10.1007/978-3-319-64218-5_42

19. Ozcan-Top, O., Demirörs, O.: Assessment of agile maturity models: a multiple case study. In: Woronowicz, T., Rout, T., O'Connor, R.V., Dorling, A. (eds.) SPICE 2013. CCIS, vol. 349, pp. 130–141. Springer, Heidelberg (2013). https://doi.org/10.1007/978-3-642-38833-0_12

20. Silva, F.S., Soares, F.S.F., Peres, A.L., de Azevedo, I.M., Pinto, P.P., de Meira S.R.L.: A reference model for agile quality assurance: combining agile methodologies and maturity models. In: 9th International Conference on the Quality of Information and Communications Technology, Guimaraes, pp. 139–144 (2014) https://doi.org/10.1109/quatic.2014.25

21. Leppänen, M.: A comparative analysis of agile maturity models. In: Pooley, R., Coady, J., Schneider, C., Linger, H., Barry, C., Lang, M. (eds.) Information Systems Development. Springer, New York (2013). https://doi.org/10.1007/978-1-4614-4951-5_27

22. Henriques, V., Tanner, M.: A systematic literature review of agile and maturity model research. Interdisc. J. Inf. Knowl. Manag. 12, 53–73 (2017). https://doi.org/10.28945/3666

23. Schmidt, T.S., Paetzold, K.: Maturity assessment of teams developing physical products in an agile manner. In: International Conference on Engineering, Technology and Innovation (ICE/ITMC), Funchal, 2017, pp. 351–360 (2017). https://doi.org/10.1109/ice.2017.8279907

24. Beck, D., Cowan, C.: Spiral Dynamics: Mastering Values, Leadership, and Change. ISBN 1-55786-940-5 (1996)

25. Fontana, R.M., Reinehr, S., Malucelli, A.: Agile compass: a tool for identifying maturity in agile software-development teams. IEEE Softw. 32(6), 20–23 (2015). https://doi.org/10.1109/ms.2015.135

26. Poth, A.: Effectivity and economical aspects for agile quality assurance in large enterprises. J. Softw.: Evol. Process 28(11), 1000–1004 (2016)

27. Hartmann, D., Dymond, R.: Appropriate agile measurement: using metrics and diagnostics to deliver business value. In: AGILE 200, pp. 6–134 (2002). https://doi.org/10.1109/agile.2006.17

28. Doherty, B., Jelfs, A., Dasgupta, A., Holden, P.: Defect analysis in large scale agile development: quality in the agile factory model. In: Joint Conference of the International Workshop on Software Measurement and the International Conference on Software Process and Product Measurement (IWSM-MENSURA), p. 180 (2016). https://doi.org/10.1109/iwsm-mensura.2016.034

29. Poth, A., Kottke, M., Riel, A.: Scaling agile on large enterprise level - systematic bundling and application of state of the art approaches for lasting agile transitions. In: Annals of Computer Science and Information Systems, vol. 18, pp. 851–860 (2019). ISSN: 2300-5963

30. Wiesche, M., Jurisch, M.C., Yetton, P.W., Krcmar, H.: Grounded theory methodology in information systems research. MIS Q. 41(3), 685–701 (2007). https://doi.org/10.25300/MISQ/2017/41.3.02

31. Stacey, R.D.: Strategic Management and Organisational Dynamics: the Challenge of Complexity, 3rd edn. Prentice Hall, Harlow (2002)
32. Wheelan, S.A., Hochberger, J.M.: Validation studies of the group development questionnaire. Small Group Res. **27**, 143–170 (1996)
33. Erkutlu, H.: The impact of organizational culture on the relationship between shared leadership and team proactivity. Team Perform. Manag. **18**(1/2), 102–119 (2012). https://doi.org/10.1108/13527591211207734

# Release Planning in a Hybrid Project Environment

Kristina Marner[1]([⊠]), Sven Theobald[2], and Stefan Wagner[3]

[1] Dr. Ing. h.c. F. Porsche AG, Porschestraße 911, 71287 Weissach, Germany
kristina.marner@porsche.de
[2] Fraunhofer IESE, Fraunhofer-Platz 1, 67663 Kaiserslautern, Germany
sven.theobald@iese.fraunhofer.de
[3] Universität Stuttgart, Universitätsstraße 38, 70569 Stuttgart, Germany
stefan.wagner@iste.uni-stuttgart.de

**Abstract.** *Context*: Even regulated domains like the automotive domain increasingly adopt agile software development. However, traditional sequential processes are still in use and have to coexist with the new development approaches. Collaboration between agile and hybrid projects within complex traditional product development processes is challenging, especially regarding the creation and synchronization of a qualification phase plan. *Objective*: The aim of this study is to motivate research related to the combined use of agile and traditional paradigms in release planning in the automotive domain and to report challenges from industry. *Method*: We introduce and motivate the research topic and discuss related work based on the results of a small literature study. Further, an online survey with 56 respondents from an automotive Original Equipment Manufacturer was conducted. *Results*: There is a clear research gap regarding release planning for combined agile and traditional projects. The state-of-the-practice survey identified challenges, such as a lack of transparency regarding the status quo of related projects. *Conclusions*: The research gap as well as the challenges from industry should motivate further research on this topic, in order to improve release planning processes in this specific context.

**Keywords:** Automotive · Agile method · Challenges · Hybrid development process · Hybrid project environment · Product development process · Qualification phase · Release planning · Traditional process

## 1 Introduction

Agile software development approaches promise many benefits like increased transparency, a faster response to change or a shorter time to market [1]. Nowadays, they have become the most commonly used software development approach, especially in information systems domains [1]. Companies from the strongly regulated automotive domain realize these benefits. Most companies have already started their evolutionary bottom-up transition to agility [2] by using agile development in pilot projects. In reality, these agile projects often use hybrid processes [3]. How does a hybrid environment look like? Automotive domains are situated in a hybrid project environment with two conflictive parts. On the one hand, there are processes with many milestones

© Springer Nature Switzerland AG 2020
A. Przybyłek and M. E. Morales-Trujillo (Eds.): LASD 2019/MIDI 2019, LNBIP 376, pp. 19–40, 2020.
https://doi.org/10.1007/978-3-030-37534-8_2

planned long time in advance, before the projects go live and serve the production and the distribution. On the other hand, there is the operational level. On this operational level, the projects try to act in a way that fits best to their project character. The majority of teams in regulated domains prefer adopting single agile practices [2] or strongly adapting existing agile methods like Scrum instead of adopting methods in their pure form [4].

Nonetheless, traditional approaches like waterfall or the V-model are still predominant in the automotive domain. Within these domains, the adoption of agile practices is hard to achieve and even not always desired [5]. This inevitably leads to a mixture of different processes ranging from completely traditional processes to agile adaptations. With these so called hybrid development approaches [3, 6], it becomes more and more complex to handle the interfaces [7] between all involved methodologies.

Especially in the automotive domain, the complexity of software and systems is constantly increasing [8]. Causes are increasing connectivity, increasing distribution of functionality to control units inside the car as well as new technologies like connected services or cloud services. Due to their complexity, automotive projects are large projects with many subprojects and suppliers. One of the many challenges in such projects is to speed up the software release cycles [5]. Creating and updating a common release plan that considers all dependencies is challenging, even more when multiple parties work with different processes and timelines. Agile approaches can cause chaos in release planning, because the two paradigms differ largely.

Thus, we want to motivate the investigation of release planning in the context of system development with coexisting agile and traditional projects and propose the following high-level goal: Identify and analyze challenges in qualification phase planning in order to identify improvements in the context of system development with coexisting agile and traditional projects from the perspective of an automotive original equipment manufacturer (OEM). The research questions below are possible ways to investigate the research field:

- What are challenges concerning qualification phase planning in a hybrid project environment?
- What are the challenges of agile projects that are embedded in a traditional development context?
- What are the challenges of traditional projects, having to synchronize with agile projects?
- What are solutions for the identified challenges?
- How should a release planning process look like to optimize synchronization in a hybrid project environment?

This work extends a previous publication [9]. The contribution of this paper is to detail and motivate the research topic by presenting an extended background and related work. We extended the results of the survey study [9] with the data from 17 additional respondents, and provide more insights into the comments of participants. By presenting these updated results, we highlight common challenges that show the need to investigate potential solutions and come up with a suitable release planning process in a hybrid project environment.

The remainder of this paper is structured as follows: The background and related work is presented in Sect. 2. Section 3 presents the research approach of the survey study, and the results are presented in Sect. 4. We conclude our work and outline future research in Sect. 5.

## 2 Background and Related Work

In this section, we present the background of our research and the related work. First, the hybrid project environment is presented together with our understanding of release planning. Afterwards, we provide insights into the agile initiative of an automotive OEM and present the identified related research.

### 2.1 Hybrid Project Environment

In the automotive domain, a hybrid project environment consists of two conflicting parts (see Fig. 1). There is the strategic framework on one side consisting of processes with many milestones planned a long time in advance before projects related to production and distribution go live. This strategic framework (shown in the upper part of Fig. 1) represents the time and content requirements, such as the product development process and thus defines a superordinate process. The Qualification Phase (QP) is the repetitive integration and testing process of an Electronic Control Unit (ECU) network, its sensors and actuators. This phase is typically defined at the beginning of a project. The maturity level is determined to release the ECU network for further testing, usage, and development. The maturity levels provide information about the development progress of functions and ECUs in relation to the target state.

The Additional Qualification Phase (AQP) is an extra qualification phase with a reduced testing scope if the level of maturity is found to be insufficient and refers to a reduced scope of ECUs. The reduced test scope refers to the inadequate target state and is defined application-specifically. An AQP is not planned in advance but established depending on the quality level of the QP. An AQP has to be executed only in case of low quality. For this reason, an AQP is not represented in Fig. 1. The selection of the test cases and the duration of the tests depend on the errors identified during the QP.

On the other hand, there is the operational level: the development of ECUs and associated software. Here projects are performed in the way that best fits the project's character (see bottom part of Fig. 1). On this level, projects are developed in an agile, hybrid or traditional way. However, all projects have one milestone in common, which triggers them to serve the next release. Represented by the grey milestone. Reality demonstrates that coordination and synchronization of these two parts no longer works successfully (symbolized by the different colors of the flashes).

A solution has to be found that synchronizes both levels and which enables coordinated release planning.

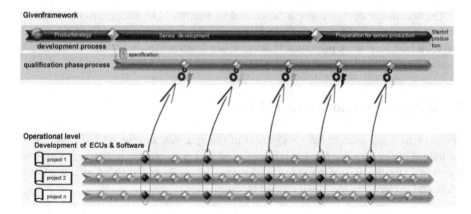

**Fig. 1.** Coordination between strategic and operational level

## 2.2 Release Planning

Release planning, in an agile way, contains all decisions to feature content of the next releases and deals with planning to develop the features [10]. Several aspects need to be considered in order to guarantee a successful release:

- Planning: Planning the content that is supposed to be realized in the next release is challenging, since the work has to be distributed on several teams. It is certainly not easy to come up with a reliable plan upfront, so that all planned content can be integrated in the end.
- Coordination: The dependencies between several teams need to be considered and managed. Transparency is necessary to know the relevant stakeholders and to synchronize work with them.
- Integration: Integrating the results from several teams into the final product. Sometimes, errors are only found when integrating, causing bug fixing and additional integration effort.
- Testing: Fully testing the results of all teams individually is already a challenge, but also the integrated product needs to be checked in order to assure all parts work together like expected.

The automotive domain is a strongly regulated domain. Therefore, this combination cannot start in a green field, as strategic frameworks define different phases of the development process.

## 2.3 Agile@Porsche

The benefits of agile development methods have also arrived at Dr. Ing. h.c. F. Porsche AG. For a stepwise introduction of agile practices, a set-up team called Agile@porsche was established. This team consists of representatives corresponding to the individual departments, such as development, marketing or controlling.

The Agile@Porsche team agrees upon common objectives and activities to strengthen an agile organization. Six dimensions characterize the Porsche-specific approach of agility (see Fig. 2) [11].

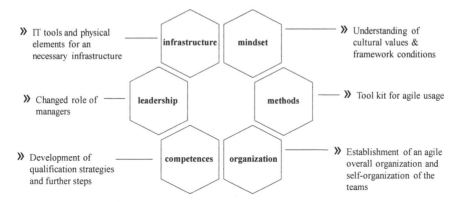

**Fig. 2.** Six dimensions of agility at Porsche [11]

The first dimension contains a defined understanding of cultural values and framework conditions and provides the basis. The second dimension includes a tool kit for the use of agile methods. This tool kit comprises various methods and practices that can be applied in projects. Organization is the topic of the next dimension that ensures the development of an agile overall structure and the self-organization of individual teams. The development of qualification strategies and the taking of relevant steps for an agile establishment is specified in the fourth dimension that is named competences. The fifth dimension called leadership is characterized by a changing role of leadership. The management has to learn handing responsibility over to the developers. For this purpose a definition of new roles is required and necessary. In an agile environment, the team makes the decisions and a vertical commitment is needed. The usage and implementation of agile practices is only feasible with a suitable environment. For this purpose, a dedicated infrastructure consisting of different IT-tools and physical elements is required and seen as a fundamental condition.

Guidelines for the practical implementation of these six dimensions can be found in a document [11] that offers a standardized definition of agility and a common understanding of agility at Porsche. The transition to a holistic agile organization will be implemented step by step. The state of the practice of using agility results in implementing agile methods in larger scaled projects and the development of supporting processes and organizational structures for anchoring. For the near future, the company targets at having an efficient coexistence of traditional and agile teams.

## 2.4    Related Work

To investigate how the proposed research topic is already covered by research, we investigated the related work. Besides considering the sources, the authors already knew, a small literature review was conducted. We defined three aspects (c.f. Fig. 3) based on our research goal and tried to identify related work about release planning that in addition covers at least one of those aspects:

1. Release Planning in Systems Engineering
2. Release Planning in the automotive domain
3. Release Planning in a hybrid project environment

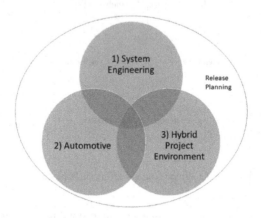

**Fig. 3.** Research aspects

For each category, we defined a search string (see Fig. 4) and searched on Scopus[1]. We assessed the resulting list of literature based on the title and included every literature that seemed to address any of our categories. This final list of papers was then mapped to the three categories and checked for relevancy.

1) TITLE-ABS-KEY ( ( "product release" OR "release planning" OR "release management" ) AND ( "System engineering" OR "System development" OR "systems development" OR "systems engineering" ) )
2) TITLE-ABS-KEY ( ( "product release" OR "release planning" OR "release management" ) AND ( automotive OR automobile OR car ) )
3) TITLE-ABS-KEY ( ( "product release" OR "release planning" OR "release management" ) AND ( "hybrid project environment" OR ( agile AND traditional ) OR "hybrid projects" ) )

**Fig. 4.** Search strings

In the following, we present related work and analyze research gaps. There is a research gap considering this hybrid project environment where projects with different development paradigms meet. The HELENA study [3] investigates the combined use of agile and traditional practices in hybrid processes, but does not consider the coexistence of agile and hybrid projects and their synchronization. Theobald et al. [7]

---

[1] www.scopus.com.

investigates and classifies problems at the interface of agile and traditional environment. Our work in this paper can be classified in the problem field "project planning" at the interface "project-team". We could only identify one source dealing with release planning in a hybrid project environment. [12] identified "an obvious gap in the research of release planning in large-scale agile software development organizations" in a literature review.

There is some work on release planning in the automotive domain. [13] describes software release and configuration management in the automotive domain. [14] define requirements to control and monitor dependencies with other release processes with the help of workflow support. [15] define requirements for IT-support to improve release management in the automotive domain. [16] identified key aspects of release planning in the context of software and system development projects and also captured the state of the practice for release planning in industry. There is no explicit work on release planning in systems engineering, but the contributions dealing with an automotive context mostly also cover release planning in systems engineering.

There is literature dealing with release planning in agile software development projects: single project as well as scaled projects. [17] evaluates the methods that are used by companies to plan for new software releases. [18] presents a case study where the agile release planning process in a scaled Scrum environment was evaluated. [19] describes the practice qualification phase planning and presents a case study of multi-team agile release planning with the help of this practice. [20] conducted a systematic literature study to identify agile release engineering practices. [21] conducted a literature study to report on software release planning models.

The focus of the majority of publications on release planning models aim at several kinds of mathematical models and simulations [22], which are ineffectual in complex industries [23]. Practitioners said that these approaches are either too simple to generate a benefit or so difficult that they cannot reconstruct the whole process created [24, 25].

In total, there is no direct related work that considers release planning in coexisting traditional and agile processes in the automotive domain. Some work deals with agile release planning, but none of the identified sources deals with the hybrid project environment that is targeted. In order to better understand release planning in such a hybrid project environment, we conducted a survey study at an automotive case company [9] and present the updated results in the following sections.

## 3  Research Approach

The research approach is presented including the research questions and design, the data collection and analysis procedure, the research site and participants, as well as the threats to validity.

### 3.1  Research Questions

The survey study aims to answer the following research question: What are the challenges and consequences of the qualification phase in an automotive hybrid project environment? To answer this question, three research questions were defined:

- RQ1. What are challenges concerning the qualification phase in a hybrid project environment?
- RQ2. What are the specific challenges of agile projects embedded in a traditional development context?
- RQ3. How could agility address the identified challenges?

## 3.2  Research Design

To answer the research questions, we selected a two-step research approach. First, we set up an exploratory, qualitative interview study within a German automotive OEM. An interview guide for identifying challenges and problems with regard to the release planning process was specified. The interview guide was tested in a pilot interview. Emerging issues, such as vague phrases, were addressed before the qualitative interview study was conducted. In the second step, an online survey questionnaire was built to validate the challenges identified from the qualitative interview study in detail.

The data collection instrument was a questionnaire that contained 31 open and closed questions structured into six categories (cf. Table 1).

**Table 1.**  Survey questionnaire

| Category | ID | Question |
|---|---|---|
| Context | 1 | What is your current role? [free text] |
| | 2 | How long have you been working in that role? [free text] |
| | 3 | What are you working on in your project? [E/E ECU, software component, function, connect service, vehicle project] |
| | 4 | Please select a sector to classify your project. [powertrain electronics, body electronics, infotainment, project is safety-critical, others] |
| | 5 | What kind of development method do you use? (agile, hybrid, or traditional) [use of adapted agile methods, hybrid methods, traditional approaches] |
| | 6 | If you are using agile or hybrid methods, please specify the method. [free text] |
| Qualification phase | 7 | What do you think about the current number of qualification phases (incl. additional qualification phase)? [too high, adequate, too low] |
| | 8 | How often are you able to generate current software versions ready to deliver? [never, seldom, often, always] |
| | 9 | Do you receive feedback about the qualification phase on time? [never, seldom, often, always] |
| | 10 | How often should a qualification phase take place in order for you to be ready to deliver? [every week, once a month, every 3 months, at larger intervals] |
| | 11 | Would additional releases in terms of partial composites with reduced test scope be helpful for safeguarding dependent ECUs? [yes, partially, no] |

*(continued)*

**Table 1.** (*continued*)

| Planning | 12 | Is an initial planning of content possible? [never, seldom, often, always] |
|---|---|---|
| | 13 | Does an initial planning of content make sense? [never, seldom, often, always] |
| | 14 | How often is the content of the initial planning still up-to-date at the beginning of a qualification phase? [never, seldom, often, always] |
| | 15 | How difficult is it to get planning information for the relevant counterparts? [very difficult, difficult, easy, very easy] |
| | 16 | To what extent do management decisions, external influencing factors, or externally determined decisions influence your development process? [no impact, weak impact, strong impact, very strong impact] |
| Integration | 17 | To what extent does bug fixing affect the timely implementation of planned functionalities for the next qualification phase? [no impact, weak impact, strong impact, very strong impact] |
| | 18 | It is inevitable that software versions are released that are suboptimal concerning quality or content. [yes, partially, no] |
| | 19 | What kind of activities dominate your daily routine during a qualification phase? [free text] |
| | 20 | Rate the following statement: Additional qualification phases are necessary. [yes, partially, no] |
| | 21 | Rate the following statement: Additional qualification phases are reasonable. [yes, partially, no] |
| Coordination | 22 | Is the status of development transparent to you at any time? [yes, partially, no] |
| | 23 | Is the status of development of your stakeholders transparent to you at any time? [yes, partially, no] |
| | 24 | How important is the transparency of the development status of your relevant counterparts to you? [totally unimportant, unimportant, important, very important] |
| | 25 | Rate the following statements: <br> - Stakeholder/Interfaces are known [Disagree, rather disagree, rather agree, agree] <br> - Quality of coordination is good. [Disagree, rather disagree, rather agree, agree] |
| Testing | 26 | Development can no longer handle the high number of bug reports. [Disagree, rather disagree, rather agree, agree] |
| | 27 | Problem resolution management can no longer handle the high number of bug reports. [Disagree, rather disagree, rather agree, agree] |
| | 28 | What are the reasons for the high number of tickets? [free text] |
| | 29 | Do all planned changes to the ECU network have to be fully tested for each qualification phase? [yes, partially, no] |
| | 30 | Do all types of tests have to be performed for every ECU for each qualification phase? [yes, partially, no] |
| | 31 | When do all ECUs have to be fully tested? [every qualification phase, depending on the changes, not mandatory] |

The categories and questions were derived from the insights gained in the previous interviews and match the four aspects of release planning (c.f. Sect. 2.2). The questions were originally written in German. The questionnaire went through four review cycles by an independent researcher as well as by a specialist from the case company. The authors discussed the review comments and improved the questionnaire.

In the first category, we elicited the "Context", such as role and experience of the participant, as well as project type, area, and the development method used (traditional vs. agile). The second category, "Qualification Phase", aimed at evaluating how many qualification phases are feasible. The third category, "Planning", was for evaluating the need to have an initial plan as well as external influences on such a plan. At a certain point in the development process, an initial planning of the functional scope of an ECU must be submitted for each release. In addition to general ECU information, deviations from the required functional, network and diagnostic maturity levels must also be specified. We examined the need for additional qualification phases in the fourth category "Integration". Integration is an upstream part of the actual process and represents the integration of one or more ECUs into a whole network. Transparency of the status quo and the quality of coordination were the focus of the fifth category, "Coordination". Finally, we covered all questions related to "Testing" in the last category, trying to evaluate which kind and intensity of tests are necessary and if and why there are so many bug reports. The test phase focuses on the execution of the qualification phase and is therefore a main activity.

### 3.3   Data Collection and Analysis Procedure

To identify the main challenges, the first researcher conducted 26 semi-structured interviews, which took between 30 and 60 min each. The information from each interview was incorporated into later interviews. Because these interviews did not allow for quantitative results, an online survey was conducted to confirm the challenges and to draw a more complete picture by consulting different participants. This allows for quantitative results, but gave every participant the chance to provide further qualitative results by sharing their experiences.

During the first run of the online survey (results presented in [reference]), 95 potential participants were selected based on their roles, to cover all perspectives. Then the participants were invited via an email motivating the goal of the study and outlining the contents and the time expected to answer the questionnaire. A reminder email was sent after one week. Also, one of the participants forwarded the questionnaire to an additional group of 25 people. The survey was open from November to December 2018 and resulted in 55 respondents of which 39 completely filled out the whole questionnaire.

In addition to [9], we run the online survey a second time. Reasons were to give everyone who missed the first round an opportunity to share their experiences, and to increase the number of respondents in order to increase the validity of the results. The survey was opened up at the end of February 2019 for a duration of two weeks. Afterwards, combined with the results of the first round [9], we ended up with 94 respondents, of which 56 completely filled out the questionnaire.

After extracting the data from the online survey tool into an Excel document, we analyzed the answers for completeness. There were 56 complete responses, meaning all six pages of the questionnaire had been answered and thus the survey had been officially finished. In addition, there were 38 incomplete answers where the questionnaire was not finished. Of these 38 incomplete answers, 11 respondents only finished the first category (Context), while 20 respondents did not even finish the first questions. Only three respondents finished the second category (Qualification Phase), two respondents stopped after category 3 (Planning) and 4 (Integration) each. Although we had access to the incomplete data sets, we decided to only consider the complete data sets for further analysis. Afterwards, we conducted a descriptive analysis of the individual questions and analyzed the textual answers to identify common opinions.

### 3.4    Research Site and Participants

This study was conducted at Dr. Ing. h. c. F. Porsche AG, a manufacturer that builds sports cars for everyday driving. The division EE within Dr. Ing. h. c. F. Porsche AG in Weissach, Germany, is responsible for the development process of electronic systems and its integration into the development process of the complete vehicle. For achieving this goal, transparent development processes and hence accurate release planning are essential.

The target population of our survey included all roles involved in the qualification phase process of automotive products where the subprojects differed in terms of the development approaches used, including agile as well as traditional methods. The sample selected consisted of stakeholders from Dr. Ing. h. c. F. Porsche AG involved in release planning activities. The participants were expected to be motivated enough to answer the comprehensive questionnaire because they anticipated improvements based on the findings that reflect their current situation.

### 3.5    Threats to Validity

As the results only represent one specific case, it might not be possible to generalize them. However, the fact that the case company has the same framework conditions (regulated domains, complex supplier relationships and high safety requirements) as similar OEMs, others could benefit from the findings. The issues that were identified in the earlier interviews were addressed in the questionnaire, whereas new survey participants did not have a chance to add more individual problems during the online survey. There might be a bias concerning the stakeholders who participated. Some roles are overrepresented, while other relevant roles were not represented by many participants. This might have led to results that are skewed towards the opinion of certain roles. Nonetheless, many different roles participated in the study, providing answers from many perspectives. As in all surveys, non-response bias could have led to missing the opinions of certain participants. The second round of the interview study was conducted at a later point of time, which could have led to a difference in the perception of the participants. However, a comparison of results of the first with the second round showed that the answers of all participants followed the same trend.

# 4 Survey Results

This section contains the demographics and context of the respondents, followed by the presentation and discussion of the results of this work structured along the research questions.

## 4.1 Context

The respondents' professional experience in their current role (Q1) was slightly below six years on average, with a minimum of one year and a maximum of 20 years (Q2). 18 respondents (32%) had management roles related to projects, products, functions, integration, testing, quality, data, processes, or other related disciplines. 22 participants (39%) represented the operational level. The remaining respondents had roles with responsibilities related to the environment of qualification phases (n = 16; 29%).

The respondents described their working environment using one or more categories (Q3). Most participants reported working in vehicle projects (n = 29), development of E/E components (n = 23), development of functions (n = 22), development of software components (n = 17), and connected services (n = 16). Others (n = 7) dealt with IT backend, cross-project integration, distributed functions, or quality.

27% (n = 15) of the respondents answered that their project was safety-critical. Most participants assigned their project to the area of infotainment (n = 26), followed by electronics for car bodies (n = 14) and electronics for engines (n = 8). Regarding the 25 individual answers, ten participants reported working on crosscutting topics (Q4).

Most respondents reported using traditional development or project management approaches such as the V-model or sequential approaches (n = 34). Only twelve respondents used adapted agile methods, and ten persons used hybrid approaches, which was defined as strongly adapted agile methods or use of only single agile practices (Q5). This showed that about 40% of the participants were using agile concepts at the time.

Agile implementations were based on Scrum or the Porsche-specific adaption of agile methods. One person even reported scaled agile and lean at the unit level combined with an adapted Scaled Agile Framework (SAFe). Single agile practices like daily standups, user stories, backlogs, retrospectives, or the Scrum Master role were used in traditional projects. Some respondents reported using both agile and traditional approaches at different project levels. One answer stated that agile was being used at the team level together with the V-model for whole projects, while another respondent reported using a sprint-like approach within the V-model due to highly dynamic changes in requirements. Another respondent indicated the use of different development paradigms in different life cycle phases (Q6).

## 4.2 RQ1: Current Challenges

In the following, the current challenges concerning the qualification phase in a hybrid project environment will be presented and discussed along the categories of the survey questionnaire.

**(1) Qualification phase.** The majority of all participants (n = 30; 54%) stated that the current number of releases (p.a.), including all additional qualification phases (AQPs) and special qualification, is too high (Q7). On the other hand, there are 14 participants that claim that this number is too low, while another 12 perceive this amount as the right number of releases. An analysis of the comments field of this question shows results relating to the regulated defined number of releases. It emerged from the free text that the regular number of QPs (without AQPs and special qualifications) is appropriate. Nevertheless, AQPs and special qualifications are inevitable in the project phase relating to the start of series production. The developers confirmed their opinion and asked for a higher number of qualification phases. The management group agreed with the regulated defined numbers.

Further information concerning the ordinary number of qualification phases was given by the group of developers using agile methods. For the majority of those participants, the absolute number of qualification phases is too low to use agile methods properly. They complained about the too great distance between two QP to integrate and test the new version more quickly.

The next issue concerned the delivery results (Q8). 52% of the survey participants answered that the required deliverable is seldom available in the required quality. On a closer look of these 52%, n = 12 of the management level answered that the deliverable is seldom available. In contrast, 46% of all participants replied that it is always (11%) or at least most of the time (35%) possible to create a delivery version for every requested release. Hence, there is a different perception of the definition of 'required quality' and what exists in reality.

45% of all participants (n = 25) answered that they mostly receive feedback about qualification phases on time (Q9), while ten participants (18%) claim to always be informed in time. A minority never receives feedback on time (n = 7; 12%), another 14 participants only do seldom (n = 14; 25%). A deeper analysis of the answers related to this question showed that it depends on the stakeholder and its required feedback. The management level wants to have early feedback in order to be able to intervene in time. However, the operational level needs feedback about the testing results in more detail, which takes time. Receiving feedback on time and in the required quality depends on different expectations and fixed targets.

The next question dealt with identifying a suitable number of qualification phases with regard to being able to generate a releasable software version (Q10). Half of the participants (n = 29; 52%) stated that qualification phases should take place at least each quarter of the year. Six participants (11%) said that the QP should take place each week, 14 participants (25%) wanted the QP to take place once a month. Only seven participants (12%) said that the QP should take place less often than each quarter of a year. In the comments, the participants emphasize that a regular QP should target testing on vehicle level. Therefore, a QP should serve the qualification of the whole vehicle network. In order to avoid big bang integration, smaller integration loops should be carried out in advance in order to achieve the greatest possible maturity for the QP.

In the last question (Q11) of this category, 50% of participants called for additional qualification phases with reduced test scopes. Only five participants (9%) said that such additional QPs would not be helpful, the remaining 23 respondents (41%) agreed in parts. On a closer look, 68% of all participants of the operational level want to have a higher number of QPs on condition that not the whole scope has to be tested. Nonetheless, this statement raises concerns, since the operational level answered in Q8 and Q10 that they are not always able to release good quality with the regular number of QPs.

**(2) Planning.** This category highlights the characteristics around planning. The first question (Q12) aimed at evaluating the feasibility of initial planning at the beginning of the project. 48% of the participants in our study reported that initial planning is mostly or always possible, and the others (52%) answered that such a plan is rarely or never possible. At the beginning of a project, the decisions for or against a supplier have sometimes not been made yet. That is one reason why it is difficult to generate an initial planning. Another person replied that requirements for functions are the results of testing, which is done further on in the development process.

In a further question, the participants were asked if such initial planning would be meaningful (Q13). A majority (n = 34; 61%) stated that planning at the beginning of a project is mostly (20%) or always (41%) reasonable because it is a resilient starting point for further steps. On a closer inspection, only 18% of all developers are in favor of an initial planning. The other half do not consider planning effective. Participants also mentioned the existing change management process as an argument for initial planning, which permits updates at any time.

The next question (Q14) regarding this topic dealt with the projected content before the next release in terms of timeliness. The results show that scheduled content is frequently impossible to implement in practice (80%). No participant stated that the content is still up to date at the start of a new release, only 11 participants (20%) claimed it is up to date most of the time. The majority of the participants stated that awareness still exists for high quality in planning. Planning updates have to pass a committee, which is one reason why change requests are not implemented in the current release. Also some areas, such as the area "connected car", are very dynamic, which is another reason for the bad current state of planning, which is not up-to-date.

Receiving information about planning details from the relevant stakeholders is perceived as challenging (Q15). Most of the respondents replied that obtaining information on time is difficult (59%) or very difficult (14%), because there are no regulated tasks nor a consistent workflow for changing the relevant information. The remaining participants perceived it to be easy (23%) or very easy (3%) to receive planning information.

Another issue is the impact of management decisions during the development cycle (Q16), which implies that these cannot be implemented easily. A significant majority of the respondents rated the influence of external decisions on the course of development as strong (50%) or very strong (43%) and reported that the development of new functionality suffers from having to deal with unexpected changes demanded by management. Some respondents complained about management decisions that change the backlog priority and have severe effects on further procedures. Only four participants perceive the influence to be weak (7%), no participant stated that there is no influence.

**(3) Integration.** This category contains the results relating to the challenges of software and hardware integration during a development cycle. During a qualification phase, new software versions are tested at different levels of integration. The test results and even bug fixing have a great impact on the subsequent procedure (Q17). Most of the participants answered that bug fixing has a strong effect (50%) or very strong effect (29%) on their timely implementation related to the next release. Only three participants (5%) claimed that there is no influence. The remaining 16% reported a weak influence. 73% of the operational level stated that debugging has a strong effect on the upcoming tasks. Since the project plan does not consider an extra buffer, fixing bugs can even lead to delays of the next scheduled functions.

This non-existing hold is one of the main reasons for bad quality releases (Q18). Almost all interviewees admitted that delivering software versions with high quality is infeasible (46%) or partly infeasible (50%) when they also have to provide the content planned for the next release. The results considered for integration have low maturity, due to the increasing pressure of costs and deadlines.

Another question in this category dealt with the activities during a qualification phase (Q19). The main activities or tasks linked to the respective role are: Management is engaged in coordination and ensuring the scheduled scope with regard to the next release. At the operational level, tracking of test results and analysis of upcoming bug tickets are the main concerns. Both groups have to handle the subsequent deliveries.

For this reason, additional qualification phases (AQP) have been established subsequent to the original deadline. We wanted to know if such AQPs are necessary (Q20) and reasonable (Q21). 64% of all participants considered AQPs necessary, 29% partly necessary and there were only 7% of participants that claimed that AQPs are not necessary. After taking a closer look, 60% the operational level call for AQPs as a necessary action. 41% of all participants were convinced that AQPs are reasonable, 30% stated that they are partly meaningful. There were 29% of respondents that claimed that AQPs are not meaningful. However, 27% of the operational level considered AQPs to be of partly use. The main reasons given by the participants for subsequent integrations were poor software quality, lack of adherence to delivery dates on the part of the suppliers, poor scheduling without buffering, and no complete bug fixing from the previous qualification phase.

**(4) Coordination.** Transparency and coordination were the relevant aspects in this category (Q22). We asked whether the current development status of the respondents' own team or dependent teams is sufficiently transparent. Only 28% of all participants (n = 9) reported that their own development is transparent. The majority of respondents rated transparency as only partially existent (n = 30; 54%) or non-existent (n = 10; 18%).

The next question (Q23) dealt with the transparency of the status of projects by relevant stakeholders and relevant counterparts. Here, only 14% (n = 8) of the respondents answered that the development status of other projects is transparent for them. Most participants (n = 27; 48%) reported partial transparency, while 38% (n = 21) reported a lack of transparency. Reasons for the lack of transparency were missing time and coordination mechanisms, and the use of outdated content of the release plans. The free text fields reveal that developers agree that generating transparency is a management task.

The transparency of the status quo of a certain development project is very important and closely linked to the quality of a release (Q24). 93% of the respondents supported the statement that having a transparent software version at any time is important (45%) or very important (48%). Transparency is necessary due to the complexity, dependency, and connectivity of software engineering.

Another question aimed at getting information about the communication structures within the company and involved persons from the release planning process (Q25). The participants had to rate whether they knew their interfaces and relevant stakeholders and whether the quality of the coordination was good. This rating had to be done for several interfaces: within the team, between team and testing, within the case company, within the company group, as well as towards external suppliers. The results presented in Fig. 5 (bottom figure) demonstrate that communication quality decreases with longer communication paths: Communication within a project was perceived as good, but the quality was perceived as decreasing in communication within the company and even worse in communication with suppliers (internal means company group and external suppliers). Similarly, the relevant stakeholders and interfaces of the wider project context were reported less known than those within the team (see Fig. 5, top figure).

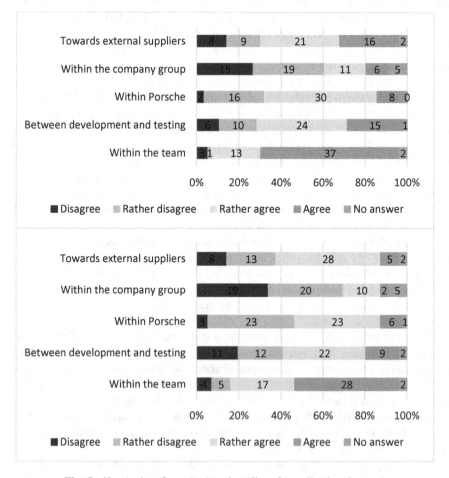

**Fig. 5.** Known interfaces (top) and quality of coordination (bottom)

**(5) Testing**. This category assesses the testing situation. The first question aimed to evaluate whether the number of bug reports is still controllable by development (Q26) or problem resolution management (Q27). Overall, the majority of the participants agreed (20%) or rather agreed (36%) that development is able to control the high number of bug reports. The remaining respondents had a tendency to disagree (25%) or disagreed (19%). Concerning problem resolution management, most participants disagreed (21%) or had a tendency to disagree (39%) that resolution management is able to cope with the number of bug reports. The minority of the participants agreed (14%) or rather agreed (25%).

Furthermore, the participants were asked about reasons for the high number of bug reports/tickets (Q28). The survey revealed that identifying errors is usually not done before the upcoming release due to insufficient development time, cost, and deadline pressure. It was reported that the intensity of testing by the supplier was not adequate. Other reasons given for the high number of error tickets were the rising complexity of the product itself, a lack of coordination within the team, and inadequate requirements engineering. Generally, it can be stated that the quality before a qualification phase is insufficient and questionable, endangering the success of the qualification phase.

Software changes may have severe effects on interfaces, which is why tests have to be done. The need for testing the software changes to the full extent for every qualification phase (Q29) was not seen by 13% of the respondents, who claimed that this is not necessary. Most respondents (55%) said that changes have to be tested to the full extent for every planned release. The remaining 32% partially agreed that testing is always necessary and specified in the comments specific situations where more testing was necessary or less testing was acceptable. Some stated that the scope of testing depends on the number of changes made or on the development phase. One respondent commented that it is not possible to test all changes; another one said that full testing is always necessary because cross-dependencies only become visible by testing within a release. Only 16% of the respondents agreed that all types of tests have to be performed in every release cycle (Q30). 36% disagreed with this statement and about half of them (48%) partially agreed. The participants further pointed out that conducting all tests is not feasible or that the necessary types of tests are predefined in the test strategy and depend on the change itself. Others reported that regression tests are often sufficient, or that full releases need to be tested more accurately than partial releases.

To save testing effort, it is important to know when comprehensive testing (including all types of tests) of all ECUs needs to be done (Q31). 79% of the respondents answered that testing needs to be done dependent on the software, hardware, or functional changes. Some respondents (16%) claimed that the ECUs have to be tested once per qualification phase, either at the beginning or at the end. 5% said that testing is not always necessary. One participant commented that due to the high product complexity and low software quality, all ECUs have to be tested as an integrated system with all possible tests, or at least with good regression tests. Another one claimed that comprehensive testing is not possible for all system parts, but major parts can be covered with a good testing strategy.

### 4.3    RQ2: Agile-Specific Challenges

Existing vehicle development processes emerged at a time when agility was not present yet and were formalized based on traditional development methodologies. Due to the regulations, strict production deadlines and the complexity in vehicle development, the need to have formal processes will remain. However, the potential to integrate agile processes must be evaluated in order to exploit the benefits of agility. New technologies such as cloud services implicate a stronger customer focus, to be able to respond more flexibly to customer needs, which results in conflicts with the slow and unresponsive traditional development. Innovation is happening fast in the automotive domain, and companies have to react in time to stay competitive.

Iterative cycles are already incorporated into many processes, but other concepts of agile methods initially designed for small teams are more difficult to integrate or synchronize with the existing rigid processes. The OEMs are currently performing a balancing act between fixed framework conditions and scope for flexibility. On the one hand, legal requirements, standards and production requirements must be observed and on the other hand, developers want to act more freely without being restricted by guidelines. The results of this survey indicate that this is not a simple procedure.

The survey revealed that if departments are already working with agile methods, they only use them to a certain extent. Our initial expectation was that agile methods are commonly used at least in fields such as connected car, with its digital services and shorter development cycles. The differences between our expectations and reality may be caused by the lack of a common understanding of agile methods. This is confirmed by the inconsistency of the answers by the respondents, who considered additional qualification phases necessary but at the same time did not demand more qualification phases. The reason for this may be a lack of knowledge about agile methods.

There is also a lack of suitable means of communication for short, regular exchanges aimed at establishing transparency between all participants. Such possibilities for fast feedback would also increase the overall quality of voting and benefit the flow of information. Respondents from agile projects reported that the length of release cycles is too long and does not suit agile approaches.

The fact that management decisions have such a strong influence on the further course of development illustrates that decisions are made at higher levels of hierarchy. In an optimal agile environment, the development team makes the decisions. Based on the priorities set by the Product Owner and the requirements dependencies identified by the development team, a Scrum team knows best how to achieve the best solutions. At the beginning of each iteration, they commit to a product increment that is valuable and achievable. If management forces decisions upon the team during an iteration, results can be expected to be suboptimal.

However, this is only the point of view of a single team. If each single team cannot meet their commitments, the qualification phase of an integrated product is going to raise problems. One reason is that the release plan, which considers dependencies between different projects, gets unofficially changed without being updated. That means the developers change their release plans on the operational level without having the change approved and without informing the affected interfaces.

## 4.4    RQ3. Improvements with Agile Methods

There are many challenges that are predestinated to be solved with agility. The survey revealed that transparency and coordination are highly important for a successful qualification phase. Some of the interviewees stated that the communication path in their department is too long, which causes loss of time and a lack of coordination. This argument is supported by the fact that some participants reported not knowing their interfaces and relevant stakeholders, resulting in bad synchronization and integration structures. By using agile development and by having small working groups with no typical hierarchy, interface management as well as short communication paths could become possible [26].

Currently, additional qualification phases are started to fix the remaining bugs or to finish some functionalities that had been planned for the previous release cycle. Due to the increased effort for these activities, the planned results for the next release cycle cannot be fully achieved, pushing a wave of additional efforts, e.g., for coordinating additional qualification phases, through the whole project. Increased transparency regarding the content that was finished in an iteration can be achieved with a definition of done and by incorporating time-boxed sprints. At the end of each sprint, the status quo is assessed, and unfinished requirements can be planned for the next sprint.

Another characteristic of sprints is that requirements are usually not changed, especially not from outside the team. This would also help to stabilize the release plan, which would help to achieve higher-quality products delivered for integration by each single team. Sprints are usually short iterations of several weeks. Respondents from agile projects reported that the length of release cycles is too long, and that they would prefer receiving feedback earlier. This issue leads to work overload and defined timelines not being achieved, which ultimately leads to lower software quality. In addition, development costs increase due to many additional qualification phases. By using agile methods and more intermediate steps, including regular assessments of the project state, discrepancies could be identified earlier.

Agile teams use face-to-face communication and daily standups to synchronize their work in order to achieve their sprint goal. In a scaled environment, so-called Scrum-of-Scrums are scaled daily standups where representatives of different teams synchronize their development status and plan their dependencies. The Scaled Agile Framework (SAFe) uses an architectural runway to coordinate architectural decisions between the single development teams to facilitate integration.

Continuous integration is commonly used in agile projects and could be of benefit in qualification phases. Integrating smaller work products incrementally can replace a larger and more complex final integration and provides early transparency about the finished content of the release as well as raising awareness of dependencies.

In general, regular retrospectives can be held at the end of each sprint, helping the team to raise issues impeding their work and improve their development process. Conducting retrospectives together with relevant stakeholders and dependent projects helps to continuously improve collaboration between teams.

## 5  Conclusion and Future Work

Agile development has its origins in the information systems domain. Organizations from regulated domains like the automotive domain also want to benefit from agility. Due to regulations and the complexity of systems, traditional sequential processes are still in place and have to be synchronized with the coexisting agile and hybrid development approaches. Qualification phases of traditional, hybrid as well as agile projects are difficult. Release planning in such a hybrid project environment needs to be improved. In this research, we presented this research topic by formulating research goal and questions and by detailing the research background. An investigation of related work showed that there is a research gap concerning this topic. We elicited the state of the practice from 56 respondents of a German automotive Original Equipment Manufacturer. The identified challenges, such as lack of transparency, show the problems related to release planning in this specific context. We outlined how agile concepts could improve some of the identified challenges and thus provided recommendations for practitioners.

In future work, the survey questionnaire can be adapted to collect experiences outside the case company, in order to check whether there are similar problems at other automotive companies or even companies from other regulated domains that are developing complex systems in a hybrid project environment. Finally, solutions for the identified challenges need to be identified in order to come up with a suitable release planning process in the context of co-existing traditional and agile approaches.

## References

1. VersionOne: the 13th annual state of agile report (2019). www.collab.net
2. Diebold, P., Zehler, T.: The right degree of agility in rich processes. Managing Software Process Evolution, pp. 15–37. Springer, Cham (2016). https://doi.org/10.1007/978-3-319-31545-4_2
3. Klünder, J., et al.: HELENA Study: reasons for combining agile and traditional software development approaches in German companies. In: Felderer, M., Méndez Fernández, D., Turhan, B., Kalinowski, M., Sarro, F., Winkler, D. (eds.) PROFES 2017. LNCS, vol. 10611, pp. 428–434. Springer, Cham (2017). https://doi.org/10.1007/978-3-319-69926-4_32
4. Diebold, P., Theobald, S.: How is agile development currently being used in regulated embedded domains? J. Softw. Evol. Process 30(8), e1935 (2018). https://doi.org/10.1002/smr.1935
5. Hohl, P., Münch, J., Schneider, K., Stupperich, M.: Forces that prevent agile adoption in the automotive domain. In: Abrahamsson, P., Jedlitschka, A., Nguyen Duc, A., Felderer, M., Amasaki, S., Mikkonen, T. (eds.) PROFES 2016. LNCS, vol. 10027, pp. 468–476. Springer, Cham (2016). https://doi.org/10.1007/978-3-319-49094-6_32
6. Kuhrmann, M., et al.: Hybrid software and system development in practice: waterfall, scrum, and beyond. In: Proceedings of the 2017 International Conference on Software and System Process, pp. 30–39 (2017). https://doi.org/10.1145/3084100.3084104
7. Theobald, S., Diebold, P.: Interface problems of agile in a non-agile environment. In: Garbajosa, J., Wang, X., Aguiar, A. (eds.) XP 2018. LNBIP, vol. 314, pp. 123–130. Springer, Cham (2018). https://doi.org/10.1007/978-3-319-91602-6_8

8. Broy, M.: Challenges in automotive software engineering. In: Proceedings of the 28th International Conference on Software Engineering, pp. 33–42. ACM (2006). https://doi.org/10.1145/1134285.1134292

9. Marner, K., Theobald, S., Wagner, S.: Real-Life challenges in automotive release planning. In: Proceedings of the Federated Conference on Computer Science and Information Systems, pp. 831–839 (2019). https://doi.org/10.15439/2019f326

10. Ruhe, G., Saliu, M.O.: The art and science of software release planning. IEEE Softw. **22**(6), 47–53 (2005)

11. Dr. Ing. h.c. F. Porsche AG: Methodenleitfaden für agiles Arbeiten bei Porsche (guidelines for agility at Porsche) (2018)

12. Heikkilä, V.T., Paasivaara, M., Rautiainen, K., Lassenius, C., Toivola, T., Järvinen, J.: Operational release planning in large-scale scrum with multiple stakeholders–a longitudinal case study at F-Secure Corporation. In: Information and Software Technology, vol. 57, pp. 116–140 (2015). https://doi.org/10.1016/j.infsof.2014.09.005

13. Sax, E., Reussner, R., Guissouma, H., Klare, H.: A Survey on the State and Future of Automotive Software Release and Configuration Management. Karlsruhe Reports in Informatics, 11 (2017). https://doi.org/10.5445/ir/1000075673

14. Bestfleisch, U., Herbst, J., Reichert, M.: Requirements for the workflow-based support of release management processes in the automotive sector. In: Proceedings of the 12th European Concurrent Engineering Conference ECEC 2005 (2005)

15. Müller, D., Herbst, J., Hammori, M., Reichert, M.: IT support for release management processes in the automotive industry. In: Dustdar, S., Fiadeiro, J.L., Sheth, Amit P. (eds.) BPM 2006. LNCS, vol. 4102, pp. 368–377. Springer, Heidelberg (2006). https://doi.org/10.1007/11841760_26

16. Lindgren, M., Land, R., Norström, C., Wall, A.: Key aspects of software release planning in industry. In: Proceedings of the 19th Australian Conference on Software Engineering, pp. 320–329 (2008). https://doi.org/10.1109/aswec.2008.4483220

17. Danesh, A.S., Ahmad, R.B., Saybani, M.R., Tahir, A.: Companies approaches in software release planning-based on multiple case studies. JSW **7**(2), 471–478 (2012). https://doi.org/10.4304/jsw.7.2.471-478

18. Heikkilä, Ville T., Paasivaara, M., Lassenius, C., Engblom, C.: Continuous release planning in a large-scale scrum development organization at ericsson. In: Baumeister, H., Weber, B. (eds.) XP 2013. LNBIP, vol. 149, pp. 195–209. Springer, Heidelberg (2013). https://doi.org/10.1007/978-3-642-38314-4_14

19. Heikkilä, V., Rautiainen, K., Jansen, S.: A revelatory case study on scaling agile release planning. In: Proceedings of the 2010 36th EUROMICRO Conference on Software Engineering and Advanced Applications, pp. 289–296 (2010). https://doi.org/10.1109/seaa.2010.37

20. Karvonen, T., Behutiye, W., Oivo, M., Kuvaja, P.: Systematic literature review on the impacts of agile release engineering practices. Inf. Softw. Technol. **86**, 87–100 (2017). https://doi.org/10.1016/j.infsof.2017.01.009

21. Ameller, D., Farré, C., Franch, X., Rufian, G.: A survey on software release planning models. In: Abrahamsson, P., Jedlitschka, A., Nguyen Duc, A., Felderer, M., Amasaki, S., Mikkonen, T. (eds.) PROFES 2016. LNCS, vol. 10027, pp. 48–65. Springer, Cham (2016). https://doi.org/10.1007/978-3-319-49094-6_4

22. Svahnberg, M., Gorschek, T., Feldt, R., Torkar, R., Saleem, S.B., Shafique, M.U.: A systematic review on strategic release planning models. Inf. Softw. Technol. **52**, 237–248 (2010). https://doi.org/10.1016/j.infsof.2009.11.006

23. Carlshamre, P.: Release planning in market-driven software product development: provoking an understanding. Requir. Eng. 7(3), 139–151 (2002). https://doi.org/10.1007/s007660200010

24. Jantunen, S., Lehtola, L., Gause, D.C., Dumdum, U.R., Barnes, R.J.: The challenge of release planning. In: Proceedings of the Fifth International Workshop on Software Product Management, pp. 36–45 (2011). https://doi.org/10.1109/iwspm.2011.6046202

25. Benestad, H.C., Hannay, J.E: A comparison of model-based and judgment-based release planning in incremental software projects. In: Proceedings of the 33rd International Conference on Software Engineering, pp. 766–775 (2011). https://doi.org/10.1145/1985793.1985901

26. Spiegler, S.V., Heinecke, C., Wagner, S.: Leadership gap in agile teams: how teams and scrum masters mature. In: Kruchten, P., Fraser, S., Coallier, F. (eds.) XP 2019. LNBIP, vol. 355, pp. 37–52. Springer, Cham (2019). https://doi.org/10.1007/978-3-030-19034-7_3

# Identification of the Agile Mindset
# and Its Comparison to the Competencies
# of Selected Agile Roles

Jakub Miler[1]([✉]) and Paulina Gaida[2]

[1] Faculty of Electronics, Telecommunications and Informatics,
Gdańsk University of Technology, Gdańsk, Poland
jakub.miler@pg.edu.pl
[2] Omida Finance sp. z o.o, Gdańsk, Poland
paulina.gaida@gmail.com

**Abstract.** In this paper we present the results of the identification and evaluation of the elements of an agile mindset as well as its comparison to the competence models for the roles of Scrum Master, Product Owner and agile analyst. We have identified 70 unique agile mindset elements from literature and 5 interviews with experts. Based on an opinion survey among 52 agile practitioners we evaluated the importance of 26 selected elements of the agile mindset to the effectiveness of an agile team. The competence models contain 29 competencies of a Scrum Master, 16 competencies of a Product Owner and 40 competencies of an agile analyst, divided into behavioral, technical and contextual ones. We discuss which agile mindset elements are important to each agile role. This paper is an extended version of the paper titled "On the Agile Mindset of an Effective Team – An Industrial Opinion Survey" presented at the 3rd International Conference on Lean and Agile Software Development LASD 2019 [28].

## 1 Introduction

Agile Manifesto [1] together with the principles behind the Agile Manifesto [2] founded a set of driving values and key principles for the agile software development. Agile practitioners emphasize that effective performance of an agile team requires not only a given set of procedures, techniques and rituals, but, above all, a particular attitude, way of thinking and behavior of both the individuals and the entire team – a so called 'agile mindset' [3, 4].

Working in agile teams requires many non-technical and social competencies related to communication, organization, business, improvement and many more [5]. These are not the typical strong competencies among software engineers [6], which is why they require support of Scrum Masters, mentors and coaches to develop deep understanding of the fundamentals of Agile. Agile mindset, by addressing all of these competence areas and by suggesting important factors to the effective teamwork, supports practitioners in mastering Agile in their projects [4]. Altogether, developing the proper agile mindset contributes to the increasing success of agile software projects [7].

A. Przybyłek and M. E. Morales-Trujillo (Eds.): LASD 2019/MIDI 2019, LNBIP 376, pp. 41–62, 2020.
https://doi.org/10.1007/978-3-030-37534-8_3

The principles behind the Agile Manifesto themselves [2] recommend such attitudes and behaviors as focus on customer satisfaction, openness to change, face-to-face communication, sustainable development, simplicity, self-organization and improvement by frequent reflection. The agile methods such as Scrum [8], Kanban [9], SAFe [10] and other elaborate these principles further on, however the evolution of the IT industry since the Agile Manifesto calls for deeper and more current insight into the concept of 'being and working agile'. In our research, we assume the definition of 'an agile mindset' as a set of one's attitudes, behaviors and ways of thinking that enhance their and their team's effectiveness in working following the agile values and principles to the benefit of the customers.

The importance of particular elements of an agile mindset may depend on the role in an Agile team. The tasks and responsibilities of Scrum Masters, Product Owners, developers, analysts, architects, and testers remain different and possibly require a different way of thinking. The relation of agile mindset elements to the recommended competencies of particular roles may provide additional dimension to the concept of practical agile mindset.

This research aims at studying the elements of the agile mindset, their importance to the effectiveness of an agile team and their relation to Agile Principles and preferred competencies of selected agile roles. We have formulated the following research questions:

- RQ1: What agile mindset should the members of an agile team have in general?
- RQ2: What is the importance of the particular agile mindset elements to the effectiveness of an agile team?
- RQ3: What are the most important elements of the agile mindset to the effectiveness of an agile team?
- RQ4: What is the relation of the important agile mindset elements to the principles behind Agile Manifesto?
- RQ5: What agile mindset elements are recommended for the roles of Scrum Master, Product Owner and agile analyst?

The main contribution of this paper is the broad identification of the elements of agile mindset, the preliminary evaluation of their importance to the effectiveness of an agile team as well as mapping the selected agile mindset elements onto the competencies of the selected agile roles. This extends the reviewed literature with deeper understanding of the concept of 'agile mindset', the relative importance of its elements in an entire team and the importance of these elements to the roles of Scrum Master, Product Owner and agile analyst.

The paper is structured as follows. Section 2 presents our research method of identification and evaluation of the agile mindset elements as well as the methods of constructing the competence models. Section 3 reports the results of the identification and evaluation of the agile mindset based on the literature review, the interviews with experts, and the survey. Section 4 presents the competence models of Scrum Master, Product Owner and agile analyst. Section 5 shows the comparison of the agile mindset, the agile principles and the competence models, and discusses the observations. Section 6 discusses threats to the validity of this research as well as reports on the analysis of confounding variables. Section 7 sums up the conclusions.

## 2   Research Method

Our research comprised three steps: (1) identification of the elements of an agile mindset and their categorization, (2) selection and evaluation of the relative importance of the agile mindset elements to the effectiveness of an agile team, (3) comparison of the evaluated agile mindset elements to the principles behind Agile Manifesto and competencies of Scrum Master, Product Owner and agile analyst.

The first step involved the review of current literature and the interviews with experts from industry. The literature review covered mainly grey literature (books, blogs, portals), as the scientific databases such as Scopus or Web of Science provided very few results. We have focused on Internet sources reporting on industrial practice or written by agile practitioners and published by renowned publishers or portals. In total, we analyzed 11 literature sources.

To identify the agile mindset elements more thoroughly, we have carried out 5 structured interviews with industry experts with 2 to 5 years of experience in agile teams. They mostly worked as developers and Scrum Masters with various agile methods. The characteristics of the interviewed experts are given in Table 1. Experience is given in years.

**Table 1.** Characteristics of the experts interviewed on the agile mindset [28]

| ID | Position | Exp. | Methods |
|----|----------|------|---------|
| A | Developer | 3 | Scrum |
| B | Developer, tester | 2 | Kanban |
| C | Developer | 2 | Scrum |
| D | Scrum Master, Agile Coach | 5 | Scrum, Kanban, XP |
| E | Scrum Master | 3 | Scrum, Kanban, Scrumban |

The interviews were carried out in late May – early June 2018 in a form of face to face meetings. Experts A to C were not provided the interview questions in advance, which resulted in limited answers. Thus, experts D and E were sent the questions before the interview, which allowed them to think over their answers and generally resulted in more original insight into the subject matter. We have applied the following interview guide:

I.  Preliminary questions:
   (a)  For how long have you been working in agile teams?
   (b)  What methodology are you using in your projects (Scrum, Kanban, XP - Extreme Programming, others)?
   (c)  What is your role in the team (developer, tester, Scrum Master, etc.)?
II. General questions about the philosophy of agility:
   (a)  What is agility for you?
   (b)  What does "agile mindset" mean for you?

III. Questions about agile mindset elements (at least 3 elements from each question):
   (a) Which beliefs do you think are necessary to have the agile mindset?
   (b) What are the most important values for a person with the agile mindset?
   (c) What principles should be followed by a person with the agile mindset?
IV. Questions about the importance of agile mindset elements (at least 5 elements from each question):
   (a) What are the most important attitudes, rules and behaviors at the interpersonal level in an agile team?
   (b) What are the most important attitudes, rules and behaviors in the work organization of an agile team?
   (c) What are the most important attitudes, rules and behaviors when dealing with customers in an agile team?
V. Questions about the impact of agile mindset on work efficiency:
   (a) What attitudes, behaviors and beliefs have the greatest impact on the efficiency of agile teams (name at least 5)?
   (b) Has your team worked inefficiently for reasons related to the agile mindset? What were these reasons?
   (c) Do you think it is necessary to have the agile mindset to work effectively in an agile team? Why?

Categorization of the identified agile mindset elements was done a posteriori based on keyword analysis in the results of the literature review. The same categorization was used for the interview results. The final list of identified agile mindset elements was elaborated by summing the sets of elements in the literature review results and interview results in each category, followed by merging the duplicates. We have noted the number of times each element was mentioned in the literature and the interviews (i.e. number of literature sources and number of experts, respectively, see Tables 2, 3, 4 and 5).

The total number of identified agile mindset elements exceeded the capacity of a practical survey, so we had to select a subset of elements for further evaluation. As we aimed at one question per agile mindset element, we wanted to select no more than 30 agile mindset elements based on their frequency in sources (which is not equivalent to importance, however). We have decided to include the elements found in at least 6 out of 11 literature sources or provided by at least 2 out of 5 experts. These thresholds assume the majority of literature sources and some minimal agreement of the experts. Such thresholds favor the elements given by the experts, but this was our deliberate decision. Finally, such criteria resulted in 26 agile mindset elements selected for further evaluation. Other elements may be investigated in a separate study.

To evaluate the relative importance of the selected agile mindset elements to the effectiveness of an agile team, we have run a survey among agile practitioners in the IT industry. The survey was built on-line with Google Forms and distributed via e-mail, Facebook, forums etc. Respondents were asked to give their opinion on the degree to which a particular agile mindset element enhances the effectiveness of an agile team in the Likert-type 6 level scale of 0 to 5, where 0 meant "no impact" and 5 meant "key impact". The answers were optional which accounted for the cases of respondents' indecision or insufficient knowledge. The survey was organized by agile mindset categories. Additionally, we asked about the respondents' experience and their role in agile teams. Although basic Likert scale is ordinal, we used the Likert-type interval scale with assigned values of 0 to 5 in the survey and the data analysis [11].

For the comparison we used the competence models of Scrum Master, Product Owner and agile analyst elaborated by Miler and his students between 2013 and 2017.

The Scrum Master's competence model was proposed by Wielemborek and Miler in 2016 [29]. This model is based on data extracted from 9 literature sources. The selected competencies were evaluated with an industrial opinion survey between June 2015 and July 2016. 56 respondents evaluated the importance of each competence to the Scrum Master's work in an ordinal scale of "key", "major", "minor", "negligible" with additional "I don't know" escape answer. The evaluation of importance was given as the summed percentage of "key" and "major" answers.

The competence model of a Product Owner was proposed by Jaszewski and Miler in 2013 [30]. This model is based on literature and covers the perspectives of other team members, the goals and responsibilities of this role, the tasks, the problems, the context of Scrum, social interactions, and particular artifacts and events of Scrum. This model has not been evaluated with a survey. The assessment of relative importance of particular competencies is based on their definition, contents and relations to other competencies.

The competence model of an agile analyst was proposed by Klima and Miler in 2017 [31]. This model is based on competencies identified with 5 interviews with experts with at least 10 years of experience in IT. 40 selected competencies were evaluated with the survey in August and September 2017. 50 participants evaluated the usefulness of each competence in an interval scale of 1 to 5 with additional "I don't know" escape answer.

The mapping of Agile principles and competencies of the models followed the keyword analysis and studying the definition of the particular competences in the source models.

## 3    The Agile Mindset

### 3.1    Identification of the Agile Mindset Elements

We have found the following literature on the topic of agile mindset using generic search engines such as Google:

1. "Agile Project Management: Managing for Success", a book by Crowder and Friess [12],
2. "The Agile Enterprise: Building and Running Agile Organizations", a book by Moreira [13],
3. "Being Agile: Your Roadmap to Successful Adoption of Agile", another book by Moreira [14],

4. "The Agile Mindset – Making Agile Processes Work", a book by Broza [4],
5. "Five Agile Factors: Helping Self-management to Self-reflect", a research paper by Stettina and Heijstek [15],
6. "Learning Agile: Understanding Scrum, XP, Lean and Kanban", a book by Stellman and Greene [16],
7. "What Exactly is the Agile Mindset?", an on-line article by Susan McIntosh for InfoQ portal [17],
8. "What does it mean to have an agile mindset?", an on-line article by Leanne Howard for AgileConnection portal [18],
9. "It's All About the Mindset", an on-line article by Parvatam for Scrum Alliance portal [19],
10. "Fixed Mindset versus Agile Mindset", an on-line article by Godugu for Scrum Alliance portal [20],
11. "Agile Is Not a Process, It's a Mindset", an on-line article by Rich for AgileConnection portal [21].

We have identified four categories of the agile mindset elements:

1. support for business goals,
2. relationships within the team,
3. individual features,
4. organization of work.

The first category, denoted by G symbol, focuses on the product value and relations with the customer. The second category, denoted by the T symbol, covers the issues of collaboration and relations within the agile team. The third category, denoted by the I symbol, tackles the behavior and attitude of an individual in an agile team. Finally, the fourth category, denoted by the O symbol, involves the aspects of methods, techniques and rules.

Studying the literature, we identified 58 distinct elements of the agile mindset. The list of these elements can be found in [28]. The 5 interviews with experts A to E provided 16, 18, 16, 17, and 16 agile mindset elements, respectively. Repeating elements were merged. In total, we identified 39 unique agile mindset elements with the interviews. Again, the list of these elements can be found in [28]. Finally, we merged the lists of agile mindset elements identified from literature and with the interviews.

The resulting list of unique agile mindset elements comprises 70 entries: 7 in the 'support for business goals' category, 20 in the 'relationships within the team' category, 24 in the 'individual features' category, and 19 in the 'organization of work' category. The elements in particular categories are shown in Tables 2, 3, 4 and 5. Each element is given a unique identifier prefixed with the category symbol. We provide the literature sources and the identifiers of experts who mentioned a particular element. $n_L$ column presents the number of literature sources, while $n_E$ column presents the number of experts mentioning each element.

**Table 2.** Identified agile mindset elements in the 'support for business goals' category

| ID | Element | Literature | Experts | $n_L$ | $n_E$ |
|---|---|---|---|---|---|
| G1 | Continuous delivery of a valuable product in short intervals | [4, 12–14, 16, 17, 19] | A | 7 | 1 |
| G2 | Cooperation with the customer based on partnership | [16] | B, C, D | 1 | 3 |
| G3 | Attitude towards customer satisfaction and needs | [12–14, 16, 18] | B, D | 5 | 2 |
| G4 | Belief that a working product is the basic measure of progress | [12–14] | – | 3 | 0 |
| G5 | Continuous cooperation with the customer | [4, 13, 14] | – | 3 | 0 |
| G6 | Accurate knowledge of who the customer is and what are their needs | [14] | – | 1 | 0 |
| G7 | No assumption that the customer is always right | – | A | 0 | 1 |

**Table 3.** Identified agile mindset elements in the 'relationships within the team' category

| ID | Element | Literature | Experts | $n_L$ | $n_E$ |
|---|---|---|---|---|---|
| T1 | Mutual trust | [4, 12–16, 19, 20] | A, B, C, D, E | 8 | 5 |
| T2 | Direct communication - face to face conversations | [4, 12–16, 19] | B, D | 7 | 2 |
| T3 | Focus on achieving common goal | [12–15, 18, 19] | A, C, E | 6 | 3 |
| T4 | Helping each other | [12, 14, 15] | B, C, D, E | 3 | 4 |
| T5 | Sincerity | [14, 21] | A, B, C, E | 2 | 4 |
| T6 | Mutual respect | [4, 14, 15, 17, 19] | A, B, D | 5 | 3 |
| T7 | Mutual listening | – | A, B, C | 0 | 3 |
| T8 | Equality in the team | [14] | B, C, D | 1 | 3 |
| T9 | Searching for a solution to the problem instead of finding the guilty | [18] | A, B | 1 | 2 |
| T10 | Team responsibility | [14, 16] | C, E | 2 | 2 |
| T11 | Taking into account the opinions of other people | [13, 15] | A | 2 | 1 |
| T12 | Respecting the experience and skills in all team members | [13, 14] | – | 2 | 0 |
| T13 | Listening to the opinions of other people | [14, 15] | – | 2 | 0 |
| T14 | Treating team members as people, not a resource | [14, 20] | – | 2 | 0 |
| T15 | Openness to others | [14, 20] | – | 2 | 0 |
| T16 | A relaxed atmosphere | [19, 20] | – | 2 | 0 |
| T17 | Sense of security | [4] | – | 1 | 0 |
| T18 | Focus on people instead of on processes | [16] | – | 1 | 0 |
| T19 | Not blaming each other | [16] | – | 1 | 0 |
| T20 | Not covering up the failures | [18] | – | 1 | 0 |

**Table 4.** Identified agile mindset elements in the 'individual features' category

| ID | Element | Literature | Experts | $n_L$ | $n_E$ |
|---|---|---|---|---|---|
| I1 | Continuous improvement and learning | [4, 12–18, 20] | B, C, E | 9 | 3 |
| I2 | Openness to change | [4, 12–14, 16–18, 20] | A, B, C, D, E | 8 | 5 |
| I3 | Being motivated | [12–14, 16, 19, 20] | A, B | 6 | 2 |
| I4 | Positive attitude | [18, 19] | A, B, E | 2 | 3 |
| I5 | Openness to criticism and feedback | – | A, D | 0 | 2 |
| I6 | Openness to others | – | C, D | 0 | 2 |
| I7 | Treating failure as an opportunity to learn, learning from mistakes | [4, 16, 17, 20, 21] | – | 5 | 0 |
| I8 | Creativity, innovation | [13, 18, 19] | D | 3 | 1 |
| I9 | Ability to accept failure and deal with it | [17, 18, 21] | – | 3 | 0 |
| I10 | Willingness to constantly acquire knowledge | [15, 18] | B | 2 | 1 |
| I11 | Taking risks | [4, 17] | – | 2 | 0 |
| I12 | Pragmatism | [18] | B | 1 | 1 |
| I13 | Assertiveness | [14] | – | 1 | 0 |
| I14 | Focus on the task being performed | [4] | – | 1 | 0 |
| I15 | A sense of pride in the job | [17] | – | 1 | 0 |
| I16 | Not giving up | [18] | – | 1 | 0 |
| I17 | Inquisitiveness | [18] | – | 1 | 0 |
| I18 | Individual initiative | – | B | 0 | 1 |
| I19 | Courage | – | B | 0 | 1 |
| I20 | Commitment | – | D | 0 | 1 |
| I21 | Being a visionary | – | D | 0 | 1 |
| I22 | Understanding the need for change | – | E | 0 | 1 |
| I23 | Responsibility | – | E | 0 | 1 |
| I24 | Understanding the significance of retrospectives | – | E | 0 | 1 |

**Table 5.** Identified agile mindset elements in the 'organization of work' category

| ID | Element | Literature | Experts | $n_L$ | $n_E$ |
|---|---|---|---|---|---|
| O1 | Self-organization | [4, 12–16, 19] | A, C, D, E | 7 | 4 |
| O2 | Maintaining a steady pace of work | [4, 12–14, 16, 20] | A, E | 6 | 2 |
| O3 | Ability to collaborate | [4, 12–14, 16, 17, 20] | – | 7 | 0 |
| O4 | Sharing knowledge and results | [12–14, 18–20] | C | 6 | 1 |
| O5 | Asking questions in case of insufficient knowledge | [20] | B, C, D | 1 | 3 |
| O6 | Finishing the current task before taking the next one | [21] | A, C, E | 1 | 3 |

*(continued)*

**Table 5.** (*continued*)

| ID | Element | Literature | Experts | $n_L$ | $n_E$ |
|----|---------|-----------|---------|-------|-------|
| O7 | Transparency in decision-making and actions | [4, 12, 14, 20, 21] | C, E | 5 | 2 |
| O8 | Simplicity and maximization of unnecessary work, simplifying tasks | [4, 12–14, 16] | – | 5 | 0 |
| O9 | Ability to make decisions together | [12–15] | – | 4 | 0 |
| O10 | Interdisciplinarity | [12–14] | – | 3 | 0 |
| O11 | Attitude towards working in short iterations with small increments | [14, 16] | – | 2 | 0 |
| O12 | Applying retrospectives to identify areas for improvement | [14, 16] | – | 2 | 0 |
| O13 | Understanding the purpose and vision of the task before taking it | [4, 15] | – | 2 | 0 |
| O14 | Focus on cross-functional teams | [15] | E | 1 | 1 |
| O15 | Expressing feedback on the work of other people | [15] | – | 1 | 0 |
| O16 | Estimating the results for a given timeframe | [16] | – | 1 | 0 |
| O17 | Determining possible tasks instead of looking for excuses | [18] | – | 1 | 0 |
| O18 | Focus on one task instead of many at once | [21] | – | 1 | 0 |
| O19 | Focus on the tasks performed | – | D | 0 | 1 |

Table 6 shows the number of agile mindset elements in each category identified in the literature and the interviews, the number of unique elements in our final list as well as the number of elements selected for the evaluation survey.

**Table 6.** Summary of the agile mindset identification and selection

| Category | Literature | Interviews | Unique | Survey |
|----------|-----------|-----------|--------|--------|
| Support for business goals | 6 | 4 | 7 | 3 |
| Relationships within the team | 19 | 11 | 20 | 10 |
| Individual features | 15 | 16 | 24 | 6 |
| Organization of work | 18 | 8 | 19 | 7 |
| Total | 58 | 39 | 70 | 26 |

## 3.2   Evaluation of the Selected Agile Mindset Elements

Based on the criteria presented in Sect. 2, we have selected 26 elements of agile mindset for further evaluation with the opinion survey. We selected the top 3 elements in the "support for business goals" category, top 10 elements in the "relationships within the team" category, top 6 elements in the "individual features" category, and top 7 elements in the "organization of work" category. Additionally, we observed that 13 elements in the "individual features" category as well as 8 elements in the "organization of work" category were mentioned only in one source, be it literature or interview.

The evaluation survey was carried out in late June and early July 2018. The questionnaire was divided into 5 sections: an introductory section and 4 sections with the agile mindset elements to evaluate grouped by their categories. In total, 52 respondents took part in the survey. Figure 1 shows the distribution of the respondents' experience with agile. Most of the respondents (52%) had at least 2 years of experience.

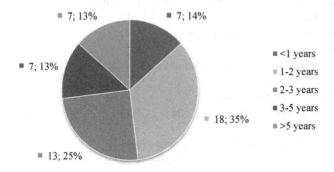

**Fig. 1.** Distribution of agile experience of the survey respondents

Figure 2 shows the distribution of respondents' roles in agile teams. Most of them worked as developers (about 60%), while others worked mostly as Scrum Masters.

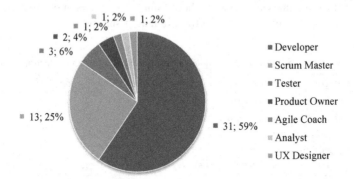

**Fig. 2.** Distribution of roles of the survey respondents

Table 7 presents the evaluation of the importance of selected agile mindset elements to the effectiveness of an agile team according to the respondents' opinion. E shows the mean evaluation of an agile mindset element in the Likert-type scale of 0 to 5 with standard deviation; n gives the sample size. The sample size slightly differs for some elements due to the option to skip an element in the survey. The elements are ordered by their decreasing evaluation.

**Table 7.** Evaluation of the importance of agile mindset elements to the team effectiveness [28]

| No. | ID | Element name | E | n |
|---|---|---|---|---|
| 1 | T9 | Searching for a solution to the problem instead of finding the guilty | 4.44 (0.79) | 52 |
| 2 | I3 | Being motivated | 4.44 (0.69) | 52 |
| 3 | T4 | Helping each other | 4.40 (0.63) | 52 |
| 4 | T7 | Mutual listening | 4.37 (0.71) | 51 |
| 5 | T3 | Focus on achieving common goal | 4.29 (0.77) | 52 |
| 6 | I5 | Openness to criticism and feedback | 4.23 (0.82) | 52 |
| 7 | O4 | Sharing knowledge and results | 4.21 (0.86) | 52 |
| 8 | T6 | Mutual respect | 4.11 (0.91) | 52 |
| 9 | T1 | Mutual trust | 4.10 (0.96) | 51 |
| 10 | T5 | Sincerity | 4.09 (0.97) | 52 |
| 11 | I1 | Continuous improvement and learning | 4.08 (1.00) | 52 |
| 12 | O7 | Transparency in decision-making and actions | 4.08 (1.03) | 52 |
| 13 | O1 | Self-organization | 4.04 (0.88) | 52 |
| 14 | I2 | Openness to change | 4.00 (1.02) | 52 |
| 15 | G1 | Continuous delivery of a valuable product in short intervals | 3.96 (1.04) | 52 |
| 16 | G3 | Attitude towards customer satisfaction and needs | 3.92 (0.83) | 52 |
| 17 | G2 | Cooperation with the customer based on partnership | 3.88 (0.97) | 52 |
| 18 | I6 | Openness to others | 3.88 (0.97) | 52 |
| 19 | O6 | Finishing the current task before taking the next one | 3.86 (1.06) | 52 |
| 20 | I4 | Positive attitude | 3.84 (0.77) | 52 |
| 21 | O3 | Ability to collaborate | 3.81 (0.90) | 52 |
| 22 | O5 | Asking questions in case of insufficient knowledge | 3.74 (1.06) | 51 |
| 23 | T2 | Direct communication - face to face conversations | 3.69 (1.26) | 52 |
| 24 | T8 | Equality in the team | 3.42 (1.28) | 52 |
| 25 | T10 | Team responsibility | 3.23 (1.31) | 52 |
| 26 | O2 | Maintaining a steady pace of work | 3.04 (1.34) | 52 |

It can be seen that the top evaluated elements achieved the evaluation of about 4.5 out of 5. 14 out of 26 elements achieved the evaluation of 4.0 and above. They can be considered the recommended agile mindset elements from our survey. The lowest evaluated elements obtained the score of less than 3.5. However, it should be noted that the standard deviation of the evaluations of the last 4 elements is the highest of our study (about 1.3). Other elements were evaluated with the standard deviation of 0.69 to 1.06.

The top 5 evaluated agile mindset elements are: "Searching for a solution to the problem instead of finding the guilty", "Being motivated", "Helping each other", "Mutual listening", and "Focus on achieving common goal". They belong only to two categories: "relationships within the team" and "individual features". This suggests that effective agile teamwork requires a specific attitude towards the team and other people as well as proactive and open mind of the individuals. This corresponds with the "growth mindset" concept from Dweck [3].

The 5 least important mindset elements in our survey are: "Asking questions in case of insufficient knowledge", "Direct communication - face to face conversations", "Equality in the team", "Team responsibility", "Maintaining a steady pace of work". They are related to organizational issues as well as shared responsibility and equality. This suggests that agile mindset is not about particular detailed practices or rituals. This is consistent with earlier findings [21–24].

We have also calculated the mean evaluation of all agile mindset elements in particular categories which is presented in Table 8. It can be observed that "individual features" are evaluated as the most important category. Next is "relationships within the team", followed by "support for business goal". "Organization of work" scored the lowest mean evaluation of all categories. The number of samples n differs greatly due to different number of elements in each category.

**Table 8.** Mean evaluation of the agile mindset categories [28]

| Category | E | n |
|---|---|---|
| Support for business goals | 3.92 (0.95) | 156 |
| Relationships within the team | 4.02 (1.07) | 518 |
| Individual features | 4.08 (0.91) | 312 |
| Organization of work | 3.83 (1.09) | 363 |

## 4  Competence Models

### 4.1  Scrum Master

The original definition and evaluation of the competence model for the role of Scrum Master is presented in [29]. The competencies were divided into three groups following the competence model of a project manager [32]:

- behavioral – attitudes, traits of personality, soft skills (prefix B),
- technical – doing certain tasks within the team, hard skills (prefix T),
- contextual – doing tasks outside the team on an organization level (prefix C).

Tables 9, 10 and 11 present the behavioral, technical and contextual competencies of a Scrum Master, respectively. E gives the evaluation of importance of each competence, while N denotes the number of answers (close to sample size). The competencies are ordered and numbered by decreasing evaluation of importance.

**Table 9.** Scrum Master's behavioral competencies

| ID | Competence | E | N |
|---|---|---|---|
| SM.B1 | Communication | 100% | 55 |
| SM.B2 | Building relationships | 98% | 55 |
| SM.B3 | Vigilance | 95% | 55 |
| SM.B4 | Involvement | 89% | 54 |
| SM.B5 | Assertiveness | 89% | 55 |

*(continued)*

**Table 9.**  (*continued*)

| ID | Competence | E | N |
|---|---|---|---|
| SM.B6 | Flexibility | 87% | 55 |
| SM.B7 | Supporting the team | 87% | 55 |
| SM.B8 | Emotional control | 85% | 55 |
| SM.B9 | Inspiration | 82% | 55 |
| SM.B10 | Logical and abstract thinking | 78% | 55 |
| SM.B11 | Dynamism in actions | 76% | 55 |
| SM.B12 | Influencing the team | 73% | 55 |
| SM.B13 | Initiative | 65% | 55 |
| SM.B14 | Creativity | 62% | 54 |
| SM.B15 | Self-reliance | 60% | 54 |

**Table 10.**  Scrum Master's technical competencies

| ID | Competence | E | N |
|---|---|---|---|
| SM.T1 | Defending and protecting the team | 89% | 54 |
| SM.T2 | Solving conflicts | 87% | 55 |
| SM.T3 | Organizing and moderating Scrum meetings | 87% | 54 |
| SM.T4 | Negotiating | 84% | 55 |
| SM.T5 | Consistent implementation of the Scrum process | 82% | 54 |
| SM.T6 | Sharing knowledge | 78% | 55 |
| SM.T7 | Time management | 78% | 55 |
| SM.T8 | Planning | 71% | 55 |
| SM.T9 | Professional knowledge about the project | 60% | 55 |

**Table 11.**  Scrum Master's contextual competencies

| ID | Competence | E | N |
|---|---|---|---|
| SM.C1 | Continuous education | 89% | 54 |
| SM.C2 | Understanding Scrum principles | 82% | 55 |
| SM.C3 | Scrum implementation and adaptation | 75% | 54 |
| SM.C4 | Training | 60% | 54 |
| SM.C5 | Promoting Scrum | 56% | 55 |

## 4.2   Product Owner

The definition of the competence model for the role of Product Owner is presented in [30]. The competencies were divided into two groups following the competence model of a project manager [32]:

- behavioral – attitudes, traits of personality, soft skills (prefix B),
- technical – doing certain tasks within the team, hard skills (prefix T).

Tables 12 and 13 present the behavioral and technical competencies of a Product Owner, respectively. E gives the evaluation of importance of each competence in a scale of 1 to 5, where 1 is the lowest importance and 5 is the highest. The importance was derived from the number of activities the competence supported, denoted by "act." and the number of other competencies depending on a given competence, denoted by "dep.". The idea is that the higher the number of supported activities and the higher the number of dependant competencies, the higher the importance of a competence. The competencies are ordered and numbered by decreasing evaluation of importance.

**Table 12.** Product Owner's behavioral competencies

| ID | Competence | E | Act. | Dep. |
|---|---|---|---|---|
| PO.B1 | Communication skills | 5 | 11 | 5 |
| PO.B2 | Creating product vision | 4 | 8 | 6 |
| PO.B3 | Decisiveness | 2 | 6 | 4 |
| PO.B4 | Inspiration | 2 | 6 | 3 |
| PO.B5 | Leadership | 2 | 6 | 3 |
| PO.B6 | Responsibility | 1 | 6 | 2 |
| PO.B7 | Negotiating | 1 | 4 | 3 |

**Table 13.** Product Owner's technical competencies

| ID | Competence | E | Act. | Dep. |
|---|---|---|---|---|
| PO.T1 | Product backlog management | 5 | 14 | 6 |
| PO.T2 | Requirements management | 4 | 9 | 5 |
| PO.T3 | Taking care of the product value | 3 | 8 | 4 |
| PO.T4 | Customer relationship management | 3 | 6 | 5 |
| PO.T5 | Business context | 2 | 6 | 4 |
| PO.T6 | Project measurement | 2 | 6 | 3 |
| PO.T7 | Planning | 2 | 6 | 3 |
| PO.T8 | Product domain specialist | 2 | 6 | 3 |
| PO.T9 | Project administration | 1 | 5 | 2 |

### 4.3  Agile Analyst

The definition and evaluation of the competence model for the role of agile analyst is presented in [31]. The competencies were divided into two groups following the competence model of a project manager [32]:

- behavioral – attitudes, traits of personality, soft skills (prefix B),
- technical – doing certain tasks within the team, hard skills (prefix T).

Tables 14 and 15 present the behavioral and technical competencies of an agile analyst, respectively. E gives the mean evaluation of importance of each competence in a Likert-type interval scale of 1 to 5, where 1 is the lowest importance and 5 is the highest. N shows the number of responses, which is close to sample size. The competencies are ordered and numbered by decreasing evaluation of importance.

**Table 14.** Agile analyst's behavioral competencies

| ID | Competence | E | N |
|----|------------|---|---|
| A.B1 | Ability to ask questions | 4.64 (0.53) | 50 |
| A.B2 | Being able to admit mistakes and looking for solutions | 4.56 (0.79) | 50 |
| A.B3 | Effective reasoning from available information | 4.56 (0.58) | 50 |
| A.B4 | Understanding other points of view | 4.52 (0.61) | 50 |
| A.B5 | Establishing relationships with ease, building and maintaining good customer relationships | 4.48 (0.79) | 50 |
| A.B6 | Adjusting the means of communication to the partners' expectations, using the right levels of abstraction, listening and understanding the needs of the interlocutors | 4.47 (0.65) | 49 |
| A.B7 | Negotiating to agree mutually beneficial solutions, relaxed requirements, faster delivery, lower estimates | 4.37 (0.70) | 49 |
| A.B8 | Ability to work out a compromise, reconciling the expectations of stakeholders | 4.30 (0.91) | 50 |
| A.B9 | Distance and the ability to look from the outside | 4.29 (0.82) | 49 |
| A.B10 | Willingness and openness to change, ability to work in changing conditions | 4.26 (0.80) | 50 |
| A.B11 | Close cooperation with all parties involved, uniting the client and the team | 4.23 (0.86) | 48 |
| A.B12 | Openness to other design proposals and acceptance of team decisions | 4.20 (0.88) | 50 |
| A.B13 | Loyalty and honesty in order to maintain good relations | 4.18 (0.88) | 49 |
| A.B14 | Decisiveness | 4.10 (0.91) | 50 |
| A.B15 | Product focus, product-oriented approach | 4.06 (0.82) | 50 |
| A.B16 | Working in a methodical manner, being disciplined and requiring discipline from the team, concentration in chaos | 4.02 (1.01) | 49 |
| A.B17 | Empathy towards the client and team | 4.00 (1.11) | 50 |
| A.B18 | Building the team's commitment as a whole and a sense of responsibility for the product, motivating | 3.78 (1.10) | 49 |
| A.B19 | Moderating discussions and meetings | 3.73 (0.98) | 48 |
| A.B20 | Positive attitude towards people, willingness to spend time with them | 3.67 (1.23) | 49 |

**Table 15.** Agile analyst's technical competencies

| ID | Competence | E | N |
|----|------------|---|---|
| A.T1 | Collecting feedback and passing it on to the team | 4.77 (0.47) | 48 |
| A.T2 | Sharing knowledge with the team and stakeholders | 4.60 (0.76) | 50 |
| A.T3 | Setting priorities for requirements and tasks | 4.56 (0.73) | 50 |
| A.T4 | Defining functional and non-functional requirements | 4.43 (0.68) | 49 |
| A.T5 | Creating understandable, unambiguous and easy-to-maintain documentation | 4.42 (0.88) | 50 |
| A.T6 | Having knowledge of the business domain | 4.40 (0.70) | 50 |
| A.T7 | Presentation of the product to stakeholders, conducting demos or product reviews with the client | 4.31 (0.92) | 49 |
| A.T8 | Decomposition of business requirements into system functions | 4.27 (0.92) | 48 |

*(continued)*

**Table 15.**  (*continued*)

| ID | Competence | E | N |
|---|---|---|---|
| A.T9 | Defining scenarios (epics) | 4.16 (0.80) | 49 |
| A.T10 | Knowledge of software life cycle | 4.16 (0.89) | 50 |
| A.T11 | Communication with programmers and understanding the technical language of the team | 4.12 (0.87) | 50 |
| A.T12 | Defining user stories | 4.10 (1.09) | 50 |
| A.T13 | Product and sprint backlog management | 4.09 (1.10) | 47 |
| A.T14 | Knowledge of issue management tools, creating documentation (JIRA, Confluence, WIKI) | 3.98 (1.00) | 50 |
| A.T15 | Modeling of diagrams and business processes according to notation (BPMN, UML) using tools (EA, Visual Paradigm, Visio, Draw.io) | 3.88 (1.11) | 49 |
| A.T16 | Good knowledge of development methodology (Scrum, PRINCE2, Kanban) | 3.71 (1.15) | 49 |
| A.T17 | Knowledge of programming technologies on min. basic level, general knowledge about application architecture | 3.52 (0.97) | 50 |
| A.T18 | Creating acceptance tests (UATs) | 3.26 (1.14) | 46 |
| A.T19 | Knowledge of SQL and databases | 3.20 (1.34) | 50 |
| A.T20 | Ability to install the application on a local (development) environment and update the version | 2.48 (1.13) | 50 |

## 5   Comparison and Discussion

We have mapped the elements of agile mindset in our study onto the 12 principles behind the Agile Manifesto [2] as well as the competencies of Scrum Master, Product Owner and agile analyst presented in Sect. 4. We analyzed the relative position of the agile mindset elements that map directly onto these principles and competencies. The results are shown in Table 16. "No." indicates the relative importance of the elements based on our survey. P# shows the Agile principle number mapped to an element, while SM, PO, and AA columns give the identifiers of the mapped Scrum Master's, Product Owner's and agile analyst's competencies, respectively.

**Table 16.**  Comparison of agile mindset, agile principles and competence models

| No. | ID | Agile Mindset Element | P# | SM | PO | AA |
|---|---|---|---|---|---|---|
| 1 | T9 | Searching for a solution to the problem instead of finding the guilty | | | | A.B2 |
| 2 | I3 | Being motivated | 5 | SM.B4 | | |
| 3 | T4 | Helping each other | | SM.B7 | | |
| 4 | T7 | Mutual listening | | | | A.B6 |
| 5 | T3 | Focus on achieving common goal | | | PO.B2 | A.B7 |
| 6 | I5 | Openness to criticism and feedback | | SM.B8 | | A.T1 |
| 7 | O4 | Sharing knowledge and results | | SM.T6 | | A.T2 |
| 8 | T6 | Mutual respect | | | | |

(continued)

**Table 16.** (*continued*)

| No. | ID | Agile Mindset Element | P# | SM | PO | AA |
|-----|-----|-----------------------|-----|-----|-----|-----|
| 9 | T1 | Mutual trust | 5 | | | A.B11 |
| 10 | T5 | Sincerity | | | | A.B13 |
| 11 | I1 | Continuous improvement and learning | 12 | SM.C1 | | |
| 12 | O7 | Transparency in decision-making and actions | | | PO.B3 | A.B14 |
| 13 | O1 | Self-organization | 11 | SM.B15 | | |
| 14 | I2 | Openness to change | 2 | SM.B6 | | A.B10 |
| 15 | G1 | Continuous delivery of a valuable product in short intervals | 1, 3, 7 | | PO.T3 | |
| 16 | G3 | Attitude towards customer satisfaction and needs | 1 | | PO.T3 | A.B15 |
| 17 | G2 | Cooperation with the customer based on partnership | 4 | SM.B2 | PO.T4 | A.B5 |
| 18 | I6 | Openness to others | | | | A.B4 |
| 19 | O6 | Finishing the current task before taking the next one | | | | |
| 20 | I4 | Positive attitude | | | | A.B20 |
| 21 | O3 | Ability to collaborate | | SM.B12 | | A.B12 |
| 22 | O5 | Asking questions in case of insufficient knowledge | | | | A.B1 |
| 23 | T2 | Direct communication - face to face conversations | 6 | SM.B1 | PO.B1 | A.T11 |
| 24 | T8 | Equality in the team | | | | |
| 25 | T10 | Team responsibility | | | PO.B6 | A.B18 |
| 26 | O2 | Maintaining a steady pace of work | 8 | SM.T7 | PO.T7 | A.B16 |

It can be seen that only the I3 agile mindset element mapped to the 5th Agile principle was evaluated very high (position 2, score 4.44). Elements mapped to most of the Agile principles were evaluated in the middle range (positions 9 to 17, score 4.10 to 3.88). However, the agile mindset elements T2 and O2 mapped to 6th and 8th principle respectively were evaluated very low (position 23 and 26 (last), score 3.69 and 3.04). Remaining two Agile principles were mapped to the agile mindset elements that were excluded from the survey.

This mapping shows an interesting discrepancy between what our respondents think is important to "being agile" and what the creators of the Agile Manifesto pointed out as the principles of Agile. We can hypothesize that this indicates insufficient understanding of Agile by our respondents, partial or flawed implementation of Agile in the respondents' teams or companies, or even a shift in practical agility from the 18 years old principles of Agile. This may also be specific to Polish IT industry and have some cultural background. Definitely, it calls for more research.

The comparison of the agile mindset to the competence models shows that only 3 agile mindset elements are recommended for all three studied roles. These are: G2 Cooperation with the customer based on partnership, T2 Direct communication - face to face conversations, and O2 Maintaining a steady pace of work. All of them also mapped to Agile principles. These elements may constitute "the core of Agile" based on our multiple studies.

It can be observed that the agile mindset related to the competencies of the Product Owner is nearly entirely contained within the agile mindset related to the competencies of the agile analyst. The G1 'Continuous delivery of a valuable product in short intervals' element is the only exception. The Product Owner's point of view focuses more on delivering the business value of the product. Nearly all behavioral competencies of agile analyst are mapped to the evaluated agile mindset elements.

Another interesting observation is that the agile mindset elements related to the competencies of a Scrum Master contains some unique elements different from the sets of elements related to the roles of Product Owner and agile analyst. The unique elements are: I3 Being motivated, T4 Helping each other, I1 Continuous improvement and learning, and O1 Self-organization. They are rather highly evaluated in our survey (top half). This may result from a considerable number of Scrum Masters in our survey sample.

It should also be noted that most of the competencies mapped onto the agile mindset elements belong to the behavioral type. This is expected as this type of competencies represents attitudes, behaviors, or traits of personality which is very close to the understanding of the concept of a mindset.

## 6 Threats to Validity

### 6.1 Threats to Construct and Internal Validity

We have identified and reduced the following threats to the construct and internal validity of this research related to the interviews and the survey: (a) interview moderator's bias and influence on experts, (b) misinterpretation of the interview outputs, (c) learning and tiring of the survey respondents, (d) forced answers to the survey, (e) subjective mapping of elements to principles and competencies.

We have controlled the interview moderator's bias and their influence on experts with the structure of the interview. Each interview followed the same protocol (Sect. 2). To minimize misinterpretations, the interviews were recorded, transcribed and thoroughly analyzed while relistening to the recordings, if necessary. The results of each interview have been coded separately and only then merged together.

The survey questions were not randomized to minimize the impact of learning and tiring of the respondents due to the limitation of the Google Forms tool. However, the survey was conveniently divided into 5 sections and contained only 26 evaluation questions. The survey also allowed the respondents to skip the evaluation of a particular agile mindset element when unsure.

We followed the keyword analysis method while building the mapping between the agile mindset elements, the agile principles and the competencies of the analyzed roles. When in doubt, we referred to the detailed definition of a competence in the source model. Additionally, in some cases we allowed some principles and competences to be mapped onto more than one agile mindset element.

## 6.2 Threats to External Validity

We have identified the following threats to the external validity of the interviews and the survey: (a) low number of interviewed experts and survey respondents, (b) insufficient experience of interview experts and survey respondents, (c) interview experts and survey respondents as a convenience sample, (d) interview experts and survey respondents sample limited to Polish IT industry, (e) competence models with limited validation.

We have interviewed 5 experts from the industry. The interviewed experts had 2 to 5 years of experience in Agile. We aimed at covering various roles in an agile team and experiences with various agile methods. We engaged 2 Scrum Masters with broad experience (see Table 1) Altogether, the input from experts supplemented the list of 58 agile mindset elements from the literature by 22 new elements (38%), which can be considered a substantial contribution (see Table 6).

We have collected data from 52 respondents in the survey, which definitely exceeded the typical threshold sample size of 30 for the choice of the statistical tests [11]. 52% of the respondents had at least 2 years of experience. 13.5% of the respondents had more than 5 years of experience (see Fig. 1). The respondents represented various roles in the agile team, which covered diverse points of view (see Fig. 2). Moreover, we have analyzed the impact of the respondents' experience and role as the confounding variables on the validity of our results, which showed marginal impact (Sect. 6.3).

Our survey sample is not statistically random – it is a convenience sample, although we invited the respondents through various channels like personal and business contacts, interest groups, social media, and recommendations. This method provided for a fairly diverse group of experts and respondents with different experience. The experts and respondents used many agile methods such as: Scrum, Kanban, Scrumban, Extreme Programming, SAFe.

The survey was in Polish and possibly attracted most of the respondents among the peers of one of the authors (P. Gaida) working in the Tricity region of Poland, so the results it may exhibit some cultural or regional bias, which needs to be studied further. Comparison of the perception of the concept of agile mindset in Poland and other countries may bring valuable insights.

We have asked our respondents only for their (self-declared) experience in agile and their role in an agile team. We have not collected other data such as company size, age, industry sector or type of projects they worked on. Thus, our study provides only preliminary insight into the conceptual structure of the agile mindset.

We have compared the evaluated agile mindset elements to the competence models of Scrum Master, Product Owner and agile analyst. However, the models were built based on limited number of sources and evaluated with a relatively small survey samples. The surveys were conducted in Poland, which, again, may expose the data to some cultural or regional bias.

## 6.3    Analysis of Confounding Variables

We have analyzed the respondents' experience and role as confounding variables in the evaluations of agile mindset elements. The detailed results are presented in [28]. We have used the t-Student test for independent pairs. Treating our data as interval, this test is suitable for such analysis [11]. We assumed equal variances of the grouped samples and the confidence level of 95% ($\alpha = 0.05$).

The tests showed that the impact of both experience and role on nearly all of the evaluations could not be considered statistically significant with the assumed confidence level of 95% and sample size of 52. However, two agile mindset elements stood out. The evaluation of I6 element "Openness to others" exhibited statistically significant difference in the evaluation depending on respondents' experience. It was evaluated much higher by the respondents with less than 2 years of experience compared to those with more than 2 years of experience (4.24 compared to 3.56). Our working hypothesis is that it is related to learning and gathering experience at the start of the professional career. However, "openness" in general is crucial to being agile [2].

The evaluation of T2 element "Direct communication - face to face conversations" exhibited statistically significant difference in the evaluation depending on respondents' role. It was evaluated much lower by the developers compared to the non-developers (3.39 compared to 4.14). Our working hypothesis is that they may see the meetings as (partial) waste of time that diverts them from coding. This may also indicate some overuse or misuse of meetings in the agile teams of our respondents.

Our study is based on limited data on the respondents themselves. The understanding of the agile mindset may also vary by the industry sector, company size, company culture and maturity, type of projects, national and regional culture and possibly more. Our initial set of agile mindset elements and its mappings to the competence models may be used in such further studies.

## 7    Conclusions

We have identified 70 elements of the agile mindset studying the literature and interviewing the industry experts, which answer our research question RQ1. We grouped the elements into 4 categories. Then, we have obtained an opinion-based evaluation of the importance of each agile mindset element to the effectiveness of an agile team, which answers our research question RQ2. Next, we have analyzed the evaluations to point out the most and least important elements based on the opinions of our respondents, which provides a preliminary answer to our research question RQ3. Further and more detailed study of the impact of agile mindset on the team effectiveness requires careful observation of a number of different types of projects and can be done in future research.

Finally, by mapping the evaluated agile mindset elements onto the principles behind Agile Manifesto and the competencies of Scrum Master, Product Owner and agile analyst we were able to identify the coverage, the cross-relationships and key differences between the mindsets from different points of view. This provides the answer to our research questions RQ4 and RQ5.

The detailed contribution of this paper is the identification of the elements of agile mindset, the preliminary evaluation of their importance to the effectiveness of an agile team based on an industrial opinion survey as well as the analysis of this mindset by comparison to agile principles and competencies of agile roles. This contributes to filling the gap in the literature related to the definition and scope of the agile mindset and the relative importance of its elements in the industry and education [22–25].

The evaluated list of agile mindset elements and its comparison to the agile principles and competencies of roles may be used as guidance for developers, Scrum Masters, Product Owners, and agile analysts to:

- improve the understanding of Agile,
- improve the understanding of other roles in an Agile team,
- improve the agile process and solve problems identified during retrospectives,
- educate and train both in the industry and academia,
- self-develop, in particular to switch to Scrum Master or Agile coach.

Full results of the research on the Agile mindset are available in [26]. The raw data from the agile mindset evaluation survey are available in [27].

**Acknowledgment.** This work was partially supported by the DS Funds of ETI Faculty, Gdansk University of Technology. The authors thank all the experts and respondents who took part in the interviews and the survey.

# References

1. Manifesto for Agile Software Development, agilemanifesto.org (2001)
2. Principles behind the Agile Manifesto (2001). http://agilemanifesto.org/principles.html
3. Dweck, S.C.: Mindset: The New Psychology of Success, Random House, New York (2006)
4. Broza, G.: The Agile Mindset – Making Agile Processes work, 3P Vantage Media (2015)
5. Przybyłek, A., Kowalski, W.: Utilizing online collaborative games to facilitate Agile Software Development. In: Ganzha, M., Maciaszek, L., Paprzycki, M. (eds.) Proceedings of the 2018 Federated Conference on Computer Science and Information Systems. ACSIS, vol. 15, pp. 811–815 (2018). https://doi.org/10.15439/2018f347
6. Colomo-Palacios, R., Casado-Lumbreras, C., Soto-Acosta, P., García-Peñalvo, F.J., Tovar-Caro, E.: Competence gaps in software personnel: a multi-organizational study. Comput. Hum. Behav. **29**(2), 456–461 (2013). https://doi.org/10.1016/j.chb.2012.04.021
7. The 13th annual State of Agile Report, CollabNet VersionOne (2019)
8. Schwaber, K., Sutherland, J.: The Scrum Guide. Rules of the Game (2017). Scrum.org
9. Hammarberg, M., Sunden, J.: Kanban in Action. Manning Publications, NY (2014)
10. Knaster, R., Leffingwell, D.: SAFe 4.5 Distilled: Applying the Scaled Agile Framework for Lean Enterprises, 2nd edn. Addison-Wesley Professional (2018)
11. Navidi, W.: Statistics for Engineers and Scientists, 4th edn. McGraw-Hill Education, USA (2014)
12. Crowder, J.A., Friess, S.: Agile Project Management: Managing for Success, Springer, Cham (2015)
13. Moreira, M.E.: The Agile Enterprise: Building and Running Agile Organizations. Apress, New York (2017)

14. Moreira, M.E.: Being Agile, Your Roadmap to Successful Adaption of Agile. Apress, New York (2013)
15. Stettina, C.J., Heijstek, W.: Five agile factors: helping self-management to self-reflect. In: O'Connor, R.V., Pries-Heje, J., Messnarz, R. (eds.) EuroSPI 2011. CCIS, vol. 172, pp. 84–96. Springer, Heidelberg (2011). https://doi.org/10.1007/978-3-642-22206-1_8
16. Stellman, A., Greene, J.: Learning Agile: Understanding Scrum, XP, Lean and Kanban. O'Reilly Media, USA (2015)
17. McIntosh, S.: What Exactly is the Agile Mindset? InfoQ (2016). https://www.infoq.com/articles/what-agile-mindset
18. Howard, L.: What does is it mean to have an agile mindset? Agile Connection (2015). https://www.agileconnection.com/article/what-does-it-mean-have-agile-mindset
19. Parvatam, S.: It's All About the Mindset, Scrum Alliance (2015). https://www.scrumalliance.org/community/articles/2015/december/its-all-about-the-mindset
20. Godugu, V.: Fixed Mindset versus Agile Mindset, Scrum Alliance (2015). https://www.scrumalliance.org/community/articles/2015/june/fixed-mindset-versus-agile-mindset
21. Rich, L.: Agile Is Not a Process, It's a Mindset, Agile Connection (2018). https://www.agileconnection.com/article/agile-not-process-it-s-mindset
22. Zieris, F., Salinger, S.: Doing scrum rather than being Agile: a case study on actual nearshoring practices. In: IEEE 8th International Conference on Global Software Engineering, pp. 144–153 (2013). https://doi.org/10.1109/icgse.2013.26
23. van Manen, H., van Vliet, H.: Organization-wide agile expansion requires an organization-wide agile mindset. In: Jedlitschka, A., Kuvaja, P., Kuhrmann, M., Männistö, T., Münch, J., Raatikainen, M. (eds.) PROFES 2014. LNCS, vol. 8892, pp. 48–62. Springer, Cham (2014). https://doi.org/10.1007/978-3-319-13835-0_4
24. Martin, A., Anslow, C., Johnson, D.: Teaching agile methods to software engineering professionals: 10 years, 1000 release plans. In: Baumeister, H., Lichter, H., Riebisch, M. (eds.) XP 2017. LNBIP, vol. 283, pp. 151–166. Springer, Cham (2017). https://doi.org/10.1007/978-3-319-57633-6_10
25. Gannod, G.C., et al.: Establishing an agile mindset and culture for workforce preparedness: A baseline study, Proceedings – Frontiers in Education Conference (2019). https://doi.org/10.1109/fie.2018.8658712
26. Gaida, P.: Analysis of the agile mindset for software projects, MSc thesis, supervisor J. Miler, Gdansk University of Technology, Poland (2018). (in Polish)
27. Miler, J., Gaida, P.: Survey on agile mindset and agile team effectiveness, data.mendeley.com. https://doi.org/10.17632/phvx6nts6b.1
28. Miler, J., Gaida, P.: On the Agile mindset of an effective team – an industrial opinion survey. In: Ganzha, M., Maciaszek, L., Paprzycki, M. (eds.) Proceedings of the 2019 Federated Conference on Computer Science and Information Systems. ACSIS, vol. 18, pp. 841–849 (2019). https://doi.org/10.15439/2019f198
29. Wielemborek, E.: A competence model for the Scrum Master, MSc thesis, supervisor J. Miler, Gdansk University of Technology, Poland (2016). (in Polish)
30. Jaszewski, G.: A competence model of the Product Owner in the Scrum methodology, MSc thesis, supervisor J. Miler, Gdansk University of Technology, Poland (2013). (in Polish)
31. Klima, M.: Evaluation of the role of analyst in the Scrum projects, MSc thesis, supervisor J. Miler, Gdansk University of Technology, Poland (2017). (in Polish)
32. IPMA, IPMA Competence Baseline, ed. 3, (2006)

# Adapting Agile Practices to Security Context – Practitioners' Perspective

Katarzyna Łukasiewicz[1(✉)] and Sara Cygańska[2]

[1] Gdańsk University of Technology, ul. Narutowicza 11/12,
80-233 Gdańsk, Poland
katlukas@pg.edu.pl
[2] IHS Markit, ul. Marynarki Polskiej 163, 80-868 Gdańsk, Poland
sara.cyganska@ihsmarkit.com

**Abstract.** In this paper we explore the problem of introducing agile practices to projects dealing with systems with high security requirements. We also propose an approach based on AgileSafe method and OWASP ASVS guidelines, that could support such introduction. What is more, we present the results of two surveys aimed at analyzing IT practitioners' views on applying agile methods to security reliant systems as well as evaluating the set of agile security-oriented practices which are a part of the proposed approach. This paper is an extended version of the paper "Security-oriented agile approach with AgileSafe and OWASP ASVS" that was published as a part of LASD 2019 conference proceedings [36].

**Keywords:** Agile · Security · Software development methods

## 1 Introduction

The concern for providing secure systems has become increasingly important throughout the years. With the rapid progress in the IT domain, expansion of the internet solutions and the level of general computer science knowledge, the problem with security is no longer restricted to government organizations and banking, it involves even small companies that store any private data or engage in the IoT projects.

At the same time, the changing markets and need for flexibility encourages many companies to adopt agile approach [1]. While such approach is known for its benefits concerning effectiveness and client satisfaction [1], when it comes to the security aspect the potential advantages are not that obvious. The core agile methods, such as Scrum [2], eXtreme Programming [3] or Kanban [4] do not mention explicitly security-oriented practices. On the other hand, most of the readily available security frameworks were created with a more disciplined approach in mind.

Taking into consideration the unflagging popularity of agile methods and an increasing concern for security in the IT domain, an approach that would allow to incorporate more security-oriented practices into agile software development would be of value [5].

The goal of the research described in this paper was to identify security-focused agile practices, evaluate their usability and impact so that the positively assessed

A. Przybyłek and M. E. Morales-Trujillo (Eds.): LASD 2019/MIDI 2019, LNBIP 376, pp. 63–81, 2020.
https://doi.org/10.1007/978-3-030-37534-8_4

practices could be incorporated into an OWASP ASVS [6] compliant process, as a part of AgileSafe method [7].

## 2   Background

### 2.1   Agile Methods

Ever since the announcement of the Agile Manifesto [8], the agile methods have been growing increasingly in popularity. The reports of the benefits experienced by numerous companies [9, 10] encouraged the trend to shift from traditional, plan-driven methods to the agile ones. What is important, this shift has not only concerned small and evolving companies which are considered a target of the agile approach. Bigger organizations with larger teams or corporate structures have also sought the ways to incorporate agile approach, which resulted in methods such as SAFe [11] or DevOps [12].

### 2.2   Security Frameworks and Standards

Since the 1990's there have been attempts to formalize guidelines and standards concerning software security. In 1999 ISO [13] proposed Common Criteria for Information Technology Security Evaluation – ISO 15408 [14]. Recognizing the value of unified security standard, governments of Canada, France, Germany, Netherlands, United Kingdom and United States were involved in the creation of this document. The main goal of ISO 15408 was to present formal criteria for security assessment of computer systems. There are other standards that address more specific security concerns such as ISO 27032 [15] and NIST Cybersecurity Framework (NIST CSF) [16] which focus on cybersecurity.

While providing vital information and formal methods to assess security in computer systems, these standards are not directly applicable to agile software development processes. Agile methods are not inherently equipped with security assurance practices. Should such methods be applied in their basic forms, they would struggle to provide conformance evidence for security standards. At the same time, adding traditional security-oriented practices to agile software development process might weigh it down and advantages of the agility could be lost. This opens a room for researching towards a solution which enables to meet the recommendations and to follow the related best practices of secure software development processes while still not backing down from being agile unless it is necessary.

### 2.3   OWASP ASVS

The name of the OWASP Application Security Verification Standard (OWASP ASVS) comes from the organization with same name, which created it - The Open Web Application Security Project [17]. OWASP is a non-profit organization whose goal is to improve software security. Its mission is defined as improving the visibility of the security problem, both among individuals and organizations, so that they can make decisions on this subject consciously [17]. The organization operates as an open community in which anyone interested in security issues can participate. It publishes tools and documents that are available under open licenses. Due to the lack of connection with commercial companies, OWASP describes itself as impartial.

OWASP ASVS is directed both to people involved directly in the development process (developers, architects, testers, security experts) as well as their clients. Its two main goals are to help creating and maintaining secure software and help in defining requirements between service providers and their clients. A straightforward language and accessibility make it a practitioners' friendly standard.

The standard distinguishes three levels of requirements for various purposes and the degree of security provided: Level 1: Opportunistic, Level 2: Standard and Level 3: Advanced.

OWASP ASVS has been chosen for this research based on its versatility, open access and popularity among practitioners [18]. The domain of web applications is at the forefront of security issues, with frequent news about major security breaches [19]. For this reason, catering a solution that would allow combining agile security practices with OWASP ASVS requirements could be of interest to many organizations.

### 2.4    Related Work

Attempts to address the new hybrid approach for security aware agile development are carried out in various ways. One of the ideas is to create new, extended methodologies based on the existing agile ones. An example of this is the Secure Scrum method 20, which extends Scrum. It's been created as an extension to Scrum to support the security assurance. This method presents some valuable practices (such as S-Tag and S-Mark) but focuses only on Scrum and does not address the norms and standards conformance aspect.

Other propositions include frameworks that can be used with any agile methodology - this approach has been used by the aforementioned AgileSafe method but in the safety aspect as well as the method proposed by Veracode. It involves performing Veracode services on user's code to detect vulnerabilities. The service is offered in the cloud and the details of the tests are not visible to the users. Veracode allows security verification to be carried out in several different ways.

The operation of this type of solution is based on the observation that agile methodologies are a set of certain practices. It is possible, therefore, to extend them to new practices, as long as they do not conflict with the existing ones.

## 3    AgileSafe

The need for hybrid approaches that would allow reconciling regulatory requirements with agile practices is not exclusive to the security context. Safety-critical software development is another, if only more so, highly constrained domain. In the safety context, quite similarly to the security one, norms and standards are vital to ensure the level of trust and quality of high-integrity systems. In order to enable safety-critical software companies to adopt hybrid agile approach while satisfying the regulatory requirements of applicable standards, AgileSafe [21] method has been proposed.

It presents a framework for collecting and suggesting the most suitable agile practices for a given project, as well as the means for managing and monitoring conformance with the applicable regulatory requirements. In this article we present how AgileSafe can be adapted to the security aspect of software development projects and support introduction of hybrid agile approach to such projects while ensuring the compliance with security norms and standards, using OWASP ASVS as an example.

## 3.1   Overview

As shown in the Fig. 1, as an input to AgileSafe takes the characteristics of a project in which the new approach will be implemented (Project Characteristics) as well as a list of regulations (Regulatory Requirements), which the project needs to comply with.

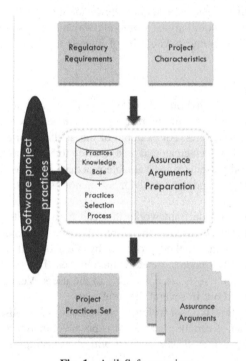

**Fig. 1.**  AgileSafe overview

Based on this information, the user is guided through the process of practices suggestion as well as the process of preparing a set of assurance arguments [22] that will help the user to maintain conformance with given norms and standards. As a result, the user obtains a tailored Project Practices Set, which would suit best a project with given characteristics and regulation restrictions as well as a set of assurance arguments to monitor compliance with the chosen regulations.

## 3.2  Project Practices Knowledge Base

The information about practices available in AgileSafe, their capability to answer given Project Characteristics and Regulatory Requirements, is kept in the Practices Knowledge Base. Each practice is described using the same template that is then translated into OWL and managed using Protégé tool [23].

An example of a practice description and its capability (type of project for which it works best) for different project factors is presented in the Fig. 2.

At the moment of this research, there were 50 software development practices in the Practices Knowledge Base, including safety-oriented ones.

## 3.3  Assurance Arguments

In order to ensure that the Regulatory Requirements will be met when applying the new agile approach, AgileSafe uses a set of assurance arguments. The highest level of abstraction is represented by Practices Compliance Argument (and its template Practices Compliance Argument Pattern). It is created separately for each standard added to the method and collects all of the practices from Practices Knowledge Base that have a potential to answer the standard's requirements. Such practices are arranged accordingly in the argument structure for a given standard requirements. Based on these arguments, Project Practices Compliance Arguments are created for each standard that a given project need to comply with, leaving only these practices that will be used in this project. Project Compliance Argument serves as an argument for collecting actual artifacts of the planned practices that serve as evidence in a conformance process. The arguments structure is presented in the Fig. 3.

## 3.4  AgileSafe in the Security Context

The potential of applying AgileSafe to the projects concerned with security issues has already been presented in [24] based on a case study for clinic appointment/queue management system and IEC 62443-4.1 standard [25]. The promising results of this case study allowed to form another step to further adapt AgileSafe method to cater for security-critical projects and present hybrid security-oriented practices to the Practices Knowledge Base.

# 4  Security-Oriented Agile Practices

In order to propose agile security practices that could extend the Practices Knowledge Base of the AgileSafe method, a review of the scientific literature and articles on blogs and industry portals was carried out.

## 4.1  Identification of Security-Oriented Agile Practices

While there are many well-known security-oriented practices such as threat modelling or attack trees, in this research we wanted to expand this list and focus on less obvious, agile inspired practices, to enrich the Practice Knowledge Base of AgileSafe method.

| Id | 1 | |
|---|---|---|
| Name | **Abuser stories** | |
| Description | *Abuser stories are a way of documenting system security requirements. They describe how the system might be attacked and how assets might be put in risk.* | |
| | *Procedure: Abuser stories are similar to regular user stories - informal and lightweight. They should be written by customers cooperating with developers. The reason is different field of expertise that makes them likely to notice different security issues. Good starting point for writing Abuser stories may be considering system assets. Everything that has value to customer and is accessible by the system might become a target of attack. Another beneficial approach is to try to identify possible attackers, as they characteristic determine nature of attack. Customer industry history is a good resource for such speculations – it contains information that can help identify popular motivations and attack techniques.* | |
| | *Abuser stories should be assigned a value corresponding with user story scores. Their score should be estimated considering how much damage can be done and probability of successful attack. Abuser story and user story scores should be equal when successful attack described in abuser story devaluates benefits from user story. Assigned scores might be changed as the conditions change (e.g. environment change). Abuser stories should be chosen for sprints to mitigate risks created by developing user stories.* | |
| Discipline | Architecture | No |
| | Deployment | No |
| | Development | Yes |
| | Environment | No |
| | Project Management | Yes |
| | Requirements | Yes |
| | Test | No |
| Capability | Factor | Values |
| | Team Size | A – Under 10 developers; B – From 10 to 50 developers; |
| | Geographical Distribution | A – Co-located; B – Same building; C – Some working from home; D – Within driving distance; E – Globally distributed |
| | Domain Complexity | A – Straightforward; B - Predictable; C – Quickly changing; D – Complicated; E – Intricate/Emerging |
| | Organisational Distribution | A – Collaborative; B – Different teams; |
| | Technical Complexity | A – Homogenous; B - Multiple technology; C – New technology; D - System/embedded solutions; E – Heterogeneous/Legacy |
| | Organisational Complexity | A – Flexible, intuitive; B – Flexible, structured; C – Stable, evolutionary; |
| | Enterprise Discipline | A – Project focus; B – Mostly project focused; C – Balanced; D – Mostly enterprise focused; E – Enterprise focus; |

**Fig. 2.**  Abuser Stories practice description

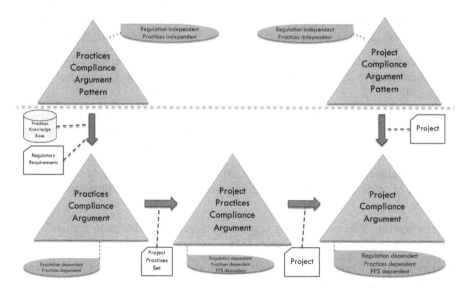

**Fig. 3.** AgileSafe assurance arguments

The first step to identify the practices was to develop queries that allowed finding suitable sources. The following queries: "secure agile practices", "xp security", "scrum security" were selected through the elimination and trial searches. The search was carried out in the IEEE Xplore digital library, ResearchGate portal and Google Scholar and Google search engines. The initial selection of articles was performed based on the following criteria: titles, summaries (if available) and access to the entire text. The sources were selected based on the fact whether they addressed the subject of security in agile methodologies. The next step was to inspect them for the presence of the agile practices. For further analysis, those articles that described such practices or those that only mentioned them were selected, provided they contained a reference to the source with further information about the practice. A similar selection process was carried out for articles found on the basis of sources obtained in the previous step. As a result, 10 articles were selected to be used in further work [20, 26–28, 30–34].

## 4.2 Selected Practices Description

Based on the articles identified in the research, 10 hybrid agile security-oriented practices were identified:

**Abuser Stories.** They describe, using a form similar to regular User Stories, how the system might be attacked and how assets might be put in risk. They should be estimated in accordance to how much damage they may potentially cause and probability of a successful attack [26].

**Evil User Stories.** This practice describes actions of malicious user (e.g. "As a hacker I want to steal payment information of other clients, so I can sell it."). They may be used as a starting point for threat modelling [27].

**Misuse Cases.** They are negative use cases. They illustrate behavior not wanted in the system, that can cause a security breach and can be described using UML diagrams [28].

**Protection Poker.** This is a software security game intended to create a list of each requirement relative security risk. It derives form Planning Poker technique of estimation [29].

**Second Delivery.** This is a process, that aims to integrate security related solutions to the project that already satisfies functional requirements. It is based on XP methodology [30].

**Security Engineer.** It calls for adding an expert role, that brings up-to-date security knowledge to developers' team. His insight is useful during multiple phases and actions in project.

**Security Sprint.** This is a practice inspired by Scrum. It's similar to regular Sprint except that it focuses on security issues [31].

**Security-Focused Code Reviews.** Such reviews should be performed for every story separately – no story can be completed without security review, fixing findings from review and then passing re-review [32].

**S-Mark and S-Tag.** Originating from Secure Scrum, they are a way to document identified security issues in Scrum Backlog by creating system of tags (security issues) and markings for stories related to respective tags [20, 34].

**Spikes.** They are a way to include security analysis and design within Scrum. They accommodate activities that don't produce customer-valued product, like security analysis or system designing [33].

## 5 Surveys

In order to evaluate the usability and accessibility of the selected security-oriented agile practices in projects with high security requirements two surveys were conducted. The first one (Survey A), analyzing more general security in agile aspects, was focused on gaining information about expected average user awareness of problems and chances related to using agile approach in such projects. The second survey (Survey B) tackled 10 specific agile security-oriented practices, asking the respondents to rate their respective ease of use and security enhancement potential.

Subjects chosen to participate in the surveys were 24 IT practitioners (both development and operations) from 7 different software companies, ranging from small to corporate ones, from Poland and UK. The questionnaire was distributed mostly by emails and direct messages in social networks, eliminating probability of acquiring responses from random, unrelated to the field respondents. The survey was created using Google Forms infrastructure, utilizing both open and closed questions. The respondents were also provided with the practices detailed descriptions.

## 5.1   Survey A

First three survey questions were used to evaluate participants' experience in agile methods and security related topics. The next two questions assessed benefits and problems related to using agile practices in projects with security requirements. Then respondents were asked about their preferred methodology. All of 24 participants answered those questions.

First question was about years of experience in agile methodologies. The results are presented in the Fig. 4. Almost half of participants declared 1–3 years of experience in agile. Less than ¼ had experience of up to 1 year. Almost 40% had been working with agile methodologies for more than 3 years. Those results suggest that most of the survey participants had at least basic knowledge about agile.

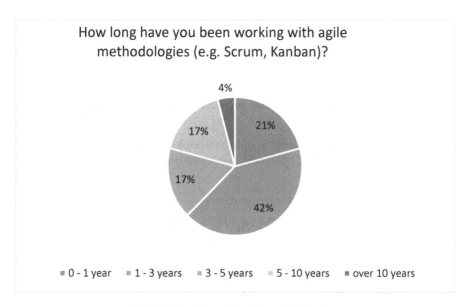

**Fig. 4.** Experience in agile methodologies

The second question, which results are presented on Fig. 5, was about experience in security reliant projects. Similarly, to the previous questions result, largest group had 1–3 years of experience. ¼ of participants declared experience shorter than 1 year. 17% had more than 3 years of experience, but none had more than 10 years. According to those results participants should have had some knowledge about security related issues.

The third question was about participation in projects with security requirements and utilized methodologies. 75% of respondents participated in such project and out of those 83% used agile methodologies, 11% used traditional methodologies, and 11% worked with different solutions (e.g. hybrid methodologies). For agile practices users, results are shown on Fig. 6. Among agile participants the most popular methodology was Scrum, then Kanban ex-aequo with agile methodologies modification. 13% of

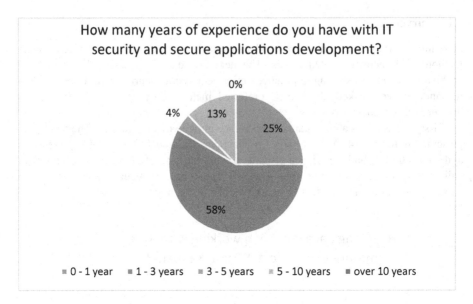

**Fig. 5.** Experience with security and secure applications development

respondents didn't mention any specific agile methodology. It's worth noting, that none of the respondents who used traditional methodologies had less than 3 years of experience in security.

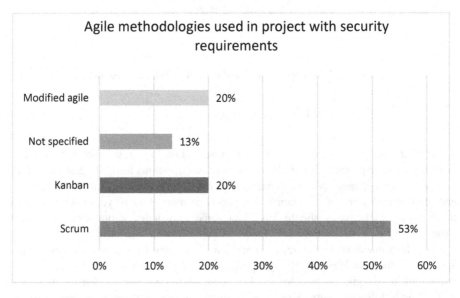

**Fig. 6.** Agile methodologies used in project with security requirements

The next question was an open one about threats related to use of using agile practices in projects with security requirements. The most popular answers were:

- problems with documentation and conforming to security standards (21%),
- allowing client to prioritize features (17%),
- using User Stories to express security requirements (17%),
- using TDD (due to problems with defining appropriate tests) (17%),
- slowing down development (17%),
- pressure to release product early (13%),
- difficulty to keep some parts of the system secret (13%).

Half of respondents mentioning slow down blamed for it security requirements and only some noticed that it's not dependent on the methodology. Among other mentioned threats were uneven level of knowledge in the team, lot of refactoring and usage of external tools. Also, worth noting is the fact that 17% of the respondents didn't come up with any problem – all of them had less than 3 years of experience in security.

Fourth question was complementary to the third one – it was about the benefits of using agile practices in projects with security requirements. The most popular answers where:

- frequent deployments, pair programming (25%),
- increased speed of development (25),
- increasing security knowledge level in the team – better communication (21%),
- User Stories and Backlog to document security requirements and raise awareness of security issues (21%),
- fast security patches release (17%),
- continuous integration (17%),
- addressing changes in requirements (17%).

Among other answers were also TDD, DDD, preventing errors and rising team awareness. 17% of respondents didn't see the difference in benefits for security and non-security projects and 4% didn't see a possibility to use agile practices in projects with security requirements at all.

Respondents were also asked about their preferred methodology for security related projects. Results are presented on Fig. 7. The vast majority chose agile methodologies, but most did not provide any justification except for curiosity. In that group the most popular was Scrum, then Kanban and their modified versions. The rest didn't mention any specific agile method. 17% of all respondents would use more traditional approach (e.g. V model or Waterfall) due to importance of documentation and planning for security. 75% of them had less than 3 years of experience in both agile and security. 8% would use hybrids of traditional and agile solutions. 4% of participants would match the methodology to project characteristic and the same amount answered that it makes no difference to the developer.

The results of the first survey showed that a lot of projects with security requirements are currently developed using agile methodologies, despite the fact that they are not perfectly suited for the task. Traditional methods created to fit this very purpose are rarely used anymore among the respondents of the survey. Also, most of the participants would like to use agile methodologies for future projects. This shows the need to

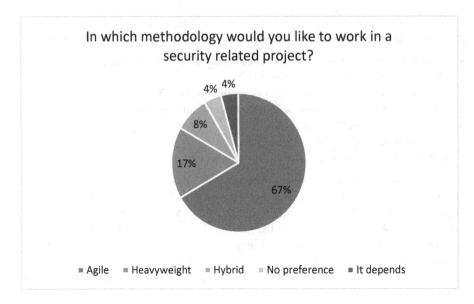

**Fig. 7.** Methodology choice for security related project

develop new, more agile methods of secure software development. The threats that respondents noticed in agile practices were mostly related to using unmodified versions of those practices, not adjusted to security needs – a place for improvement in this area is clearly visible. Also, it's important to notice that a lot of participants had little or no knowledge of security issues, despite their study and work in IT field. That calls for an effort to popularize the topic among both students and professionals.

## 5.2   Survey B

For each practice two closed questions were asked about its ease of use and if it's improving security in the project. In total, 15 of the participants made their choices in those questions. Also, each practice was open to comments from the respondents. The results are presented in the Figs. 8 and 9.

**Abuser Stories.** None of respondents chose negative answer for this practice security improvement potential and not many had doubts about its positive influence. But 27% believed it would not be easy to use - as the reason they mostly described difficulty in estimating attack probability. Despite this fact, this practice has potential benefits in the projects wanting to comply with OWASP.

**Evil User Stories.** This practice was also positively rated in terms of security improvement. What's more, only 20% expressed doubts or were undecided about its ease of use. Those results categorize it as both efficient and easy to get started with. Respondent commented on possible threat to project agility in case of creating a large number of evil user stories.

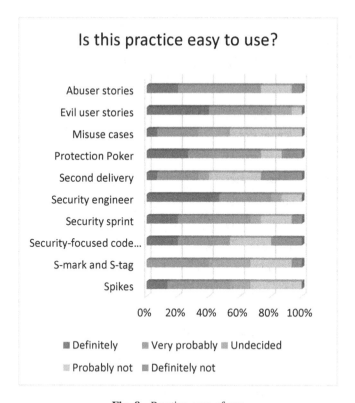

**Fig. 8.** Practice ease of use

**Protection Poker.** Majority of respondents found this practice easy to use – among the benefits they listed possible automation of prioritization. The doubts of 27% of surveyed were similar to those for Abuser Stories practice – difficulty in estimation of attack ease and probability. Another noticed difficulty is the necessity for security experts to participate in the process. Despite that problems only 7% didn't rate the practice positively in terms of security.

**Second Delivery.** This practice didn't occur as easy to use to most respondents (60%). A lot of them were concerned about the need to re-implement huge parts of system in order to satisfy security requirements. 67% of answers in question about security were positive, but considering its difficulty, this practice might not cause some problems in actual development process. Also, a significant problem with security was noticed. During the first development unexpected security flaws might be introduced to the system that are not addressed in the second delivery.

**Security Engineer.** Most of respondents (80%) rated this practice positively in terms of easiness to use, as it wouldn't require additional amount of work from the team and it would be beneficent to have an expert that is not writing the code himself. Among listed problems were difficulty in finding the suitable person for this role and risk of putting all of responsibility for security on one person. Despite those issues, rating in

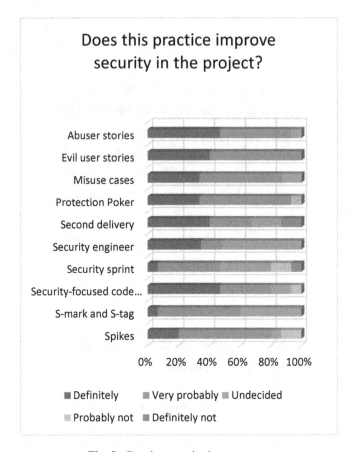

**Fig. 9.** Practice security improvement

security improvement area was very positive, with only 7% of participant undecided and none rating it negatively.

**Security Sprint.** The majority of respondents (67%) rated this practice as easy to use, but doubts were expressed that it could lead to development work duplications. Also, the question was asked about the case in which not enough security tasks are defined to fill the whole sprint. 47% of answers were positive in terms of security improvements, but as much as 33% of participants were undecided. This can indicate that practice description should be clarified when added to the Knowledge Base.

**Security-Focused Code Reviews.** Opinions on this practice's ease of use are divided – the results for definitely and definitely not are equal (20%). Among mentioned problems were difficulty with finding a suitable expert and a lot of additional effort required for conducting such reviews. Despite that, most of respondents decided that this practice improves security in the project (80%). But the expected improvement seems not to be worth the effort required.

**S-Marks and S-Tags.** None of the respondents found this practice definitely easy to use, and 40% decided it's probably easy to use. Considering amount of answers "Undecided" in both questions, this practice might be too complicated to take up without previous training. Practice gained no negative rating in terms of security, but concerns were raised that it might be possible to lose track of some tags and marks and therefore omit some security issues in development. Also, the question was asked about support in existing project management tools, which could solve tracking problem.

**Spikes.** Although the majority of respondents (53%) rated this practice as easy to use, 33% doubted it – some commented that it's difficult to understand. However, in terms of security, most of participants expressed no concern about its influence on project security. A question was also asked about other practices that can be used in security projects development. Only two answers were provided – bug bounty and security hackathon. This shows that it's not a common knowledge among developers.

The results show that, although not all practices are easy to use, most of them serve their purpose well by explicitly requiring some security assurance activities. Some of those that scored lowest in terms of easiness might be improved by description clarification, training or providing supporting tools.

## 6  OWASP Assurance Argument

Because of the positive results of practices security assurance evaluation, the next step was to add them to the Practices Knowledge Base. The selected practices were analyzed according to the AgileSafe practice description template and incorporated into the knowledge base. An example of such description is presented in Fig. 2. Newly added security practices were assessed with respect to their OWASP conformance potential. An example of such assessment is presented in the Fig. 10.

OWASP ASVS requirements has been added to the method and based on the Practices Compliance Assurance Argument Pattern, were mapped to the Practices Compliance Assurance Argument using NOR-STA tool [35]. An excerpt of this argument is presented in the Fig. 11.

All of the OWASP ASVS requirements were successfully mapped into the structure. The practices that were able to answer specific requirements were attached with a relevant rationale in the NOR-STA tool. None of the requirements were left without a practice that might be able to provide conformance.

It is worth noting that there was not one practice that would sufficiently address all of the OWASP ASVS requirements, which means that in a project wishing to comply with the standard, implementing a combination of the analyzed practices would be needed.

The prepared Practices Compliance Argument has been accepted as a part of the AgileSafe potential extension for security assurance domain. Based on this argument, depending on a given project's Project Characteristics, a new hybrid approach with OWASP ASVS compliance potential could be suggested.

| Id | 1 | | |
|---|---|---|---|
| Name | **Abuser stories** | | |
| Used in: | Name of the Regulation and regulatory requirement | General Practice | Fact |
| | OWASP ASVS / 1.10 Verify that there is no sensitive business logic, secret keys or other proprietary information in client-side code. | Abuser stories covering attacks that use sensitive business logic, secret keys or other proprietary information in client-side code can be created. | Abuser stories document security requirements for the project. Those requirements are addressed during development. |
| | OWASP ASVS / 2.19 Verify there are no default passwords in use for the application framework or any components used by the application (such as "admin/password"). | Abuser stories covering attacks that use default passwords can be created. | Abuser stories document security requirements for the project. Those requirements are addressed during development. |
| | OWASP ASVS / 2.23 Verify that account lockout is divided into soft and hard lock status, and these are not mutually exclusive. If an account is temporarily soft locked out due to a brute force attack, this should not reset the hard lock status. | Abuser stories covering attacks that use lack of hard lock, soft lock and their mutual exclusivity can be created. | Abuser stories document security requirements for the project. Those requirements are addressed during development. |
| | OWASP ASVS / 2.27 Verify that measures are in place to block the use of commonly chosen passwords and weak passphrases. | Abuser stories covering attacks that use commonly chosen passwords and weak passphrases can be created. | Abuser stories document security requirements for the project. Those requirements are addressed during development. |
| | OWASP ASVS / 2.31 Verify that if an application allows users to authenticate, they can authenticate using two-factor authentication or other strong authentication, or any similar scheme that provides protection against username + password disclosure. | Abuser stories covering attacks that use username and password disclosure can be created. | Abuser stories document security requirements for the project. Those requirements are addressed during development. |

**Fig. 10.** Abuser stories practice assessment

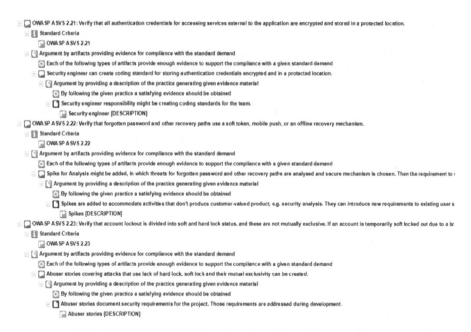

**Fig. 11.** OWASP ASVS Practices Compliance Argument excerpt

## 7  Conclusions

During the literature review, 10 security-oriented agile practices were identified. The practices were positively assessed in the conducted surveys and successfully enriched the Agile Practices Knowledge Base. The OWASP ASVS was mapped into the method and formed, along with the identified practices, the Practices Compliance Argument, which after updating it with all of the other applicable practices available in AgileSafe, might be further used to support practices selection in specific projects. A case study carried out with such projects, going through the whole practices selection process of AgileSafe might be performed as next step of the research.

## References

1. VersionOne® Releases 11th Annual State of Agile Report (2017). https://www.versionone.com/about/press-releases/versionone-releases-11th-annual-state-of-agile-report/
2. Schwaber, K., Beedle, M.: Agile Software Development with Scrum. Prentice Hall, Upper Saddle River (2002)
3. Beck, K., Andres, C.: Extreme Programming Explained. Addison-Wesley Professional, Boston (2004)
4. Anderson, D.: Kanban. Blue Hole Press, Sequim (2010)
5. Komolo, C., Gomez, M.: Incorporating security best practices into agile teams (2016). https://www.thoughtworks.com/insights/blog/incorporating-security-best-practices-agile-teams

6. Manico, J.: OWASP Application Security Verification Standard (2015)
7. Łukasiewicz, K., Górski, J.: AgileSafe – a method of introducing agile practices into safety-critical software development processes. In: Proceedings of the Federated Conference on Computer Science, vol. 8, pp. 1549–1552 (2016)
8. Agile Manifesto, Manifesto for Agile Software Development (2001). http://agilemanifesto.org
9. Drobka, J., Noftz, D., Raghu, R.: Piloting XP on four mission-critical projects. IEEE Softw. **21**(6), 70–75 (2004)
10. Lindvall, M., et al.: Agile software development in large organizations. Computer **37**(12), 26–34 (2004)
11. Knaster, R., Leffingwell, D.: SAFe Distilled: Applying the Scaled Agile Framework for Lean Software and Systems Engineering. Addison-Wesley Professional, New York (2017)
12. Kim, G., Willis, J., Debois, P., Humble, J., Allspaw, J.: The DevOps Handbook. Trade Select (2016)
13. International Organization for Standardization. About ISO - ISO. http://www.iso.org/iso/home/about.htm
14. ISO/IEC, ISO/IEC 15408-1:2009(en) (2009). https://www.iso.org/obp/ui/#iso:std:iso-iec:15408:-1:ed-3:v2:en
15. ISO/IEC, ISO/IEC 27032:2012 (2012)
16. National Institute of Standards and Technology, Framework for Improving Critical Infrastructure Cybersecurity (2014)
17. OWASP. https://www.owasp.org/index.php/Main_Page
18. OWASP users. https://www.owasp.org/index.php/Category:OWASP_Application_Security_Verification_Standard_Project#tab=ASVS_Users
19. World's Biggest Data Breaches & Hacks (2019). https://www.informationisbeautiful.net/visualizations/worlds-biggest-data-breaches-hacks/
20. Mougouei, J.D., Fazlida, N., Sani, M., Almasi, M.M.: S-Scrum: a secure methodology for agile development of web services. World Comput. Sci. Inf. Technol. J. (WCSIT) **3**(1), 15–19 (2013)
21. Łukasiewicz, K.: Method of selecting programming practices for the safety-critical software development projects. Ph.D. dissertation, Department of Software Engineering, Gdańsk University of Technology, Gdańsk, Poland (2019)
22. Górski, J., Jarzębowicz, J., Leszczyna, R., Miler, J., Olszewski, M.: Trust case: justifying trust in an IT solution. Reliab. Eng. Syst. Saf. **89**(1), 33–47 (2005)
23. Musen, M.A.: The Protégé project: a look back and a look forward. AI Matters **1**(4), 4–12 (2015). Association of Computing Machinery Specific Interest Group in Artificial Intelligence
24. Górski, J., Łukasiewicz, K.: Meeting requirements imposed by secure software development standards and still remaining agile. In: Rak, J., Bay, J., Kotenko, I., Popyack, L., Skormin, V., Szczypiorski, K. (eds.) MMM-ACNS 2017. LNCS, vol. 10446, pp. 3–15. Springer, Cham (2017). https://doi.org/10.1007/978-3-319-65127-9_1
25. IEC 62443-4-1 4-1: Secure product development life-cycle requirements
26. Peeters, J.: Agile security requirements engineering. In: Symposium on Requirements Engineering for Information Security (2005)
27. Fischer, E.A.: Federal Laws Relating to Cybersecurity: Overview of Major Issues, Current Laws, and Proposed Legislation (2014)
28. Sindre, G., Opdahl, A.L.: Eliciting security requirements with misuse cases. Requirements Eng. **10**(1), 34–44 (2005)
29. Williams, L., Meneely, A., Shipley, G.: Protection poker: the new software security "game". IEEE Secur. Priv. **3**, 14–20 (2010)

30. Aydal, E.G., Paige, R.F., Chivers, H., Brooke, P.J.: Security planning and refactoring in extreme programming. In: Abrahamsson, P., Marchesi, M., Succi, G. (eds.) XP 2006. LNCS, vol. 4044, pp. 154–163. Springer, Heidelberg (2006). https://doi.org/10.1007/11774129_16
31. Boström, G., Wäyrynen, J., Bodén, M., Beznosov, K., Kruchten, P.: Extending XP practices to support security requirements engineering. In: Proceedings of the 2006 International Workshop on Software Engineering for Secure Systems (SESS 2006). ACM, New York, pp. 11–18. http://dx.doi.org/10.1145/1137627.1137631
32. Nguyen, T.: Integrating Security into Agile Methodologies. http://www.umsl.edu/ ~ sauterv/ analysis/F2015/Integrating%20Security%20into%20Agile%20methodologies.html.htm
33. OWASP: Agile Software Development: Don't Forget EVIL User Stories. https://www. owasp.org/index.php/Agile_Software_Development:_Don%27t_Forget_EVIL_User_Stories
34. Pohl, C., Hof, H.-J.: Secure Scrum: development of secure software with scrum. In: Securware 2015: The Ninth International Conference on Emerging Security Information, Systems and Technologies (2015)
35. NOR-STA project Portal (2017). www.nor-sta.eu
36. Łukasiewicz, K., Cygańska, S.: Security-oriented agile approach with AgileSafe and OWASP ASVS. In: Proceedings of the 2019 Federated Conference on Computer Science and Information Systems, Leipzig, Germany (2019)

# Quantitative Analysis of the Scrum Framework

Ridewaan Hanslo[1]([⊠]) [iD], Anwar Vahed[2] [iD], and Ernest Mnkandla[3] [iD]

[1] Council for Scientific and Industrial Research, Pretoria, South Africa
rhanslo@csir.co.za
[2] Data Intensive Research Initiative of South Africa, Pretoria, South Africa
avahed@dirisa.ac.za
[3] School of Computing, College of Science, Engineering and Technology,
University of South Africa, Pretoria, South Africa
mnkane@unisa.ac.za

**Abstract.** Scrum provides many benefits to organizations requiring a project management framework for complex adaptive problems. Some of these benefits include improved teamwork, improved time to market, and a noticeable decrease in software defects. The primary objective of this paper is to test nineteen research hypotheses that require a quantitative analysis of the Scrum framework. In order to test these hypotheses, the findings of a survey questionnaire was used to gather response data from Scrum practitioners on their perceptions of factors affecting Scrum adoption. Exploratory factor analysis and Cronbach's alpha analysis confirmed the validity and reliability of the measuring instrument. Following these analyses, a correlation matrix was used to test the relationship strength among the different factors. The Spearman correlation analysis revealed statistically significant correlations. Multiple linear regression statistical models were developed to examine the existence of factors and constructs impacting Scrum adoption. Our findings indicate that four of the nineteen hypotheses are statistically significant. The factors Change Resistance, Sprint Management, Relative Advantage, and Complexity are shown to have a significant linear relationship to Scrum as perceived by Scrum Practitioners working within South African organizations. Future research could incorporate a larger population sample to improve the generalizability of the findings.

**Keywords:** Scrum · Agile methodologies · Conceptual framework · Multiple linear regression · Project management · Significant factors · Quantitative analysis

## 1 Introduction

Scrum is regarded as one of the most under researched Agile methodologies [1], and the majority of research literature in this field is found to be qualitative in nature [2]. This paper focuses on quantitatively analyzing the Scrum framework for constructs and factors that are hypothesized to have a significant relationship with Scrum adoption.

A previous paper on Scrum adoption challenges focused on developing a model that can be used to test and evaluate challenges to Scrum adoption [3]. The previous paper also describes the nineteen factors that are tested in our hypotheses. To test and

A. Przybyłek and M. E. Morales-Trujillo (Eds.): LASD 2019/MIDI 2019, LNBIP 376, pp. 82–107, 2020.
https://doi.org/10.1007/978-3-030-37534-8_5

evaluate these adoption challenges a narrative review was conducted on the existing Agile and Scrum adoption challenges experienced globally and by practitioners in South Africa (SA) in particular. The narrative review was used to extract and synthesize the challenges. The synthesized challenges were used as the independent variables of the model. The first iteration of the Conceptual Framework (CF) is known as the Scrum Adoption Challenges Detection Model (SACDM). This CF is a custom model adapted from the Diffusion of Innovation (DOI) theory and a study of the adoption of new technology by Sultan & Chan [12].

A previous paper entitled *"Factors that contribute significantly to Scrum adoption"* [36] described the process behind the three iterations of the CF. The online survey questionnaire serving as a Likert-type scale, gathered response data through 78 questionnaire items. A set of 207 valid responses to this survey was used to perform Exploratory Factor Analysis (EFA) and Cronbach's alpha analysis, which confirmed the validity and reliability of the questionnaire as the measuring instrument. The results from the correlational and Multiple Linear Regression (MLR) statistics were used to identify factors that have a significant linear relationship with Scrum adoption.

From these responses we were able to test the 19 hypotheses, and discuss the findings for each of the predicted statements.

## 1.1  Research Hypotheses

We collected and analyzed data to test whether the following hypotheses for the nineteen factors, could be accepted:

- *H1 - Escalation of Commitment:* There is a significant linear (negative correlation) relationship between Escalation of Commitment and Scrum adoption.
- *H2 - Experience:* There is a significant linear (positive correlation) relationship between Experience and Scrum adoption.
- *H3 - Over-Engineering:* There is a significant linear (negative correlation) relationship between Over-Engineering and Scrum adoption.
- *H4 - Communication:* There is a significant linear (positive correlation) relationship between Communication and Scrum adoption.
- *H5 - Teamwork:* There is a significant linear (positive correlation) relationship between Teamwork and Scrum adoption.
- *H6 - Specialization:* There is a significant linear (negative correlation) relationship between Specialization and Scrum adoption.
- *H7 - Sprint Management:* There is a significant linear (positive correlation) relationship between Sprint Management and Scrum adoption.
- *H8 - Change Resistance:* There is a significant linear (negative correlation) relationship between Change Resistance and Scrum adoption.
- *H9 - Training:* There is a significant linear (positive correlation) relationship between Training and Scrum adoption.
- *H10 - Recognition:* There is a significant linear (positive correlation) relationship between Recognition and Scrum adoption.
- *H11 - Quality:* There is a significant linear (positive correlation) relationship between Quality and Scrum adoption.

- *H12 - Resources:* There is a significant linear (positive correlation) relationship between Resources and Scrum adoption.
- *H13 - Collaboration:* There is a significant linear (positive correlation) relationship between Collaboration and Scrum adoption.
- *H14 - Management Support:* There is a significant linear (positive correlation) relationship between Management Support and Scrum adoption.
- *H15 - Organizational Culture:* There is a significant linear (positive correlation) relationship between Organizational Culture and Scrum adoption.
- *H16 - Organizational Structure:* There is a significant linear (negative correlation) relationship between Organizational Structure and Scrum adoption.
- *H17 - Relative Advantage:* There is a significant linear (positive correlation) relationship between Relative Advantage and Scrum adoption.
- *H18 - Complexity:* There is a significant linear (negative correlation) relationship between Complexity and Scrum adoption.
- *H19 - Compatibility:* There is a significant linear (positive correlation) relationship between Compatibility and Scrum adoption.

## 1.2   Research Limitations

There is no restriction to the geolocation of the responses within SA. However, the majority of SA's organizations and Scrum practitioners are in the provinces of Gauteng and the Western Cape. Another limitation of this study is the lack of a systematic review used to extract and synthesis adoption challenges. The narrative review results in the data being unreproducible. This study investigates Scrum adoption from the perspective of the individual Scrum practitioner perceptions, which further limits the influence of these findings on the organization's or team's decision to adopt Scrum. The last limitation is in the small sample size, which impact the generalizability of the research outcomes.

## 1.3   Research Scope

Excluded from this research, are adoption research of other Agile software development methodologies, as well as non-agile methodologies. No research was conducted outside the borders of the SA software organization, since the focus of interest is specific to the adoption factors by Scrum practitioners working in SA organizations. Within SA borders, there was no data collection from most of the nine provinces since the use of Scrum or similar methodologies occurs in provinces where such project development is most prevalent. Data collection hence mainly derived from the Gauteng and Western Cape provinces.

Implementation challenges were excluded since these challenges were considered to be beyond the scope of this research. A qualitative methodology was not used even though the respondents' opinions were recorded. The reason for this decision was that the research focus was not on the semantics of the questionnaire responses.

## 1.4    Research Significance

This paper aims to make the following research contributions on Scrum adoption:

- The use of constructs at the individual, team, organization, and technology level to identify factors that contribute significantly to Scrum adoption.
- Based on the empirical findings, provide suggestions for future research.

The remainder of this paper comprises the following sections: Sect. 2 provides background to the topic; Sect. 3 presents the research methodology including the statistical analysis techniques used to analyze and validate the data collection instrument. The results of data collection are presented in Sect. 4 and a discussion of the research findings is provided in Sect. 5. Section 6 concludes the paper and provides recommendations for extending this work.

## 2    Background

### 2.1    Software Development Methodologies

Migrating from non-agile to Agile methodologies poses many challenges. Some of these challenges are changes in management style, communication methods, and process changes within organizations [11].

Before discussing the Agile challenges presented in current literature, a non-exhaustive list of Agile methodologies used in practice, are briefly described. These methodologies provide some contextual background for Scrum.

**Adaptive Software Development.** Adaptive Software Development (ASD) was introduced by Jim Highsmith and it provides a technique to increase the success rate of developing complete, customer approved complex software and systems [18]. The cornerstones of the methodology are collaboration and team self-organization, as is evident in ASD's adaptive life cycle. The three phases of the life cycle are speculation, collaboration and learning.

**Dynamic Systems Development Method.** The Dynamic Systems Development Method (DSDM) is an Agile software development approach that does not focus primarily on system writing but instead, has a more abstract software development focus [19]. DSDM is considered to be an incremental method and is often compared to the Rapid Application Development (RAD) model which emphasizes a short development cycle [18]. DSDM follows what is termed the 80% rule, where 80% of the system is developed in 20% of the time and generating only the work required for each increment to be able to proceed to the next increment. The DSDM methodology includes steps for feasibility, business study, functional model iteration, and implementation.

**Extreme Programming.** Extreme Programming (XP) has been a widely adopted Agile software development method, and was first publicized by Kent Beck [18]. The key practices of XP are the following:

- A team of five to ten programmers work at one location with customer representation on-site.
- Development occurs in frequent builds or iterations, which may or may not be releasable, and delivers incremental functionality.
- Requirements are specified as user stories, each being a chunk of new functionality that the user requires.
- Programmers work in pairs, follow strict coding standards, and perform their unit testing.
- Customers participate in acceptance testing.
- Requirements, architecture, and design emerge over the course of the project.

XP is prescriptive in scope and customers are often readily available on-site for communication and collaboration purposes. The learning outcomes by paired programmers are invaluable, as the one developer that is not programming guides the one who is programming and this results in higher software quality in a shorter time interval [20].

**Feature-Driven Development.** Originally conceived by Peter Coad and his colleagues, Feature-Driven Development (FDD) is an Agile method for object-oriented software engineering [18]. *"A feature is a small, client-valued function expressed in the form: <action><result> <object> with the appropriate prepositions between the action, result, or object"* [21]. FDD places greater emphasis on project management than most of the other Agile methodologies, with ad hoc project management becoming inadequate as the project grows in size. FDD defines six milestones during the design and build of a feature to improve the likelihood of success of scheduled software increments [18]. The milestones for each feature are the following:

- Domain walkthrough.
- Design.
- Design inspection.
- Code.
- Code inspection.
- Promote to build.

**Lean Software Development.** Lean Software Development (LSD) is not an Agile methodology but rather a set of tools and principles that *"make the software projects leaner"* [19]. LSD draws its origins from the vehicle manufacturing industry, where productivity is measured by maximum reduction in unnecessary resource use, rather than increased throughput. Koch [19] explains that LSD is characterized by seven lean principles. LSD's principles are further expanded into 22 lean software development tools.

## 2.2 Scrum Defined

We present a description of Scrum because of its significance in the development of the CF. The quantitative analysis performed on the developed custom model includes factors such as Relative Advantage, Complexity, Compatibility, Sprint Management, and Teamwork. The significance of the relationship between these factors and Scrum are moreover influenced by the Scrum practitioner's use and understanding of Scrum.

Scrum is one of many Agile software development methodologies available. This methodology has seen exponential growth in its application over the past decade [7]. As a framework, Scrum allows organizations to improve on their project delivery objectives [17]. The Scrum guide written by Ken Schwaber and Jeff Sutherland describes this framework as lightweight, simple to understand, but extremely difficult to master [8]. Scrum embodies iterative and incremental development, and the framework comprises six artifacts, five roles, and four predominant activities [8]. The Scrum process as depicted in Fig. 1, displays some of the artifacts and activities involved in the Scrum process.

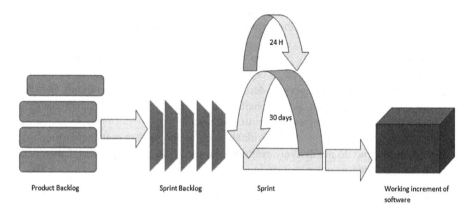

**Fig. 1.** A depiction of the components of the Scrum process.

The following lists the items within each of the three components of artifacts, roles, and activities that make up the Scrum process:

The six Scrum artifacts are:

- *Product Backlog:* The list of product items requested by the customer; for whom the software development team needs to complete. The managing of the product backlog is the responsibility of the product owner [22].
- *User Stories:* A user story is the increment of value to the customer written on a card. The product backlog is a collection of user stories [22, 23]. See Heikkila and others [22] for a detailed explanation of how product requirements are broken down into smaller and more manageable user stories and tasks, from the features and epics.
- *Backlog Sizing:* The size generation of the product backlog.
- *Sprint Backlog:* The amount of work that needs to be completed by the development team within the current sprint (the sprint is usually 30 days in length). The sprint backlog is a subset of the product backlog [23].
- *Burndown Chart:* Displays how the remaining work of the sprint task completion is progressing in graphical format.

- *Acceptance Criteria:* Seen as a secondary artifact, which provides the developer with steps to follow before a story is considered done. The acceptance criteria are created with the assistance of the product owner.

Scrum roles can be broken up into five categories as listed below:

- *Scrum Master:* This person is responsible for ensuring that the entire Scrum process team are kept informed of, and adheres to the Scrum practices. This position is seen as the Scrum mentor and its role is to also be the intermediary between the development team and the customer. The Scrum master provides the development team with the administrative support of Scrum, although a member of the development team often fills this position [24].
- *Product Owner:* The product owner is responsible for the product backlog and ensuring that the development team fulfils the requirements of the customer [22].
- *Customer:* This role is that of the organization or individual for whom the product is developed.
- *Development Team:* Usually a group of 5 to 9 members (although subgroups of these numbers may exist in large organizations with multi projects) from various professions such as developers, testers, business analysts, designers, and DevOps engineers [25]. The team is responsible for ensuring that the product backlog shrinks in size as the number of sprints increases.
- *Other Stakeholders:* These are individuals such as the project managers, directors, and sponsors who do not actively contribute towards the Scrum process. Customers are often included as other stakeholders [23].

The four activities that most Scrum teams and Scrum organizations deploy are sprint planning, daily stand-ups (Scrums), sprint reviews and sprint retrospectives. Other activities are not mentioned here, including activities that are specific to an organization and the Scrum team.

- *Sprint Planning:* This is the major four-hour long meeting which includes many of the Scrum roles. The length of the meeting might vary based on organizational preferences. The roles that must be present are the Scrum master, product owner and development team. The meeting will determine which stories to include into the next sprint and which to exclude. The sprint usually lasts for 30 days. However, this can be amended to suit the organization. What is included or excluded in the Sprint is decided between the product owner and the development team, with greater influence coming from the latter.
- *Daily Stand-ups (Scrums):* The Scrum is a brief fifteen-minute meeting for the development team and the Scrum master. The daily stand-up time of commencement during the day is irrelevant; however, it usually takes place as the first activity in the morning. Matters discussed by each member of the development team are [24]:

1. What have you done since yesterday?
2. What are you planning to do today?
3. What obstacles are preventing you from achieving your goal?

- *Sprint Review:* The review happens at the end of the sprint and gives the opportunity for the development team to present the work of the completed sprint to the customer and other stakeholders. The completed sprint is presented in the form of a demo, and the customer provides feedback.
- *Sprint Retrospectives:* Retrospectives is a time-boxed meeting for the development team and the Scrum master, to discuss ways in which the last sprint can be improved.

## 2.3    Adoption Challenges

The introduction of new methodologies typically poses challenges for individuals and organizations who make use of them [9]. The adoption of Agile methodologies creates additional challenges such as management style, software development process, and software developer resistance [2].

The challenges in the context of this paper is taken from a previous paper entitled *"Scrum Adoption Challenges Detection Model (SACDM)"* [3]. These challenges were derived from Agile, Scrum, software development methodology, and information systems literature. These challenges are encountered both within SA and globally elsewhere.

Due to Scrum research being primarily qualitative in nature [10], other Agile methodology challenges were considered as well in order to attain a more comprehensive model. Common issues such as lack of experience, the organizational culture, and lack of communication have been identified during the narrative review.

## 2.4    Theoretical Framework

Research by Chan and Thong [11], and Mohan and Ahlemann [9] explain that previous information technology adoption studies focused on the technical aspects of the innovation. These studies made use of technology adoption models, such as Technology Adoption Model (TAM). However, with complex Agile methodologies such as Scrum where collaboration between individuals within teams and organizations are important, a more inclusive model was required. The mixture of factors that affect adoption led to the selection the DOI theory as the theoretical lens for the Conceptual Framework (CF) [13].

The DOI theory is used in both organizational and individual adoption studies, with the DOI model composed of five characteristics of innovation. The five characteristics of innovation are Compatibility, Complexity, Observability, Relative Advantage, and Trialability [13].

In our custom model, as shown in Fig. 2, Compatibility, Complexity, and Relative Advantage are the three characteristics of innovation that have been retained. This decision was based on the strength of the relationship between these three characteristics and adoption behavior as identified in innovation studies [14].

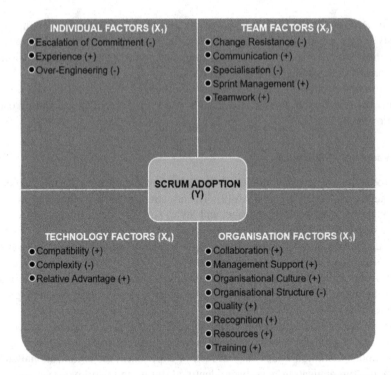

**Fig. 2.** Scrum Adoption Challenges Conceptual Framework (SACCF) [36].

## 3   Methodology

### 3.1   Research Design

The research design starts with a narrative review and the results from a survey questionnaire. This review was conducted due to the lack of quantitative literature on Scrum adoption. However, the factors of the CF were extracted and synthesized from the review of Scrum and Agile adoption challenges.

The quantitative survey design effectively operationalized the factors identified through the review as the independent variables, and Scrum adoption as the dependent variable. The online survey was used as the scale to measure the opinions of the Scrum practitioners in SA organizations [16].

The validity of the scale was tested using a pilot study, and the application of Exploratory Factor Analysis (EFA), Bartlett's test for Sphericity, and Kaiser-Meyer-Olkin (KMO). Bartlett's test for Sphericity, EFA, and KMO are discussed in the data analysis subsection. For reliability, the Cronbach's coefficient alpha was used to measure internal consistency of the scale [16].

## 3.2 Population and Sample

**Units of Analysis.** The population in this paper refers to the activities, cases, events, objects, phenomena, and subjects used for sampling [26]. The sample group (n = 207) is from the population consisting of all Scrum practitioners in SA organizations. To clarify further, Scrum practitioners in the context of this paper refers to any professional employed within a SA organization who is using Scrum while being involved in the Software Development Life Cycle (SDLC). Professionals include developers, testers, management, clients, Scrum masters, and product owners. A SA organization is any organization located within South Africa that have individuals or teams that practice Scrum as an Agile methodology.

**Sampling Method.** With reference to sampling, Floyd and Fowler [27] list five essential characteristics of a suitable sampling method:

- Deciding to select a probability or non-probability sample.
- The sample frame, and its generalization.
- The sample size.
- The sample design, and its implementation strategy.
- The response rates.

With above in mind, the sampling types that were considered for inclusion were, self-selection sampling, purposive sampling, and quota sampling. It was decided to conduct the survey using a non-probability, self-selection sampling method mainly because (a) it takes less time to complete in comparison with other methods, and (b) it presents a greater chance to obtain a more considerable number of responses.

## 3.3 Measuring Instrument

**Survey Questionnaire.** A sound survey questionnaire is defined to be one that complies with the following pertinent criteria:

- Questions are relevant and well-structured.
- The questionnaire is evaluated by means of a pilot study.
- The required response data is elicited from the sample.

The end goal of a good questionnaire is to determine what the sample's biographical details, attitudes, behavior, opinions, beliefs and convictions are toward independent variables [16]. Since the questionnaire was self-administered, it was of greater importance that the questions in the questionnaire were unambiguous, clear, understandable and straightforward [28]. The questionnaire also included ordinal measurements for ranking.

The rationale for using a questionnaire as a survey instrument can be summarized as follows:

- Inexpensive to administer.
- Less time-consuming to manage.
- Offers greater anonymity than other, e.g., face-to-face methods.

- A greater number of respondents are reachable.
- Data can be pre-coded.

**Attitude Scales.** One of the main aspects that the questionnaire focused on, was the attitude of the practitioner. *"Attitude"* for the purpose of this study is taken to be a particular mindset or disposition towards a particular issue, the issue being the so-called attitudinal object. Examples of an attitudinal object are, political issues, a single individual, a group of people or a custom [16]. The measuring scale for attitudinal aspects toward Scrum is the Likert-type scale. This scale is most popular due to its ease of compilation [16]. A seven-point Likert-type scale was used to measure the respondent's attitude toward adoption challenges of Scrum. The designed scale is as follows:

- 7 = Strongly agree
- 6 = Agree
- 5 = Agree somewhat
- 4 = Neither agree nor disagree
- 3 = Disagree somewhat
- 2 = Disagree
- 1 = Strongly disagree

The rationale for using this scale is to obtain an indication of the respondent's attitude in terms of the relationship of the independent variable with Scrum. The correlational relationship between the independent variables and the dependent variable, is evaluated by the analysis subsequently performed on the collected data.

### 3.4   Data Analysis

Exploratory Factor Analysis (EFA) is a statistical method used to describe the variability of observed variables in terms of unobserved constructs [4]. The validation of the questionnaire items against the initial 19 factors in the SACCF required a first and second order EFA to be conducted. In the first order EFA we considered the 78 survey questionnaire items to construct the newly validated 14 factors. These factors were subjected to a second order EFA in order to develop the four constructs.

The validity analysis proceeded by generating the first order EFA scores, and once these scores were summarized, the second order EFA followed. To test the sampling adequacy, the KMO measure of sampling adequacy was used. The KMO value obtained was 0.88. The Bartlett's test for Sphericity was conducted to determine if it was useful to conduct factor analysis. The Bartlett's test for Sphericity significance level was determined to be 0.00. These test results indicated that it was justifiable to conduct the EFA on the dataset.

In order to determine the number of factors derived from the individual statements, Eigenvalues greater than or near one, and the Scree plot were used. The constructs' cumulative percentage was 75.8%.

The Principal Axis Factoring (PAF) extraction method with oblique rotation was used to seek a parsimonious representation for the common variance (correlation) between variables by latent factors. The oblique rotation implemented the Oblimin with

Kaiser Normalization method since it was required to explore the correlations between the factors.

In summary, of the 78 questionnaire items, 14 factors were retained for rotation due to their Eigenvalues being greater than or near one. The first 14 factors as a collective accounted for 75.8% of the total variance.

Because of the factor loading cut-off criteria of 0.40, a total of 12 items were found to load on the first factor, and these were subsequently labelled "Organizational Behavior". Eight items loaded on the second factor, labelled "Sprint Management". Nine items loaded on the third factor, labelled "Relative Advantage". Four items loaded on the fourth, fifth, sixth, and the seventh factor respectively, labelled "Experience", "Training", "Specialization", and "Recognition". Seven items loaded on the eighth factor, labelled "Customer Collaboration". Three items loaded on the ninth factor, labelled "Compatibility". Five items loaded on the tenth factor, labelled "Over-Engineering". Three items loaded on the eleventh and twelfth factor respectively, labelled "Escalation of Commitment", and "Complexity". Eight items loaded on the thirteenth factor, labelled "Teamwork", and four items loaded on the fourteenth factor labelled "Resource Management". Table 1 shows the mapping of the initial 19 CF factors to the validated 14 factors.

**Table 1.** Mapping of the initial 19 factors to the validated 14 factors [36].

| Fourteen factors loaded from questionnaire items | Nineteen factors based on literature review |
|---|---|
| Organizational Behavior | ➢ Organizational Structure<br>➢ Management Support<br>➢ Organizational Culture |
| Sprint Management | ➢ Sprint Management<br>➢ Change Resistance |
| Relative Advantage | ➢ Relative Advantage |
| Experience | ➢ Experience |
| Training | ➢ Training |
| Specialization | ➢ Specialization |
| Recognition | ➢ Recognition |
| Customer Collaboration | ➢ Collaboration<br>➢ Quality |
| Compatibility | ➢ Compatibility |
| Over-Engineering | ➢ Over-Engineering |
| Escalation of Commitment | ➢ Escalation of Commitment |
| Complexity | ➢ Complexity |
| Teamwork | ➢ Teamwork<br>➢ Communication |
| Resource Management | ➢ Resources |

The second order EFA was conducted on the 14 factors derived from the first order EFA output. The PAF extraction method and the Oblimin with Kaiser Normalization (oblique) rotation method were used to calculate the scores. The second order EFA generated the KMO measure of sampling adequacy test result of 0.78 and a Bartlett's test for Sphericity significance level of 0.00 which made it viable to conduct an EFA. The Eigenvalues generated from the PAF extraction method resulted in 4 constructs, with the Eigenvalues greater than or near 1 and the Scree plot identifying the valid constructs. The cumulative percentage explained by the four constructs is 67.8%.

In summary, the second order EFA was applied to the 14 factors calculated in the first order EFA. The PAF method was used to extract the factors, followed by the Oblimin with Kaiser Normalization (oblique) rotation method. Of the 14 input factors, only four factors were retained for rotation, because of their Eigenvalue being greater than or near one. The first four factors as a collective accounted for 67.8% of the cumulative variance. These four factors are consequently referred to as the four constructs of the SACCF.

## 4   Results

The previous section described the methodology used to derive to the validated factors and constructs of the CF. A statistical analysis of the results derived with this methodology, is presented in this section.

### 4.1   Statistical Techniques that Answer the Hypotheses

**Testing the Fourteen First Order Factor Relationship Strength.** Correlation analysis was used to test for the relationship strength among the different factors. The Spearman correlation analysis was conducted on all the factors as opposed to a Pearson correlation analysis, due to the skewness of the data discovered during the normality tests. The Spearman correlation analysis revealed statistically significant correlations for the relationships between Scrum Adoption and all the factors at the 0.01 level, except for Teamwork which was significant at the 0.05 level ($p = 0.018$), and Over-Engineering with no significance ($p = 0.514$), as shown in Table 2.

**Testing the Four Second Order Factor Relationship Strength.** A Spearman correlation matrix was used to test the relationship strength among the four constructs, as well as between the four constructs and the dependent variable. Once again, Spearman correlation analysis was selected, instead of a Pearson correlation analysis, due to the skewness of the data indicated by the normality tests. This analysis revealed statistically significant correlations between Scrum Adoption and the four constructs at the 0.01 level as shown in Table 3.

**Testing the Statistical Significance of the Factor Relationship.** All the normality assumptions were met when a regression analysis was conducted on the 14 factors. Tolerance values were above .01, and all the Variance Inflation Factor (VIF) values were below 10, and the assumption of non-multicollinearity was met. The Durbin-Watson statistic fell within an expected range, which suggested that the assumption of no autocorrelation of residuals was met. The assumptions of linearity and homoscedasticity

**Table 2.** Correlations among all the factors used in the study [36].

| | F1 | F2 | F3 | F4 | F5 | F6 | F7 | F8 | F9 | F10 | F11 | F12 | F13 | F14 | F15 |
|---|---|---|---|---|---|---|---|---|---|---|---|---|---|---|---|
| F1 | 1.00 | .30** | .28** | .30** | .66** | .22** | .23** | .20** | .34** | .50** | .22** | .34** | .16* | .20** | .05 |
| F2 | .30** | 1.00 | .14* | .32** | .29** | .26** | .25** | .19** | .20** | .23** | .27** | .19** | .21** | .06 | .09 |
| F3 | .28** | .14* | 1.00 | .25** | .29** | .58** | .24** | .66** | .72** | .27** | .30** | .36** | .16* | .64** | -.18* |
| F4 | .30** | .32** | .25** | 1.00 | .10 | .25** | .01 | .09 | .26** | .09 | .08 | .10 | .71** | .16* | .26** |
| F5 | .66** | .29** | .29** | .10 | 1.00 | .29** | .27** | .24** | .35** | .64** | .28** | .51** | .01 | .24** | -.02 |
| F6 | .22** | .26** | .58** | .25** | .29** | 1.00 | .28** | .65** | .51** | .23** | .21** | .26** | .10 | .39** | -.01 |
| F7 | .23** | .25** | .24** | -.01 | .27** | .28** | 1.00 | .24** | .31** | .32** | .34** | .31** | -.07 | .24** | -.23** |
| F8 | .20** | .19** | .66** | .09 | .24** | .65** | .24** | 1.00 | .55** | .24** | .16* | .34** | .07 | .48** | -.09 |
| F9 | .34** | .20** | .72** | .26** | .35** | .51** | .31** | .55** | 1.00 | .29** | .29** | .39** | .11 | .57** | -.12 |
| F10 | .50** | .23** | .27** | .09 | .64** | .23** | .32** | .24** | .29** | 1.00 | .22** | .58** | .01 | .25** | -.04 |
| F11 | .22** | .27** | .30** | .08 | .28** | .21** | .34** | .16* | .29** | .22** | 1.00 | .27** | -.02 | .30** | -.33** |
| F12 | .34** | .19** | .36** | .10 | .51** | .26** | .31** | .34** | .39** | .58** | .27** | 1.00 | .01 | .42** | -.14* |
| F13 | .16* | .21** | .16* | .71** | .01 | .10 | -.07 | .07 | .11 | .01 | -.02 | .01 | 1.00 | .13 | .28** |
| F14 | .20** | .06 | .64** | .16* | .24** | .39** | .24** | .48** | .57** | .25** | .30** | .42** | .13 | 1.00 | -.24** |
| F15 | .05 | .09 | -.18* | .26** | -.02 | -.01 | -.23** | -.09 | -.12 | -.04 | -.33** | -.14* | .28** | -.24** | 1.00 |

F1 = Scrum Adoption, F2 = Experience, F3 = Organizational Behavior, F4 = Sprint Management, F5 = Relative Advantage, F6 = Training, F7 = Specialization, F8 = Recognition, F9 = Customer Collaboration, F10 = Compatibility, F11 = Escalation of Commitment, F12 = Complexity, F13 = Teamwork, F14 = Resource Management, F15 = Over-Engineering.
N Missing 0
** Correlation is significant at the 0.01 level (2-tailed).
* Correlation is significant at the 0.05 level (2-tailed).

**Table 3.** Correlations between the four constructs and Scrum adoption [36].

|  | Scrum adoption | Individual | Organization | Team | Technology |
|---|---|---|---|---|---|
| Scrum Adoption | 1.00 | .29** | .30** | .20** | .53** |
| Individual[a] | .29** | 1.00 | .39** | .16* | .38** |
| Organization | .30** | .39** | 1.00 | .25** | .42** |
| Team[a] | .20** | .16* | .25** | 1.00 | .07 |
| Technology | .53** | .38** | .42** | .07 | 1.00 |

N Missing 0
** Correlation is significant at the 0.01 level (2-tailed).
* Correlation is significant at the 0.05 level (2-tailed).
[a] = the factor's negatively phrased questions were recoded.

were also met, since the scatterplot of standardized residual and standardized predicted value did not curve or funnel out. The normal probability plot of the residuals was approximately linear, which suggests that the assumption of normality of residuals was also met.

Of the 14 factors, MLR was conducted to examine whether Over-Engineering, Relative Advantage, Recognition, Experience, Teamwork, Specialization, Escalation of Commitment, Compatibility, Resource Management, Customer Collaboration, Complexity, Training, Sprint Management, and Organizational Behavior impact on Scrum Adoption. The overall model (predictors: Over-Engineering, Relative Advantage, Recognition, Experience, Teamwork, Specialization, Escalation of Commitment, Compatibility, Resource Management, Customer Collaboration, Complexity, Training, Sprint Management, Organizational Behavior) explained 52.9% of the variance of Scrum Adoption, which was determined to be statistically significant ($F(14, 206) = 15.40$, $p < 0.0001$).

An inspection of the individual predictors of the overall model revealed that Relative Advantage ($\beta = 0.688$, $p < 0.0001$), Sprint Management ($\beta = 0.109$, $p < 0.05$), and Complexity ($\beta = 0.041$, $p < 0.05$) are significant predictors of Scrum Adoption (as shown in Table 4). Higher levels of Relative Advantage are associated with higher levels of Scrum Adoption; higher levels of Sprint Management are associated with higher levels of Scrum Adoption, and higher levels of Complexity are associated with lower levels of Scrum Adoption.

For the four constructs, MLR was conducted to examine whether Individual Factors, Technology Factors, Team Factors, and Organization Factors impact on Scrum Adoption. The overall model explained 33.40% of the variance in Scrum Adoption, which was shown to be statistically significant ($F(4, 206) = 25.34$, $p < 0.0001$). An inspection of the individual predictors revealed that Technology Factors ($b = 0.580$, $p < 0.0001$) and Team Factors ($b = 0.126$, $p < 0.05$) are significant predictors of Scrum Adoption (see Table 5). Higher levels of Technology Factors are associated with higher levels of Scrum Adoption, and higher levels of Team Factors are associated with higher levels of Scrum Adoption.

**Table 4.** Regression coefficients of the 14 factors [36].

Coefficients[a]

| Model | | Unstandardized coefficients | | Standardized coefficients | T | Sig. |
|---|---|---|---|---|---|---|
| | | B | Std. error | Beta | | |
| 1 | (Constant) | .506 | .454 | | 1.114 | .267 |
| | Experience | −.021 | .051 | −.026 | −.419 | .676 |
| | Organizational Behavior | .000 | .062 | .000 | .003 | .998 |
| | Sprint Management[b] | .109 | .049 | .178 | 2.239 | .026 |
| | Relative Advantage | .688 | .068 | .702 | 10.168 | .000 |
| | Training | −.031 | .052 | −.045 | −.604 | .547 |
| | Specialization | .004 | .042 | .006 | .103 | .918 |
| | Recognition | −.019 | .047 | −.032 | −.410 | .682 |
| | Customer Collaboration | .118 | .062 | .151 | 1.900 | .059 |
| | Compatibility | .085 | .058 | .099 | 1.477 | .141 |
| | Escalation of Commitment | .011 | .041 | .018 | .280 | .780 |
| | Complexity | −.116 | .056 | −.146 | −2.061 | .041 |
| | Teamwork[b] | −.013 | .047 | −.021 | −.279 | .781 |
| | Resource Management | −.042 | .051 | −.059 | −.830 | .407 |
| | Over-Engineering[b] | .004 | .039 | .005 | .092 | .927 |

[a] Dependent Variable: Scrum Adoption
[b] = the factor's negatively phrased questions were recoded.

**Table 5.** Regression coefficients of the four constructs [36].

Coefficients[a]

| Model | | Unstandardized coefficients | | Standardized coefficients | T | Sig. |
|---|---|---|---|---|---|---|
| | | B | Std. error | Beta | | |
| 1 | (Constant) | 1.197 | .445 | | 2.692 | .008 |
| | Team[b] | .126 | .062 | .123 | 2.040 | .043 |
| | Technology | .580 | .064 | .566 | 9.009 | .000 |
| | Individual[b] | .016 | .053 | .019 | .303 | .763 |
| | Organization | −.033 | .054 | −.039 | −.616 | .539 |

[a] Dependent Variable: Scrum Adoption
[b] = the factor's negatively phrased questions were recoded.

## 5    Discussion of Findings

### 5.1    The Conceptual Framework Factor Loadings Affecting the Hypotheses Testing

It is important to note that initially, the SACCF had 19 factors (independent variables). However, during the validation of the scale, the Exploratory Factor Analysis

(EFA) applied to the questionnaire items extracted 14 factors. The loading of the questionnaire items to new factors meant that the initial predicted model had to be evaluated. The questionnaire items with its commonalities and corresponding factor loadings were studied and it was found that the initial 19 independent variables loaded correctly into the 14 factors. The new factor loadings, therefore, made logical sense. In Table 1, as discussed in Sect. 3, the 19 hypothesized factors are mapped to the newly validated 14 factors.

While most of the mappings in Table 1 is self-explanatory, it is necessary to give an explanation of the four factors that have more than one independent variable.

These four factors are:

- Organizational Behavior
- Sprint Management
- Customer Collaboration
- Teamwork

The term Organization Behavior (OB) is defined as the actions and attitudes of individuals that work within an organization. OB is an indication of human behavior within the organizational environment, how human behavior interacts with the organization, and the organization itself [5]. George et al. [5], also states that the manner in which managers manage others is significantly affected by OB. Given this perspective of OB, it is reasonable to load Organizational Structure, Management Support, and Organizational Culture as a single factor under the heading OB.

The loading of Sprint Management and Change Resistance into a single factor is also logically sensible since firstly, Sprint Management is a time-boxed activity. Scrum practitioners would be performing their tasks within a Scrum sprint under most circumstances although it is recognized that this may not be the case for every task performed. Consequently, if a team is resisting change, it would manifest when the change is requested or performed during the Scrum sprint. Secondly, the fourth value of Agile development, being "*responding to change over following a plan*", it is therefore appropriate that Sprint Management and Change Resistance loaded as the Sprint Management factor, since Change Resistance occurs by default, within the Sprint Management cycle [6].

The loading of Collaboration and Quality into the Customer Collaboration factor was unsurprising since Customer Collaboration entails working closely with the client in order to deliver a requested output at the expected quality. The last merged factor loading was Teamwork which consists of Teamwork and Communication. This factor loading was also a simple decision and with hindsight, these two factors had to be grouped together from the outset. The reason for this is because Teamwork requires individuals to work together to complete tasks, and communication is a critical component to complete sprint tasks within the team. It is important to note that the Resources factor has been renamed to Resource Management because resource shortage or surplus is a management related concern.

Figure 3 displays the third and final iteration of the CF. The hypothesized relationships between the independent variables and the dependent variable are shown in the parenthesis. As is evident from the diagram, the conceptual model is much more refined than the previous iterations. The Specialization factor which was previously under the team construct is now under the individual construct, and Over-Engineering which was an individual factor is now a team factor. The reason for these realignments is because Specialization or specialized skills can be narrowed down to the individual level. Over-Engineering, if encountered and allowed within a Scrum team environment, means that the team was not vigilant enough during their communication sessions to identify when an individual was doing more than what was required.

While the authors are pleased with the validated CF factors and constructs, the effect it has on the evaluation of the initial hypotheses is of concern. The authors, however, believe that while the factors have changed from 19 to 14, it should not affect the hypotheses testing. The reason why the authors believe this to be the case was evident in Table 1. In the table, the reader will note that none of the initial 19 factors are removed from the SACCF. Those that are no longer a discrete factor have merged with other factors. However, based on the factor loadings and the opinion of the authors, these merged factors make sense. As a result, the authors strongly feel that the initial 19 hypotheses can be tested as individual hypotheses. However, the reader should note that some of the initial factors are loaded into a new factor as mentioned above.

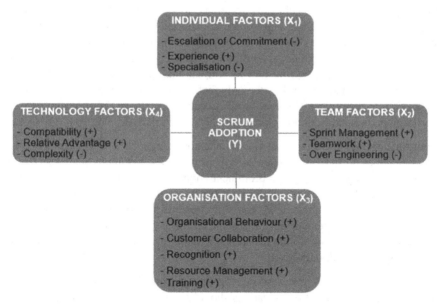

**Fig. 3.** Final iteration of the conceptual framework [36].

## 5.2 Answering the Research Hypotheses

We discuss the statistical results and whether the hypotheses, as stated in Sect. 1, can be accepted or rejected. This subsection focuses on the outcomes of the 19 hypothesized statements, and a discussion of the individual findings.

**Escalation of Commitment.** Escalation of Commitment was hypothesized to have a significant linear (negative correlation) relationship with Scrum adoption. While the research by Stray et al. [29] indicates the alarming effect of this factor on software project outcomes, with up to 40% of projects experiencing it, the regression results indicate no significant correlation with Scrum adoption. The coefficients from the MLR dictates that not only is there no significance with Scrum adoption, but the directionality of the relationship is positive. The hypothesis, that there is a significant linear (negative correlation) relationship between Escalation of Commitment and Scrum adoption, can thus be rejected.

**Experience.** The lack of experience was included as a potential barrier to Scrum adoption based on the literature of Agile challenges [30]. Mastery of skills contributes to the performance of individuals [31], which we believe, would allow the Scrum practitioner to experience a lesser challenge in understanding and adopting a project management framework such as Scrum. While there is a weak correlation with Scrum adoption, there is no significant linear relationship. The hypothesis that there is a significant linear (positive correlation) relationship between experience and Scrum adoption, can hence be rejected.

**Over-Engineering.** Over-Engineered solutions, as defined in the literature, is often due to lack of communication, and limited domain knowledge by the team executing the task [32]. It should be noted that Over-Engineering as a factor, has moved to the team construct from the individual construct of the SACCF. From the results, it can be concluded that Over-Engineering has no correlational and no significant linear relationship with Scrum adoption. It is the only factor to exhibit such a characteristic. The hypothesis that there is a significant linear (negative correlation) relationship between Over-Engineering and Scrum adoption, can hence be rejected.

**Communication.** Our view is that Communication is arguably one of the most crucial skills to have as an individual, team or organization. The results in Sect. 4 suggested that although Communication is a prominent adoption challenge, it is not statistically significant with Scrum adoption. While Communication has been loaded into the Teamwork factor as mentioned, we can still conclude, based on the research results, that Communication does not have a significant linear (positive correlation) relationship with Scrum adoption. Communication, therefore, has a very weak correlation with Scrum adoption (at the 0.05 level).

**Teamwork.** Our view is that working together to complete tasks, and achieving a common goal is what most organizations should be striving. In our opinion, a greater level of team cohesion increases the probability of successful project outcomes. It was anticipated that the Teamwork factor, which was a factor loading of the initial Teamwork and Communication factors, would have had a significant linear relationship with Scrum adoption. The reason for this view was simply because Teamwork and Communication are regarded as essential aspects of any Agile method [10]. It was surprising to note that Teamwork has no significant correlation and no notable significant linear relationship, with a p-value of 0.781. We can therefore reject the hypothesis as there is no significant linear (positive correlation) relationship between Teamwork and Scrum adoption.

**Specialization.** As mentioned earlier, due to the questionnaire item factor loadings, Specialization has been grouped under the individual factors construct. With hindsight, we completely agree with this change, as skill levels can and should be evaluated at the individual level, allowing for a more refined analysis of the factor. The reason for the inclusion of Specialization as a Scrum adoption challenge is that specialist roles in the Scrum team could hinder the successful completion of a Scrum sprint due to a lack of overlapping skills [33]. The correlation between Specialization and Scrum adoption is significant at the 0.01 level. However, the linear relationship is far from significant. We can therefore reject the hypothesis as there is no significant linear (negative correlation) relationship between Specialization and Scrum adoption.

**Sprint Management.** This factor is part of the Team construct and is generally considered an essential aspect of the sprint cycle. It is of the utmost importance that a professional Scrum practitioner in the form of a Scrum Master is appointed within organizations to facilitate the Scrum framework and sprint process. A mismanaged sprint can lead to other problems for the Scrum team [34]. The authors believe that Sprint Management should play an essential role in Scrum adoption by Scrum practitioners. Based on the research findings, Sprint Management has a significant correlation with adoption at the 0.01 level. A significant linear relationship with adoption was recorded, with a p-value $< 0.05$ and the t-statistic of 2.24. What this means is that an increase in Sprint Management relates to an increase in Scrum adoption. We accept the hypothesis of a significant linear (positive correlation) relationship between Sprint Management and Scrum adoption.

**Change Resistance.** Change resistance, as mentioned earlier, has loaded with Sprint Management. Our opinion is that this newly loaded factor is sensible since a change affecting the Scrum team usually affects their sprint planning and management. However, because of the new factor loading, it is not definitive as to whether Change Resistance on its own has a significant linear relationship with Scrum adoption. The narrative review suggests that change resistance is a re-occurring adoption challenge experienced both globally and within SA [3]. Because Change Resistance carries equal weighting under the newly loaded Sprint Management factor one can accept that Change Resistance contributes significantly to Scrum adoption. The hypothesis that there is a significant linear (negative correlation) relationship between Change Resistance and Scrum adoption, is acceptable. An increase in Change Resistance results in a decrease in Scrum adoption.

**Training.** Our view is that Training is essential for developing and up-skilling employees of an organization. The narrative review of global Agile adoption challenges demonstrated that Training, knowledge and learning, are indeed challenges to overcome. Within SA, Training was noted to be an insignificant challenge [3]. Our view is that Training could contribute to the adoption of Scrum, since Training can be regarded as a method of decreasing the challenges encountered during task completion. The results indicate that while Training has a weak significant correlation with Scrum adoption (at the 0.01 level), it does not have a significant relationship with adoption. The hypothesis being that there is a significant linear (positive correlation) relationship between Training and Scrum adoption, is rejected.

**Recognition.** This factor is under the Organizational construct (see Fig. 2). Our view is that the lack of Recognition for an individual affects their willingness (or disposition) to attempt and complete tasks. The lack of Recognition has been shown to affect the productivity levels of the individual [35]. We believe that a lack of individual Recognition affects the individual's willingness to adopt any innovation, not just Scrum, especially if the individual is not interested in the innovation. Based on the empirical findings, Recognition has a weak correlation with adoption (significant at the 0.01 level), as well as having no significant linear relationship. We reject the hypothesis because there is no significant linear (positive correlation) relationship between Recognition and Scrum adoption.

**Quality.** Quality refers to the quality of software delivered to meet client and business expectations [3]. Since the client is the receiver of the level of Quality produced, it is loaded with Collaboration to form the Customer Collaboration factor. In our opinion, the quality delivered during the project milestones can determine whether the project succeeds or fails. The narrative review identified Quality as an infrequent adoption challenge. Software quality, on the other hand, is a prominent global Scrum adoption benefit [3], suggesting that quality of software is a result of Scrum adoption. The results indicate that there is a significant correlation between Customer Collaboration and Scrum adoption. Of interest, is that Customer Collaboration is just below the $p < 0.05$ significance level, with a p-value = 0.059. More research on Customer Collaboration as an independent variable of Scrum and Agile adoption, would be helpful in order to confirm any consistency with the finding of this study. We can reject the hypothesis as there is no significant linear (positive correlation) relationship between Quality and Scrum adoption.

**Resources.** An organization requires Resources in order to generate products and services. Without a sufficient supply of Resources, for example, a lack of capital, lack of strategic direction, and inadequate resource management the organization might incur losses and setbacks. The narrative review identified a lack of documentation, budget constraints, high management overheads, and lack of infrastructure and tools as resource challenges for Scrum and Agile adoption [3]. During the second iteration of the SACCF the Resources factor has been renamed to Resource Management although the definition remains the same, as mentioned earlier. Based on the results, Resource Management was found to have no significant linear relationship although its correlation was significant. This result is unsurprising as it is difficult to conclude that poor Resource Management on its own will be pivotal in an individual to reject a framework such as Scrum. This hypothesis is rejected as there is no significant linear relationship between Resources and Scrum adoption.

**Collaboration.** The research findings for Customer Collaboration is no different to most of the factors discussed thus far. As mentioned under the Quality factor, Customer Collaboration, which includes Quality, is below the significant linear relationship threshold by a narrow margin, and it would be useful to conduct a deeper evaluation of this factor. The narrative review identified Customer Collaboration and lack of business, customer, and product owner involvement during Agile adoption as some of the biggest challenges experienced globally [3]. However, results obtained in this study indicate that Collaboration has no significant linear (positive correlation) relationship with Scrum adoption.

**Management Support.** The definition for Organizational Behavior (OB) was provided earlier in this section. Sultan and Chan [12] states that Management Support has a direct effect on innovation adoption. While not all innovations are equal, for example, Scrum requires Customer Collaboration, iterative and incremental development, while object-oriented programming as an innovation might not. We hence recognize that the statement by Sultan and Chan [12] might not necessarily hold in particular for the Scrum adoption results presented in this paper. As a newly loaded factor with Organizational Structure and Organization Culture, Management Support has an insignificant relationship with adoption. Our impression was that OB would have manifested a significant relationship should be re-evaluated in further Scrum adoption studies, perhaps with a larger population sample size. The hypothesis is rejected, since no significant linear (positive correlation) relationship between Management Support and Scrum adoption was evident in the results of this study.

**Organizational Culture.** The authors appreciate the importance of an Organizational Culture that promotes innovative thinking, as innovation adoption and implementation often depends on the culture of the organization [9]. Organizational Culture identified as one of the most common Scrum and Agile adoption challenges [3]; however, as mentioned by Hoda and others [15], literature on the influence of Organizational Culture on Scrum teams is limited. Although OB has a significant correlation with Scrum adoption, it has no relationship of linear significance. The reason for this lack of linear significance may be because teams implement Scrum even when culture is problematic, and teams continue to adopt Scrum regardless of the prevalence of such challenges within the organization. The hypothesis that there is a significant linear (positive correlation) relationship between Organizational Culture and Scrum adoption is therefore rejected.

**Organizational Structure.** We predicted that the lack of a hierarchical Organizational Structure improves the innovation adoption rate. This sentiment is aligned with findings in literature such as by Sultan and Chan [12]. However, when we consider the research findings for Scrum as innovation, the correlation significance at the 0.01 level is weak, and the MLR significance is virtually non-existent ($p = 0.998$). The hypothesis that there is a significant linear (negative correlation) relationship between Organizational Structure and Scrum adoption, is hence, rejected.

**Relative Advantage.** Relative Advantage as discussed in Sect. 2 is one of the five innovation characteristics of the DOI theory. Rogers [13] noted that Relative Advantage and Compatibility are the two characteristics of innovation which contribute the most toward adoption. We concur that Relative Advantage is an essential contributor to innovation adoption, as suggested and it was reassuring to discover that the research results supported our sentiment. The value of this finding is that it strengthens the rationale to include Relative Advantage in other innovation adoption studies. Relative Advantage has a moderate to strong correlation with adoption, significant at the 0.01 level. The coefficients taken from the regression model indicate a significant linear relationship ($p < 0.001$) with a t-statistic of 10.168. We can, therefore, accept the hypothesis by stating that there is a significant linear (positive correlation) relationship between Relative Advantage and Scrum adoption. An increase in Relative Advantage results in an increase in Scrum adoption.

**Complexity.** While Complexity, according to Kishore and McLean [14], is not one of two characteristics which contribute the most toward innovation adoption, it exhibits a relatively consistent relationship with adoption. We agree that Complexity affects an individual's decision to adopt and implement innovation. Our findings indicate that, the correlation with Scrum adoption is significant at the 0.01 level, with a linear relationship at the 0.05 significance level with a t-statistic of $-2.061$. We can, therefore, accept the hypothesis by stating that there is a significant linear (negative correlation) relationship between Complexity and Scrum adoption. An increase in Complexity results in a decrease in Scrum adoption.

**Compatibility.** Compatibility is said to be the other most important contributor, besides Relative Advantage, to innovation adoption [13]. However, research also indicates that the five characteristics of innovation adoption have characteristics of flexibility [12]. This suggests that the significance of Compatibility is dependent on several factors, including conditions such as the individual's stage of adoption, the individual's experience, and the type of innovation adopted. Although Compatibility has been shown to have a consistent relationship with adoption in other innovation research, our findings differ. The idea that these results might be due to poorly constructed questions related to the Compatibility factor was considered. However, a re-examination of the clarity and construction of the relevant questions, does not indicate that this statement holds. A possible explanation for the inconsistency of our findings with the literature, is that the decision to adopt Scrum often does not depend on the individual but the team or organization. This notion suggests that although the individual does not perceive Scrum to be compatible with them, they still end up adopting it. Compatibility has a moderate correlation with Scrum adoption ($p < 0.01$) with an insignificant linear relationship with $p = 0.141$. We reject the hypothesis since no significant linear (positive correlation) relationship between Compatibility and Scrum adoption is evident.

In summary, four of the initial 19 factors were identified as having a significant linear relationship with Scrum adoption. These four factors are Relative Advantage, Complexity, Change Resistance, and Sprint Management. The factor that came close to having a significant relationship with Scrum adoption was Customer Collaboration with $p = 0.059$. Because of the new factor loadings, both Sprint Management and Change Resistance loaded onto Sprint Management, as noted earlier. Figure 4 shows a parsimonious model of all the significant factors and their hypothesized relationship with Scrum adoption in parenthesis.

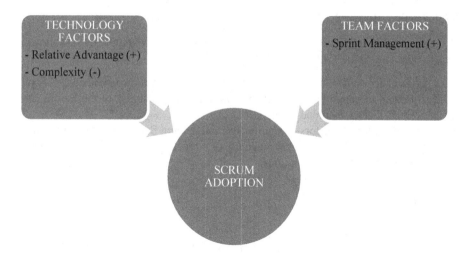

**Fig. 4.** Scrum adoption parsimonious model.

## 6   Conclusion

This paper aimed to contribute to the field of Scrum adoption by conducting quantitative analysis to test the hypotheses predicting constructs and factors of significance with Scrum. The findings in a previous paper [36] confirmed the validity and reliability of the CF.

The results of the validity and reliability of the CF allowed us to continue with a statistical analysis of the questionnaire responses. The results obtained after applying Spearman correlation analysis and MLR, revealed that three of the 14 factors have a statistically significant relationship with Scrum adoption. These three factors are Sprint Management, Complexity, and Relative Advantage. This contribution is of significance both to Scrum adoption research and to the greater body of knowledge on Agile methodologies.

### 6.1   Recommendations

The findings from this paper adds value to organizations practicing Scrum. The literature and this paper confirm the importance of the innovation's technical characteristics, namely, Relative Advantage and Complexity. In this paper, however, we also report new insights into Scrum adoption and its challenges as perceived by the individual Scrum practitioner. Based on the empirical findings, the following recommendations are made:

- Organizations that are in the adoption stage of Scrum should consider the findings in this paper, particularly the identification of Sprint Management as having a significant linear relationship with Scrum adoption.
- Organizations should look to increase their Scrum adoption success prospects by implementing strategies that also consider significant factors.

## 6.2 Further Research

Given the limited scope of this study, additional research on the topic in the following areas would contribute further knowledge to this topic:

- A systematic review of the Scrum adoption challenges experienced by Scrum practitioners to support (or debunk) the validity and reliability of the Scrum challenges and factors included in the CF.
- While we confirmed factors of significance influencing Scrum adoption through the SACCF, additional research that make use of a much larger sample, would improve the generalizability of the findings.

# References

1. Overhage, S., Schlauderer, S., Birkmeier, D., Miller, J.: What makes IT personnel adopt scrum? A framework of drivers and inhibitors to developer acceptance. In: 44th Hawaii International Conference on System Sciences. Kauai, HI, pp. 1–10. IEEE (2011)
2. Chan, K.Y., Thong, J.Y.L.: An integrated framework of individual acceptance of agile methodologies. In: PACIS 2007 Proceedings, vol. 154 (2007)
3. Hanslo, R., Mnkandla, E.: Scrum adoption challenges detection model: SACDM. In: Federated Conference on Computer Science and Information Systems (FedCSIS), Poznan, Poland, pp. 949–957. IEEE (2018)
4. Gerber, H., Hall, R.: Statistical analysis reporting template for researchers (2016)
5. George, J.M., Jones, G.R., Sharbrough, W.C.: Understanding and Managing Organizational Behavior. Pearson Prentice Hall, Upper Saddle River (2005)
6. Beck, K., et al.: Agile Manifesto. Software Development (2001). http://agilemanifesto.org/ Accessed 29 Sept 2016
7. VersionOne. 2015 9th Annual state of agile survey. VersionOne.com. http://stateofagile. versionone.com/. Accessed 26 Aug 2016
8. Schwaber, K., Sutherland, J.: The Scrum Guide. Scrum.org. (2011). https://www.scrum.org/ index.php/resources/scrum-guide. Accessed 25 Feb 2019
9. Mohan, K., Ahlemann, F.: Understanding acceptance of information system development and management methodologies by actual users: a review and assessment of existing literature. Int. J. Inf. Manag. 33(5), 831–839 (2013)
10. Noruwana, N., Tanner, M.: Understanding the structured processes followed by organisations prior to engaging in agile processes: a South African perspective. SACJ 48, 8 (2012)
11. Chan, F.K.Y., Thong, J.Y.L.: Acceptance of agile methodologies: a critical review and conceptual framework. Decision Support Syst. 46(4), 803–814 (2009)
12. Sultan, F., Chan, L.: The adoption of new technology: the case of object-oriented computing in software companies. IEEE Trans. Eng. Manag. 47(1), 106–126 (2000)
13. Rogers, E.M.: Diffusion of Innovations, 5th edn. Free Press, New York (2003)
14. Kishore, R., McLean, E.R.: Reconceptualizing innovation compatibility as organizational alignment in secondary IT adoption contexts: an investigation of software reuse infusion. IEEE Trans. Eng. Manag. 54(4), 756–775 (2007)
15. Hoda, R., Noble, J., Marshall, S.: Supporting self-organizing agile teams. In: Sillitti, A., Hazzan, O., Bache, E., Albaladejo, X. (eds.) XP 2011. LNBIP, vol. 77, pp. 73–87. Springer, Berlin (2011). https://doi.org/10.1007/978-3-642-20677-1_6
16. Welman, C., Kruger, F., Mitchell, B.: Research Methodology, 3rd edn. Oxford University Press, Cape Town (2005)

17. Dingsøyr, T., Hanssen, G.K., Dybå, T., Anker, G., Nygaard, J.O.: Developing software with scrum in a small cross-organizational project. In: Richardson, I., Runeson, P., Messnarz, R. (eds.) EuroSPI 2006. LNCS, vol. 4257, pp. 5–15. Springer, Heidelberg (2006). https://doi.org/10.1007/11908562_2

18. Pressman, R.S.: Software Engineering. A Practitioner's Approach, 6th edn. McGraw-Hill, New York (2005)

19. Koch, A.S.: Agile Software Development. Evaluating the Methods for Your Organization. Artech House, London (2005)

20. Leffingwell, D.: Agile Software Requirements: Lean Requirements Practices for Teams, Programs, and the Enterprise. Pearson Education Inc., Boston (2011)

21. Palmer, S.R., Felsing, J.M.: A practical guide to feature-driven development. Prentice Hall PTR, Upperm Saddle River (2002)

22. Heikkila, V.T., Paasivaara, M., Lassenius, C.: ScrumBut, but does it matter? A mixed-method study of the planning process of a multi-team scrum organization. In: International Symposium on Empirical Software Engineering and Measurement (ESEM), pp. 85–94. IEEE (2013)

23. Blankenship, J., Bussa, M., Millett, S.: Pro Agile.NET Development with Scrum. Apress, Berkeley (2011)

24. Bianco, C.: Agile and SPICE capability levels. In: O'Connor, R.V., Rout, T., McCaffery, F., Dorling, A. (eds.) SPICE 2011. CCIS, vol. 155, pp. 181–185. Springer, Heidelberg (2011). https://doi.org/10.1007/978-3-642-21233-8_16

25. Holzmann, V., Panizel, I.: Communications management in scrum projects. In: Proceedings of the European Conference on Information Management and Evaluation (ECIME), pp. 67–74. Academic Conferences & Publishing International Ltd. (2013)

26. Brynard, P., Hanekom, S.X.: Introduction to Research in Public Administration and Related Academic Disciplines. J.L. Van Schaik, Pretoria (1997)

27. Floyd, J., Fowler, J.: Survey Research Methods, 4th edn. Sage, Thousand Oaks (2009)

28. Gillham, B.: Developing A Questionnaire. Bloomsbury Academic, Bloomsbury (2000)

29. Stray, V.G., Moe, N.B., Dybå, T.: Escalation of commitment: a longitudinal case study of daily meetings. In: Wohlin, C. (ed.) XP 2012. LNBIP, vol. 111, pp. 153–167. Springer, Heidelberg (2012). https://doi.org/10.1007/978-3-642-30350-0_11

30. Hardgrave, B.C., Davis, F.D., Riemenschneider, C.K.: Investigating determinants of software developers' intentions to follow methodologies. J. Manag. Inf. Syst. 20(1), 123–151 (2003)

31. Brooks, R.E.: Studying programmer behavior experimentally: the problems of proper methodology. Commun. ACM 23(4), 207–213 (1980)

32. Santos, R., Flentge, F., Begin, M.E., Navarro, V.: Agile technical management of industrial contracts: scrum development of ground segment software at the european space agency. In: Sillitti, A., Hazzan, O., Bache, E., Albaladejo, X. (eds.) XP 2011. LNBIP, vol. 77, pp. 290–305. Springer, Berlin (2011). https://doi.org/10.1007/978-3-642-20677-1_21

33. Fægri, T.E.: Adoption of team estimation in a specialist organizational environment. In: Sillitti, A., Martin, A., Wang, X., Whitworth, E. (eds.) XP 2010. LNBIP, vol. 48, pp. 28–42. Springer, Heidelberg (2010). https://doi.org/10.1007/978-3-642-13054-0_3

34. Tanner, M., Khalane, T.: Software quality assurance in scrum: the need for concrete guidance on SQA strategies in meeting user expectations. In: IEEE ICAST 2013, p. 6 (2013)

35. Bishop, J.: The recognition and reward of employee performance. J. Labor Econ. 5(4, Part 2), S36–S56 (1987)

36. Hanslo, R., Mnkandla, E., Vahed, A.: Factors that contribute significantly to scrum adoption. In: Federated Conference on Computer Science and Information Systems (FedCSIS), Leipzig, Germany, pp. 821–829. IEEE (2019)

# Scientific Collaboration, Citation and Topic Analysis of International Conference on Agile Software Development Papers

Muhammad Ovais Ahmad[1,2](✉) and Päivi Raulamo-Jurvanen[3]

[1] Department of Mathematics and Computer Science, Karlstad University,
Karlstad, Sweden
`ovais.ahmad@kau.se`
[2] Faculty of Electronics, Telecommunications and Informatics,
Gdansk University of Technology, Gdańsk, Poland
[3] M3S Research Unit, University of Oulu, Oulu, Finland
`paivi.raulamo-jurvanen@oulu.fi`

**Abstract.** The International Conference on Agile Software Development (XP) was established almost sixteen years ago. Based on data from Scopus database, a total of 789 papers have been published in between years of 2002 and 2018. We employed bibliometrics analysis and topic modeling with R/RStudio to analyze these published papers from various dimensions, including the most active authors, collaboration of authorship, most cited papers, used keywords and trends of probable topics from the titles and abstracts of those papers. The results show that the first five years of XP conference cover nearly 40% of the papers published until now and almost 62% of the XP papers have been cited at least once. Mining of XP conference paper titles and abstracts result in these hot research topics: "Coordination", "Technical Debt", "Teamwork", "Startups" and "Agile Practices", thus strongly focusing on practical issues and problems faced by the practitioners in the industry. The results highlight the most influential researchers and institutions, and the collaboration between the authors in the conference papers. The approach applied in this study can be extended to other software engineering venues and can be applied to large-scale studies.

**Keywords:** Bibliometrics · Software Engineering · Publication mining · Citation analysis · International Conference on Agile Software Development

## 1 Introduction

*"Publish or perish"* is a commonly used idiom in the academic community. The phrase frames the pressure for rapid publishing to sustain or move forward in one's academic career. Research articles and other papers are being published in

© Springer Nature Switzerland AG 2020
A. Przybyłek and M. E. Morales-Trujillo (Eds.): LASD 2019/MIDI 2019, LNBIP 376, pp. 108–132, 2020.
https://doi.org/10.1007/978-3-030-37534-8_6

various venues such as conferences and journals. Such published work is taken seriously into consideration in almost all types of research funding for researchers in the academia and other research institutes. In addition, in academia, it is common to quantify the impact of published papers by analyzing the number of citations for those. Citation is one way to judge influential work and build new studies on existing research results. Citations may be helpful in observing the most popular and influential work in the field [6,21,23]. However, as pointed out by Wohlin [22], outcome and trustworthiness of the findings can be very much dependent on the actual tool(s) or source(s) used for collecting the data for the citation analysis.

Garfield put systematic effort to track the citations in scientific literature and published the Science Citation Index [7]. Further, bibliometrics methods use statistical analysis of publications to shed light on quantitative analysis [19]. Bibliometrics based identification of active authors and institutions has many benefits, e.g., in helping students and researchers to identify active and relevant institutes for their areas of interest, and in enabling employers to assess and recruit the most qualified potential researchers [1,21]. Citation analysis and bibliometrics have been used to identify influential work and researchers e.g., in Medicine, Physics, Software Engineering (SE), Social Sciences and other fields of science [1,3,10,12–15,18,21,23].

In the last decade, a number of citation and bibliometrics studies have been published in the field of SE. For instance, between 1999 and 2002, Wohlin published a series of papers with a goal of identifying the most cited papers, and invited authors of the most cited papers to contribute to a special section of the Information and Software Technology journal [22–24]. Kitchenham [16] conducted study with a focus on software metrics and identified the most cited papers published between 2000 and 2005. The study further classified the main topics, goals and empirical content of those papers [16]. Further, a number of bibliometric studies have been conducted identifying the top SE scholars and institutions in various timelines. For example, Garousi and Varma [11] present a bibliometric assessment of Canadian SE scholars and institutions. Farhoodi et al. [5] reported the most active authors in the area of development of scientific software to be located mainly in the US, followed by the Canadian and British researchers. Recently, a study by Garousi and Fernandes [8] identified and classified the top-100 highly-cited SE papers in terms of two metrics: total number of citations and average annual number of citations. In the context of agile software development, a study by Chuang, Luor and Luo [3] reported top publications, institutions, and scholars in the agile software development field from 2001 to 2012 based on the publication of such works in Science Citation Index journals. However, there are only a few citation or bibliometrics SE studies conducted in small-scale, i.e., focusing only on a selected venue or a subset of venues [8,21]. A small-scale study on a selected venue may reveal interesting insights not only into the emerging research topics within but also into the authorship of the papers, i.e., collaboration among the authors regarding the research topics.

One of the key outlets for Agile research, *"Agile Software Development Conference (XP)"*, has not been evaluated under the lens of citation analysis alone or as a sub-field of its own (processes). XP Conference (*"International Conference on Extreme Programming (XP)"*, formerly known as *"Conference on Agile Software Development (AGILE)"*) was included in a bibliometrics study of Karanatsiou et al. [15] in the general domain of SE. In that study, XP conference was the only process oriented conference [15]. In fact, XP conference is the premier Agile software development conference combining research and practice.

This paper is an extension of our previously published paper [1] entitled *"Preliminary Citation and Topic Analysis of International Conference on Agile Software Development Papers (2002–2018)"* published in 14th Federated Conference on Computer Science and Information Systems (FedCSIS 2019). This study provides an overview of the literature published in all XP conference proceedings ($n = 789$). This study helps readers to understand the development and evolution of the XP conference from three main aspects: (i) the citation landscape and the most cited papers, (ii) the most active authors, institutions and countries, in terms of number of publications, and (iii) the identification of emerging research topics in XP conference publications and use of indexed keywords. Furthermore, this paper extends our prior study [1] by comparing the results to other researches, in more detail, and by analyzing the collaboration of the authors within the XP conference papers.

This paper is organized as follows: First, we discuss the research method and the data extraction technique. Second, we present the results of the analysis including findings on authorship trends, active individuals and institutes, highly cited papers and authors, trends in the covered topics, most common keywords in the papers and collaboration of the authors within the conference. Third, we discuss the threats to validity of the study. Finally, we summarize the findings and provide recommendations for future research.

## 2    Data Extraction and Research Method

The data for the analysis was fetched from Scopus[1] on September 2nd, 2018. Scopus is claimed to be the largest abstract and citation database of peer-reviewed literature and designed to serve the needs of academic, business and government. Thus, anyone having access to Scopus data has the possibility to perform similar queries without having to have technical skills for e.g., some Application Programming Interface (API). Scopus also provides citation data and allows saving the search results to a csv-file for further analysis. We used two search queries to obtain all XP conference data from the Scopus database, see Table 1.

The first query was used with an assumption that it would provide us with all the published XP conference papers. However, the search resulted in 758 papers and it became evident that the data set did not include the papers from the year 2011. One reason was the year 2011 does not include the information about the XP conference in the Scopus database. Thus, we formulated another

---

[1] https://www.elsevier.com/solutions/scopus.

**Table 1.** Search queries for extracting papers from Scopus

| No. | Query string (as to be given in Scopus) and its explanation | Papers |
|-----|-------------------------------------------------------------|--------|
| 1 | **CONF("XP") AND DOCTYPE("cp")** <br> Select XP conference and conference papers only | 758 |
| 2 | **SRCTITLE("lecture notes in business information processing" AND VOLUME(77) AND DOCTYPE("cp")** <br> Select "Lecture Notes in Business Information Processing" <br> and only volume 77 (which includes conference papers for XP 2011) | 31 |
|  | Total | 789 |

search query to obtain the missing papers from the Scopus database. The second search query (for 2011 only) retrieved 31 papers. The two search queries together retrieved 789 papers ($758 + 31$), covering the years of 2002–2018 (published by September 2nd, 2018). The Fig. 1, shows the distribution of papers published by September 2nd, 2018.

The data acquired from Scopus (included e.g., names of the authors, title, publication year, source title, number of citations, link and abstract) were stored in a csv-file. The Scopus database also provided features to extract data for the analysis of the affiliations and countries related to the authors (analysis of the search results in Scopus) as well as the top 20 cited papers (overview of the citations in Scopus). First, the data allowed us to study the affiliations, countries and authors contributing to the research the most. Second, regarding the authors, we could count the number of papers for each author as well as the degree of collaboration among those authors. Third, the number of citations for all papers and data for the top 20 most cited papers allowed us to analyze the overall citation landscape, the highest cited papers and annual citations for the top cited papers. Additionally, we used topic modeling for the trend analysis (of the titles and abstracts in the data), see Sect. 3.4.

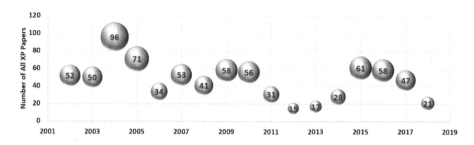

**Fig. 1.** All Publications for the XP conference in Scopus (2002–2018)

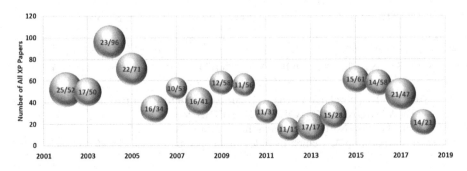

**Fig. 2.** Publications in Scopus (2002–2018), bubble size representing the number of full papers and the values within showing the number of *full* vs. *all* papers for each year.

We used MS Excel and R/RStudio for analyzing statistics and trends from the data. Many times, a table of data may serve the purpose of presenting the results, but sometimes a figure may be more descriptive or provide perspective on an issue. Thus, in addition, we used Cytoscape[2], an open source software platform, for visualizing the relationships of keywords and networks of authors in the data.

## 3   Results

The first *"XP Universe"* took place in Raleigh, North Carolina, on July 23–25, 2001. The conference hosted a number of lectures, tutorials, panel discussions, posters, workshops, and other less traditional discussions. A year later, the 2nd *"XP Universe"* and 1st *"Agile Universe"* were brought together to attract software experts, educators, and developers[3], in general. In 2003 and 2004, the two conferences, *"Extreme Programming and Agile Methods - XP/Agile Universe"* and *"Extreme Programming and Agile Processes in Software Engineering"* were organized separately, but reported together in a Springer database. In 2005, the conferences were merged and formed a single venue: *"Extreme Programming and Agile Processes in Software Engineering"*. Since 2007, the conference has been called as *"Agile Processes in Software Engineering and Extreme Programming"*.

The Scopus database search yielded 789 papers in the proceedings of XP conference published between 2002 and 2018. In the bubble chart, see Fig. 2, the year is displayed along the horizontal axis, the number of *all* conference papers is shown along the vertical axis and the total number of *"full papers"* indexed in the Scopus database is represented by the size of the bubble. The values in the bubbles, in Fig. 2, represent the number of full papers vs. the number of all papers (included in this research per year). The high number of papers for 2004 (n = 96 including 23 "full papers" that year) is explained by the fact that the two aforementioned conferences are recorded together.

---

[2] https://cytoscape.org/.
[3] http://www.xpuniverse.com/.

**Table 2.** Top 20 countries with most papers (2002–2018)

| Region | Country | Papers | Country | Papers |
|---|---|---|---|---|
| North America | United States | 116 | Canada | 57 |
| Europe | United Kingdom | 110 | Austria | 20 |
| | Italy | 81 | Netherlands | 20 |
| | Finland | 66 | Spain | 20 |
| | Sweden | 61 | Denmark | 15 |
| | Norway | 58 | Poland | 13 |
| | Germany | 50 | Switzerland | 12 |
| | Ireland | 37 | Belgium | 8 |
| Others | New Zealand | 39 | Australia | 14 |
| | Brazil | 25 | Israel | 13 |

The first five years of the XP conference cover about 38% and the first 10 years cover nearly 70% of all those papers. In XP conference, the average number of papers per year is 46.4 with a standard deviation of 20.3, using STDEV.P. The lowest number of all papers are from year 2012 ($n = 15$). The low number of papers may be an indication of rigorous selection process. Alternatively, some of the volumes include only research papers and short papers, whereas, some include e.g., abstracts of the posters or the position papers of the PhD symposium. Such variations are quite normal in various publication forums. The first values in Fig. 2 are the values from Scopus (number of all papers) and the second values represent the number of accepted full papers retrieved from the prefaces of the relevant conference books. Two of the conference proceedings, XP2014 & XP2012, did not report the number of submitted full papers. However, the acceptance rates for the conference varied between 20% (XP2011) and 49% (XP2003), arithmetic mean of the rates being 32%.

The results of the number of published papers were divided into three different regions, i.e., North America, Europe and Others, to provide visibility to XP papers country-wise. The analysis shows that majority of the XP conference papers originated from Europe and North America. The countries on the top of the contribution are: United States (116), United Kingdom (110), Italy (81) and Nordic countries (Finland (66), Sweden (61) and Norway (58)), see Table 2. Based on the contribution of those countries to XP conference papers it is reasonable to assume there exists a strong culture of agile in software development.

The Table 3 shows the most frequent contributing institutions in XP conference. It was noticed that authors have reported their affiliations in a variety of ways such as: SINTEF, SINTEF Digital and SINTEF Norwegian Inst. of Tech. However, the top three affiliations contributing to the papers are *University of Calgary*, Canada, *SINTEF*, Norway and *Free University of Bozen-Bolzano*, Italy and *Università degli Studi di Cagliari*, Italy. It is notable, that the number of

**Table 3.** Affiliations with minimum 15 papers

| Country | Affiliation | Papers | Total |
|---|---|---|---|
| Canada | University of Calgary | 39 | 39 |
| Norway | SINTEF, Norwegian Institute of Technology | 22 | 57 |
| | SINTEF Digital | 16 | |
| | Norges teknisk-naturvitenskapelige universitet | 19 | |
| Italy | Free University of Bozen-Bolzano | 29 | 57 |
| | Universita degli Studi di Cagliari | 28 | |
| New Zealand | Victoria University of Wellington | 20 | 20 |
| Sweden | Chalmers University of Technology | 17 | 17 |
| United Kingdom | Open University | 16 | 16 |

countries and affiliations is related to the number of related authors for each paper. The study of Chuang et al. [3] did not report the total number of papers per country, but reported the top publishing institutions to be from the United States, Norway and United Kingdom.

### 3.1  Authorship Trends

We studied the number of authors for the papers year-wise. The results show that 1263 unique authors contributed to the 789 papers in XP conferences until 2018. The minimum number of authors for a XP paper was one whereas maximum was nine. Majority of the XP papers in 2018 (almost 35%) have four authors. In general, about 30% of all papers have two authors, 25% have one author, and 9% of the papers have five or more authors, see Table 4. The number of authors having contributed to three or more XP papers is rather small, as most authors have contributed to just one or two papers. About 75% of the authors (944) have an authorship to just one paper and about 88% of the authors (1108) have an authorship to only one or two papers, as a single or as a co-author. Chuang et al. [3] also reported a finding of a core intellectual pool contributing to the agile research realm.

During the first three years (2002–2004) of the conference, most papers were published by a single author. For the years 2005–2009, most papers were published by two authors, and for the years 2010–2012 and 2013–2014 by three and four authors, respectively. We consider the different number of authors for the papers as an indication of increased, high (international) collaboration among the contributors. In the 1970's, the average number of authors per paper in SE was around 1.5, while after 2010, the number of authors has typically been three [8]. The average number (i.e., arithmetic mean) of authors for the papers in XP conference is 2.6.

**Table 4.** Proportion of the number of the authors per year

| Year | Number of authors | | | | | | | | |
|------|------|------|------|------|------|------|------|------|------|
|       | 1 | 2 | 3 | 4 | 5 | 6 | 7 | 8 | 9 |
| 2002 | **46.2%** | 30.8% | 9.6% | 1.9% | 5.8% | 1.9% | 1.9% | 0.0% | 1.9% |
| 2003 | **44.0%** | 30.0% | 12.0% | 6.0% | 2.0% | 4.0% | 2.0% | 0.0% | 0.0% |
| 2004 | **41.7%** | 32.3% | 13.5% | 7.3% | 1.0% | 3.1% | 1.0% | 0.0% | 0.0% |
| 2005 | 26.8% | **36.6%** | 21.1% | 9.9% | 2.8% | 0.0% | 1.4% | 1.4% | 0.0% |
| 2006 | 14.7% | **32.4%** | 17.6% | 26.5% | 8.8% | 0.0% | 0.0% | 0.0% | 0.0% |
| 2007 | 22.6% | **37.7%** | 15.1% | 17.0% | 7.5% | 0.0% | 0.0% | 0.0% | 0.0% |
| 2008 | 9.8% | **39.0%** | 29.3% | 9.8% | 4.9% | 0.0% | 4.9% | 0.0% | 2.4% |
| 2009 | 24.1% | **34.5%** | 19.0% | 13.8% | 3.4% | 1.7% | 3.4% | 0.0% | 0.0% |
| 2010 | 25.0% | 19.6% | **33.9%** | 17.9% | 1.8% | 1.8% | 0.0% | 0.0% | 0.0% |
| 2011 | 16.1% | 19.4% | **41.9%** | 19.4% | 3.2% | 0.0% | 0.0% | 0.0% | 0.0% |
| 2012 | 6.7% | 33.3% | **53.3%** | 0.0% | 6.7% | 0.0% | 0.0% | 0.0% | 0.0% |
| 2013 | 5.9% | 23.5% | 17.6% | **47.1%** | 5.9% | 0.0% | 0.0% | 0.0% | 0.0% |
| 2014 | 14.3% | 21.4% | 17.9% | **25.0%** | 10.7% | 10.7% | 0.0% | 0.0% | 0.0% |
| 2015 | 13.1% | **27.9%** | 23.0% | 21.3% | 6.6% | 3.3% | 1.6% | 3.3% | 0.0% |
| 2016 | 25.9% | **27.6%** | 25.9% | 8.6% | 5.2% | 6.9% | 0.0% | 0.0% | 0.0% |
| 2017 | 10.6% | 21.3% | **29.8%** | 23.4% | 8.5% | 4.3% | 2.1% | 0.0% | 0.0% |
| 2018 | 9.5% | 23.8% | 23.8% | **33.3%** | 9.5% | 0.0% | 0.0% | 0.0% | 0.0% |
| Total | 24.7% | 29.8% | 21.8% | 14.6% | 4.8% | 2.4% | 1.3% | 0.4% | 0.3% |

Asknes [2] studied a large body of Norwegian articles, nearly 50000 articles having at least one Norwegian address. He concluded that at an aggregated, general level the *"highly cited papers typically involve more collaborative research than what is the normal or average"* [2]. However, in our study, the correlation between the number of authors and the number of citations for a paper, considering all papers, is weak ($r = 0.13, df = 787, p = 0.0002$. However, for the set of top 20 cited papers (see Table 6), the correlation between the number of authors and the number of citations for a paper is 0.59 ($r = 0.59, df = 18, p = 0.0064$. Thus, the correlation coefficient suggests a strong positive correlation between the number of authors and the number of citations for those top 20 cited papers.

Table 5 includes the 16 most active authors in the XP conference who have minimum number of 10 papers each. Maurer F. has been the most active author compared to the other top contributors of the XP conference. There are four authors that have their most cited papers published in 2010's (the publication year for the most cited paper in parenthesis), namely Abrahamsson P. (2015), Wang X. (2015), Concas G. (2012) and Bosch J. (2012); the rest of those most cited papers have been available for ten years or more. Interestingly, in a study *"Institutions, scholars and contributions on agile software development (2001–2012)"* by Chuang et al. [3], the list of the 18 most active authors included four of the 20 most active authors in this study, namely Abrahamsson P., Dingsøyr T., Moe, N.B. and Sharp H. However, the list of the most active authors in that study [3] included also Boehm, B., Robinson H., Williams L., Dingsøyr T., Moe, N.B. and Sharp H. who were among the authors of the top 20 most cited papers in this study.

## 3.2   Citation Landscape and Most Cited Papers of XP Conference

A high citation count of a scientific work is an indication of an influential work and impact of a given paper [2,25]. Our analysis shows that 62% (n = 488) of the XP papers have been cited at least once, leaving about 38% (n = 301) as uncited papers, see Fig. 3. This is an indication of high visibility of XP conference papers. When focusing on the first ten years of the XP conference, i.e., the papers prior to 2012, nearly 65% of those papers (352/542) have been cited at least once. The findings are in line with prior studies [9,10] in which about 43% of the papers were uncited (in a study of large body of SE publications). Similarly, about 42% of the papers of "*International Symposium on Empirical Software Engineering and Measurement*" [21] were uncited.

Garfield [6] argues about citation count being the measure of *importance* or *impact* of a scientific work. He claims that a citation count is rather a measure of *utility*, i.e., usefulness of the work for a large number of people or experiments [6]. Furthermore, a citation count can also be a measure of *scientific activity* and not necessarily related to the significance of the scientific work itself [6]. As in reality, only a rather small portion of the XP conference papers retrieved from Scopus are full research papers, the high number of uncited papers is not a surprise. Thus, it can be claimed that the samples from indexed databases may not be as representative as expected for citation analysis without rigorous filtering. However, such sample papers may well be valid for analysing author activity as well as research trends and topics. The number of citations for all conference papers per year is shown in Fig. 4. The visual information in the bubble graph embeds the timeline (years in the horizontal axis), the number of all conference papers (vertical axis) and the size of the bubble shows the number of citations for the papers published that year. Pearson's correlation coefficient between years passed and the number of citations for the papers of a specific year is 0.76 with p-value 0.00041 (which is less than the significance level alpha 0.05). We can conclude that years passed and the number of citations are significantly correlated in this particular conference. Thus, some of the papers from the early years of the conference seem to have been pioneering work and fertile ground for later research.

The Table 6 shows the top 20 most cited XP conference papers (each paper having minimum 23 citations). The total number of citations for the top 20 papers covers almost 25% of all citations (680/2920) which are mainly from earlier years of XP conference (2002–2009). However, one paper is published in 2015 and five papers among the top 20 papers are published in 2002. Table 6, shows that 92% of citations (624/680) are from papers not written by the authors (of the cited paper) themselves. Such trend indicates high interest towards a

**Table 5.** Most active authors with minimum 10 papers

| Author | # | Years (papers) | Citations | | | | 1st or 2nd author[c] |
|---|---|---|---|---|---|---|---|
| | | | Total | Avg. | Max[a] | % of All[b] | |
| Maurer F. | 29 | 2011 (2), 2010 (4), 2009 (5), 2008 (5), 2007 (6), 2006 (2), 2005 (1), 2004 (1), 2002 (3) | 178 | 6.14 | 27 (2007) | 6.10 | 17 (29) |
| Abrahamsson P. | 18 | 2017 (3), 2016 (2), 2015 (2) 2014 (1), 2013 (1), 2009 (4), 2008 (2), 2007 (1), 2005 (1), 2004 (1) | 85 | 4.72 | 21 (2015) | 2.91 | 8 (18) |
| Marchesi M. | 17 | 2018 (1), 2016 (2), 2015 (2), 2014 (1), 2013 (1), 2012 (1), 2011 (2), 2008 (1), 2007 (3) 2006 (1), 2004 (1), 2003 (1) | 113 | 6.65 | 29 (2004) | 3.87 | 5 (17) |
| Fraser S. | 16 | 2015 (2), 2010 (1) 2009 (1), 2008 (1), 2007 (1), 2006 (2), 2005 (2), 2004 (2), 2003 (3), 2002 (1) | 26 | 1.63 | 8 (2003) | 0.89 | 16 (16) |
| Wang X. | 14 | 2017 (3), 2016 (1), 2015 (2), 2014 (2), 2013 (1), 2010 (1), 2009 (2), 2008 (1) 2006 (1) | 56 | 4.00 | 21 (2015) | 1.92 | 7 (14) |
| Noble J. | 13 | 2015 (1), 2014 (1), 2013 (1), 2012 (1), 2011 (2), 2010 (3), 2009 (1), 2008 (1), 2007 (1), 2004 (1) | 105 | 8.08 | 28 (2007) | 3.60 | 12 (13) |
| Sharp H. | 13 | 2018 (1), 2017 (1), 2015 (1) 2014 (1), 2012 (1), 2011 (1), 2010 (2), 2008 (1), 2006 (2), 2005 (1), 2004 (1) | 215 | 16.54 | 92 (2006) | 7.36 | 10 (13) |
| Concas G. | 12 | 2014 (3), 2013 (1), 2012 (1), 2011 (2), 2008 (1), 2007 (2), 2006 (1), 2005 (1) | 69 | 5.75 | 14 (2012) | 2.36 | 9 (12) |
| Dingsøyr T. | 12 | 2018 (3), 2017 (1), 2016 (1), 2015 (2), 2013 (1), 2011 (1), 2009 (2), 2008 (1) | 71 | 5.92 | 32 (2008) | 2.43 | 7 (12) |
| Holcombe M. | 12 | 2008 (1), 2005 (8), 2004 (1), 2003(2) | 19 | 1.58 | 7 (2005) | 0.65 | 8 (12) |
| Succi G. | 12 | 2011 (2), 2009 (3), 2008 (1), 2007 (2), 2005 (2), 2004 (1), 2003 (1) | 52 | 4.33 | 18 (2008) | 1.78 | 4 (12) |
| Bosch J. | 11 | 2018 (1), 2017 (3), 2016 (1), 2015 (3), 2014 (2), 2012 (1) | 36 | 3.27 | 15 (2012) | 1.23 | 6 (11) |
| Hussman D. | 11 | 2008 (1), 2007 (2), 2006 (1), 2005 (2), 2004 (5) | 4 | 0.36 | 1 (2005) | 0.14 | 6 (11) |
| Martin A. | 11 | 2017 (1), 2008 (1), 2007 (1), 2006 (1), 2005 (3), 2004 (3), 2003 (1) | 28 | 2.55 | 12 (2005) | 0.96 | 10 (11) |
| Moe N.B. | 10 | 2017 (2), 2016 (1), 2015 (1), 2013 (1), 2012 (1), 2011 (1), 2009 (2), 2008 (1) | 71 | 7.1 | 32 (2008) | 2.43 | 10 (10) |
| Mugridge R. | 10 | 2005 (5), 2004 (3), 2003 (2) | 16 | 1.60 | 5 (2003) | 0.55 | 8 (10) |

[a] Maximum number of citations for a single paper & publication year of that paper
[b] Percentage of the total number of citations (2920 for all publications)
[c] Number of times as first or second author in the publications
# Total number of publications

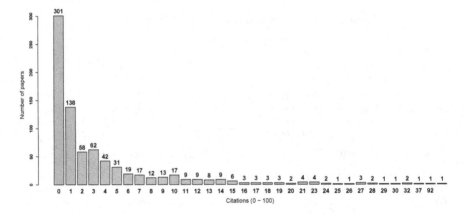

**Fig. 3.** Distribution of citations (0–100 at the time) for the papers

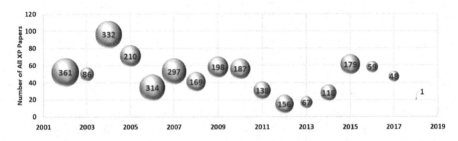

**Fig. 4.** Distribution of citations per year for all papers (2002–2018)

study from the research community, although self-citations may sometimes be expected and worthwhile (e.g., when building on previous results of one's own research). Typically, a paper is cited the first time during the year of its publication or during the following year. However, the two top cited papers, *"Empirical findings in agile methods"* by Lindvall et al. (2002) and *"Towards a framework for integrating agile development and user-centred design"* by Chamberlain et al. (2006), have been published over ten years ago, and have received the most citations since 2015. Chamberlain et al. (2006) had only a few citations right after its publication. After 2010 until 2015 the paper has received attention from both industry and academics in various fields of science, e.g., Computer Science, Mathematics, Decision science, Business, Management and Accounting, Social sciences or Psychology. In 2017, Chamberlain et al. (2006) received the most citations among the top 20 cited papers, and was the second most cited in 2018 (after Lindvall et al. 2002), at the time of the study.

**Table 6.** Top 20 cited papers (2002–2018, sorted by the column "All", All = All Citations, NS = All Citations excluding self-citations

| # | Author(s) and Title (Year) | 02 | 03 | 04 | 05 | 06 | 07 | 08 | 09 | 10 | 11 | 12 | 13 | 14 | 15 | 16 | 17 | 18 | All | NS |
|---|---|---|---|---|---|---|---|---|---|---|---|---|---|---|---|---|---|---|---|---|
| 1 | Lindvall, M., Basili, V., Boehm, B., Costa, P., Dangle, K., Shull, F., Tesoriero, R., Williams, L., Zelkowitz, M.: Empirical findings in agile methods (2002) | 1 | 2 | 4 | 8 | 8 | 6 | 6 | 5 | 6 | 8 | 6 | 6 | 4 | 6 | 9 | 9 | 6 | 100 | 96 |
| 2 | Chamberlain, S., Sharp, H., Maiden, N.: Towards a framework for integrating agile development and user-centred design (2006) |  |  |  |  |  | 1 | 2 | 2 | 5 | 8 | 9 | 7 | 17 | 12 | 10 | 14 | 5 | 92 | 89 |
| 3 | Baheti, P., Gehringer, E., Stotts, D.: Exploring the efficacy of distributed pair programming (2002) | 1 | 4 | 2 | 2 | 3 | 3 | 5 | 7 | 2 | 1 | 2 |  |  | 1 | 3 | 1 | 0 | 37 | 33 |
| 4 | Moe, N.B., Dingsyr, T.: Scrum and team effectiveness: Theory and practice (2008) |  |  |  |  |  |  |  | 1 | 3 | 4 | 3 | 5 | 2 | 6 | 4 | 4 | 0 | 32 | 28 |
| 5 | Robinson, H., Sharp, H.: The characteristics of XP teams (2004) |  |  | 4 | 3 | 1 |  |  | 3 | 3 | 2 | 1 | 6 | 3 | 3 | 1 | 1 | 1 | 32 | 28 |
| 6 | Turner, R., Jain, A.: Agile meets CMMI: Culture clash or common cause? (2002) | 1 | 2 | 1 | 2 | 3 | 2 | 1 | 4 |  |  |  | 4 | 1 | 4 | 1 | 2 | 2 | 30 | 30 |
| 7 | Mannaro, K., Melis, M., Marchesi, M.: Empirical analysis on the satisfaction of IT employees comparing XP practices with other software development methodologies (2004) |  | 2 |  | 1 | 1 | 1 | 4 | 4 | 2 | 3 | 2 |  |  |  | 2 | 3 | 4 | 29 | 27 |
| 8 | Ferreira, J., Noble, J., Biddle, R.: Up-front interaction design in agile development (2007) |  |  |  |  |  |  | 2 | 3 | 2 | 2 | 5 | 2 | 4 | 1 | 2 | 3 | 2 | 28 | 24 |
| 9 | Sfetsos, P., Stamelos, I., Angelis, L., Deligiannis, I.: Investigating the impact of personality types on communication and collaboration-viability in pair programming - An empirical study (2006) |  |  |  |  | 1 | 1 | 2 | 2 | 5 | 2 | 3 | 2 | 3 | 3 | 1 | 2 | 1 | 28 | 23 |
| 10 | Abbas, N., Gravell, A.M., Wills, G.B.: Historical roots of agile methods: Where did "Agile thinking" come from? (2008) |  |  |  |  |  |  |  |  | 2 | 3 | 4 | 4 | 1 | 5 | 3 | 2 | 3 | 27 | 27 |
| 11 | Tessem, B., Maurer, F.: Job satisfaction and motivation in a large agile team (2007) |  |  |  |  |  |  |  | 1 | 2 | 3 | 5 | 2 | 4 | 3 | 2 | 3 | 2 | 27 | 26 |
| 12 | Stotts, D., Lindsey, M., Antley, A.: An informal formal method for systematic junit test case generation (2002) | 1 | 3 | 5 | 7 |  | 4 | 2 | 1 | 1 | 1 |  |  |  | 1 |  | 1 | 0 | 27 | 27 |
| 13 | Bryant, S., Romero, P., DuBoulay, B.: The collaborative nature of pair programming (2006) |  |  |  |  |  |  | 1 | 1 | 2 | 4 | 3 | 5 | 1 | 4 | 3 | 2 | 0 | 26 | 25 |
| 14 | Hussain, Z., Milchrahm, H., Shahzad, S., Slany, W., Tscheligi, M., Wolkerstorfer, P.: Integration of extreme programming and user-centered design: Lessons learned (2009) |  |  |  |  |  |  |  | 2 | 3 | 2 | 4 | 2 | 4 | 1 | 5 | 2 | 0 | 25 | 21 |
| 15 | Haikara, J.: Usability in agile software development: Extending the interaction design process with personas approach (2007) |  |  |  |  |  |  |  |  | 3 | 2 | 3 | 2 | 3 | 1 | 4 | 5 | 1 | 24 | 24 |
| 16 | Middleton, P., Flaxel, A., Cookson, A.: Lean software management case study: Timberline Inc. (2005) |  |  |  |  |  |  |  |  | 1 | 4 | 3 | 5 | 3 | 4 | 1 | 2 | 1 | 24 | 23 |
| 17 | Diebold, P., Ostberg, J.-P., Wagner, S., Zendler, U.: What do practitioners vary in using scrum? (2015) |  |  |  |  |  |  |  |  |  |  |  |  |  | 4 | 5 | 10 | 4 | 23 | 8 |
| 18 | Melnik, G., Maurer, F.: Comparative analysis of job satisfaction in agile and non-agile software development teams (2006) |  |  |  |  |  | 1 |  |  |  | 3 | 3 |  | 5 | 4 | 1 | 3 | 3 | 23 | 22 |
| 19 | Koch, S.: Agile principles and open source software development: A theoretical and empirical discussion (2004) |  |  | 1 | 1 |  |  | 5 | 5 |  | 4 | 3 |  |  |  | 1 | 2 | 1 | 23 | 21 |
| 20 | Melnik, G., Maurer, F.: Perceptions of agile practices: A student survey (2002) | 1 |  | 1 | 4 | 1 | 1 | 4 | 2 | 5 | 1 | 2 |  |  |  |  | 1 | 0 | 23 | 22 |

**Table 7.** Top cited papers per year (2002–2018)

| Year Author(s) and Title | Cites | C-Norm[a] | #[b] |
|---|---|---|---|
| 2002 Lindvall, M., Basili, V., Boehm, B., Costa, P., Dangle, K., Shull, F., Tesoriero, R., Williams, L., Zelkowitz, M.: Empirical findings in agile methods | 100 | 6.25 | 4 |
| 2003 Lowell C., Stell-Smith J.: Successful automation of GUI driven acceptance testing | 8 | 0.53 | 17 |
| 2004 RobinsonH., SharpH.: The characteristics of XP teams | 32 | 2.29 | 12 |
| 2005 Middleton, P., Flaxel, A., Cookson, A.: Lean software management case study: Timberline Inc | 24 | 1.85 | 14 |
| 2006 Chamberlain, S., Sharp, H., Maiden, N.: Towards a framework for integrating agile development and user-centred design | 92 | 7.67 | 1 |
| 2007 Ferreira, J., Noble, J., Biddle, R.: Up-front interaction design in agile development | 28 | 2.55 | 10 |
| 2008 MoeN.B., DingsyrT.: Scrum and team effectiveness: Theory and practice | 32 | 3.20 | 7 |
| 2009 Hussain, Z., Milchrahm, H., Shahzad, S., Slany, W., Tscheligi, M., Wolkerstorfer, P.: Integration of extreme programming and user-centered design: Lessons learned | 25 | 2.78 | 9 |
| 2010 FerreiraJ., SharpH., RobinsonH.: Values and assumptions shaping Agile development and User Experience design in practice | 14 | 1.75 | 15 |
| 2011 DorairajS., NobleJ., MalikP.: Effective communication in distributed agile software development teams | 15 | 2.14 | 13 |
| 2012 StaronM., MedingW., PalmK.: Release readiness indicator for mature agile and lean software development projects | 21 | 3.50 | 5 |
| 2013 HeikkiläV.T., PaasivaaraM., LasseniusC., EngblomC.: Continuous release planning in a large-scale scrum development organization at ericsson | 12 | 2.40 | 11 |
| 2014 LiskinO., PhamR., KieslingS., SchneiderK.: Why we need a granularity concept for user stories | 12 | 3.00 | 8 |
| 2015 Diebold, P., Ostberg, J.-P., Wagner, S., Zendler, U.: What do practitioners vary in using scrum? | 23 | 7.67 | 1 |
| 2016 OrtuM., DestefanisG., CounsellS., SwiftS., TonelliR., MarchesiM.: Arsonists or firefighters? Effectiveness in agile software development | 7 | 3.50 | 5 |
| 2017 TaibiD., LenarduzziV., JanesA., LiukkunenK., AhmadM.O.: Comparing requirements decomposition within the Scrum, Scrum with Kanban, XP, and Banana development processes | 7 | 7.00 | 3 |
| 2018 OyetoyanT.D., MilosheskaB., GriniM., SoaresCruzesD.: Myths and facts about static application security testing tools: An action research at telenor digital | 1 | 1.00 | 16 |

[a]C-Norm = Citations divided by the number of years a paper has been available
[b]Rank according to column "C-Norm"

## 3.3    Highest Cited Papers Per Year

Many countries and evaluating bodies (for funding, promotions or appointments) are using figures like publication records or citation counts in decision-making [3]. Such evaluations have two sides; firstly, it is fair to see the influential and trendy work of a specific researcher, and secondly, the appropriateness of such trends or counts can be questioned on scientific grounds. Rapid growth of citations for a paper may be a sign of a popular topic, or active author(s) building on their existing research, or both. Eight of the year-wise most cited papers are the same as reported in Table 6 as the top 20 most cited papers. Those papers have been available for the public for a long period of time, from years 2002 (5), 2004 (3), 2005 (1), 2006 (4), 2007 (3), 2008 (2), 2009 (1) and 2015 (1). The average number of citations for top cited paper per year in Table 7 is 26.6, which is less than the average from top 20 most cited papers, 34 in Table 6.

To compare the general interest on the published papers, we normalized the number of citations for years, see column C-Norm in Table 7. The values for normalized citations varied between 0.53–7.67. The highest number of normalized citations, 7.67, are for the paper *"What do practitioners vary in using scrum"* by Diebold et al. (2015) which received 23 citations in three years (ranked #8 in Table 7 considering purely citations). Similarly, the paper *"Empirical findings in agile methods"* by Lindvall et al. (2002) has been available for twelve years and has 92 citations (similarly, ranked as #2 in Table 7). The paper also ranked the highest for the number of citations (100, see Table 6) and has the fourth highest normalized citation count (6.25).

Garousi and Fernandes [9] claim that newer papers will first get to be known in the communnity. According to Raulamo-Jurvanen et al. [21] the longer the paper has been available the better are the chances to be cited. However, according to our results, recent papers have received more attention in terms of citations. One reason can be that the SE community has grown over the years and recent topical papers may have a slight advantage when it comes to the number of citations per year.

We were curious to see whether the length of the title had impact on the number of citations for a paper. In the findings of Letchford et al. [17], the relationship between the lengths of paper titles and citations (across various journals) concluded a short title for a paper to be an advantage for receiving citations. However, they also noted that the evidence is not as strong when it is adjusted for the journal where the paper is published. For the XP papers, the correlation between the length of the title, either in words or in characters, and the number of citations is weak ($r = 0.03, df = 787, p = 0.415$ and $r = 0.04, df = 787, p = 0.235$, respectively). The top 5 cited papers have rather short titles (length varying from 31 to 77 in characters and from 5 to 10 in words). The median length of all titles, in characters and words is 62 and 8, respectively.

## 3.4    Topical Issues

With topic modeling, we analyzed the abstract topics in the combined text of abstracts and titles of the papers. Topic modeling is a statistical way to analyze contents of a collection of papers. First, we removed 66 papers from the original pool of 789 papers, as the data retrieved from Scopus did not include abstracts for those 66 papers. Thus, the set of papers for trend analysis included 723 papers. To have an overview of the topics covered in the papers, we combined the titles and the abstracts of the papers, converted the text to lowercase and removed all (English) stopwords from the text in R. (A stopword is a commonly used word, a useless word like "the"). For the trend analysis we utilized topic modeling and Latent Dirichlet Allocation (LDA) as described by Griffiths and Steyvers [13] with R scripts based on an approach of Ponweiser [20]. LDA is an algorithm used for classifying the text in a paper to some topics (mixture of topics) and each topic to a mixture of terms (words). Our approach was identical to the process used by Raulamo-Jurvanen et al. [21] and Garousi and Mäntylä [10]. We created a document term matrix from the corpus (using R "text2vec"[4] package), excluding words having less than two characters or appearing in less than three papers. We generated a LDA model (using R "topicmodels"[5] package) by running the topic models from 2 to 100 by one, yielding 35 as the optimal number of topics.

In the analysis of the trend slopes (by publication year) the topics gaining interest among the authors are the "hot topics" and the topics declining interest are the "cold topics". The five hottest and coldest topics, interpreted by the topic-specific words (and related titles), and 10 significant terms for each of those, are shown in Table 9a and b, respectively. The topics gaining the most interest are "Coordination" and "Technical Debt", which include issues like largescale coordination and interteam objectives as well as metrics and automation. Cold topics such as "Education", "Methods and Practices" (including pair programming) and "Testing", have been of less inspiration for the submissions during the recent years of the XP conference (Table 8).

In 2012, the key research themes in agile software development at the time, reported by Dingsøyr et al. [4], were *Case Study Methodology, Traditional Software Engineering, CMM, Project Management, Software estimation, Pair Development, Distributed Cognition, Agile methods, User-centered design, Agile methodologies* and *Patterns*. Some of those themes seem still topical, e.g., *software estimation* as "Technical Debt" and some not, like *Pair Development* or *Agile Methods* as "Methods and Practices" (see Table 9a and b). In that study, the research topics worth further research were collected from academics attending the Agile2011 conference [4]. Pair programming in educational settings and reuse of code were considered as fading topics while topics like agile across projects and across organizations and distributed agile development were considered as important topics, requiring further research. *"We concur that these are exciting research areas that can further our understanding of the effectiveness of agile methods and practices, particularly in different project/organizational contexts"* [4]. Such trend was also visible in our prior study, as "Education" and "Methods and Practices" (including pair programming) were found to be cold topics and topics like "Coordination" and "Teamwork" were among the

---

[4] https://cran.r-project.org/web/packages/text2vec/index.html.
[5] https://cran.r-project.org/web/packages/topicmodels/index.html.

**Table 8.** Hot and cold topics and number of papers for each topic

(a) Hot topics

| Coordination 24 | Technical Debt 21 | Teamwork 23 | Startups 18 | Agile Practices 30 |
|---|---|---|---|---|
| largescale | technical | meeting | startup | scrum |
| coordinate | debt | retrospective | devops | kanban |
| mechanism | metric | reflection | prototype | board |
| tailor | evolution | standup | stage | barriers |
| interteam | td | commitment | speed | wip |
| userstory | production | workshop | sprints | selforganizing |
| standard | automatic | education | monitoring | multitasking |
| story | stakeholders | scalability | pressure | automotive |
| objectives | monitored | guideline | theoretical | optimization |
| human | influencing | enhance | attempts | transformations |

(b) Cold topics

| Process Simulation 52 | Education 28 | Coaching & Experimenting 17 | Testing 21 | Methods and Practices 31 |
|---|---|---|---|---|
| xp | student | coach | acceptance | pair |
| simulation | teach | languages | executable | programmer |
| integrate | university | transition | version | experiment |
| budget | education | mock | regulations | skill |
| units | curriculum | panel | workshop | tester |
| leadership | skill | standard | testdriven | switching |
| waterfall | classroom | tutorial | packages | assist |
| events | testable | certified | technical | standard |
| tester | selforganizing | exercises | classify | structures |
| userinterface | comprehensive | shares | methodological | expectations |

hot topics [21]. Questions related to topics of interest, for both academics and practitioners in the field, should be asked from those stakeholders on a regular basis, to support the needs or interests in the industry, too.

## 3.5  Indexed Keywords

To study the published topics from another perspective, we collected the indexed keywords from Scopus. It is notable that we used the indexed keywords (not the author keywords), as in the data set the indexed keywords outnumbered the author keywords, providing more details. Additionally, there are papers that are not only missing abstracts (see Sect. 3.4) but also keywords (see Scopus e.g., a conference paper *"Agile acceptance testing"* by Pettichord and Marick from

2002). There were 720 papers with indexed keywords. The minimum number of indexed keywords for a paper was 3, the maximum was as high as 25 (for one paper) and arithmetic mean 9.4. We checked the correlation between the number of indexed keywords and the number of citations for a paper, but that correlation is weak $(r = 0.028, df = 718, p = 0.459)$.

We paired the keywords for each paper (e.g., a paper having four keywords would eventually yield 6 unique keyword pairs). Any spaces in between words of a single keyword were removed (to generate a single combined word) and those keywords were then converted to lower case and capitalized. The pairing resulted in 32131 keyword pairs which we then stored in a csv-file. We used Cytoscape for visualizing the network of the paired keywords (after removing duplicates), see Fig. 5. The lighter the background color of a keyword, the more the keyword had connections (pairs). The keyword *"software engineering"* was, unsurprisingly, the most used keyword, see Fig. 5. The nine other most used keywords were *"software design"*, *"agile software development"*, *"agile methods"*, *"computer programming"*, *"project management"*, *"computer software"*, *"agile development"*, *"extreme programming"*, *"agile"* and *"software testing"*. The keywords are rather generic, but still quite nicely represent the key research themes identified by Dingsøyr et al. [4]. However, a more detailed analysis of the keywords, to view the overall importance and reveal the topicality of the keywords, would be required to see the trends in the area of XP.

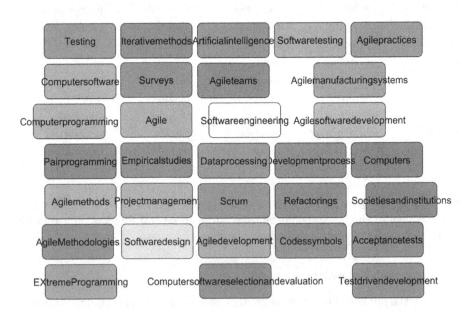

**Fig. 5.** Visualization of the most used indexed keywords (31)

## 3.6   Author Collaboration

Table 5 presents the most active authors and Table 4 the proportion of the number of authors yearly. We were also interested in analyzing the "clusters of collaboration" among the authors of the XP. The collaboration between the authors is measured with the total number of different co-authors in their papers (within the scope of the XP papers). For analyzing the collaboration, we changed the author names to lower case letters and combined the first initial(s) to make a difference between two authors with the same last name (e.g., Poppendieck M. is *"poppendieckm"* and Poppendieck T. is *"poppendieckt"*). Then, we paired the author names for the papers (just as we paired the keywords for each paper, as explained in Sect. 3.5). From observing the collaboration, we could conclude that roughly half of the authors (about 47%) have written their papers either by themselves or with just one collaborator. There are a few "clusters of authors", indicating that there are groups of researchers and/or practitioners that work together on the topic of XP. It would be interesting to study whether those different "clusters of collaboration" have e.g., focused on different topics, used different research methods or cited each other's papers in their research. (Of course, it is notable that not all papers in XP are "full papers").

The 15 "top collaborating authors" (i.e., those having the most co-published papers) have been contributing to the forum from early on and they have from 17 to 54 collaborators within the forum, see Table 9. Many of those authors have not only collaborated with different researchers and/or practitioners but have also been active publishing in the forum, see the column "*R*ank in Table 5" in Table 9. It seems the top collaborating authors have many connections, but the collaboration network among those top authors themselves has not been very active, see Table 10. There are two authors among the top collaborators that have not collaborated with any of the other top collaborators, namely Sharp H. and Dingsøyr T. On the other hand, there are three top collaborators that have collaborated with several other top collaborators: Fraser S. (9), Martin A. (7) and Eckstein J. (7). Collaboration, or lack of it among the top collaborators (and among all authors) could be due to various reasons, e.g., different affiliations or differing research interests (e.g., specific research topic-wise or research method-wise).

We selected the top three authors having the most collaboration (i.e., the most co-authors, see Table 9) and the co-authors in their XP papers. Those authors form a "cluster of collaboration", a network of 117 authors. To get an overview of their collaboration, we used Cytoscape for visualizing the network of the paired authors (after removing duplicates) for the top three authors of the Table 9: *frasers*, *abrahamssonp* and *maurerf*, see Figs. 6, 7 and 8, respectively. The lighter the background color of the author name, the more it has connections. From the figures we can observe that Fraser S. is collaborating a lot with authors that are very collaborative themselves, too, while e.g., the co-authors for Maurer F. have less connections among the other authors of the XP papers. A high number of collaboration among authors is not only a sign of interest in publishing but also implies high level of expertise in the topic. However, when

**Table 9.** Top collaborators in the papers (2002–2018)

| Author | #[a] | Since[b] | All[c] papers | Rank in Table 5[d] | # of papers in Table 6[e] | # of papers in Table 7[f] |
|---|---|---|---|---|---|---|
| Fraser S. | 54 | 2002 | 16 | 4 | — | — |
| Abrahamsson P. | 36 | 2004 | 18 | 2 | — | — |
| Maurer F. | 36 | 2002 | 29 | 1 | 3 | — |
| Marchesi M. | 29 | 2003 | 17 | 3 | 1 | 2016 |
| Wang X. | 28 | 2006 | 14 | 5 | — | — |
| Concas G. | 28 | 2005 | 12 | 8 | — | — |
| Martin A. | 23 | 2003 | 11 | 14 | — | — |
| Eckstein J. | 21 | 2002 | 8 | — | — | — |
| Hussman D. | 20 | 2004 | 11 | 13 | — | — |
| Succi G. | 20 | 2003 | 12 | 11 | — | — |
| Poppendieck M. | 19 | 2003 | 9 | — | — | — |
| Sharp H. | 19 | 2004 | 13 | 7 | 2 | 2004, 2006, 2010 |
| Dingsøyr T. | 18 | 2008 | 12 | 9 | 1 | 2008 |
| Holcombe M. | 18 | 2003 | 12 | 10 | — | — |
| Wild W. | 17 | 2004 | 6 | — | — | — |

[a]# = Number of Collaborators in the forum
[b]Published in the forum since the given year
[c]Number of papers published by the author in the XP conference (2002–2018)
[d]Rank in Table 5, active authors
[e]Number of papers in Table 6, most cited
[f]Number of papers in Table 7, most cited per year

looking at the big picture, there are clear "clusters of collaboration" among the authors implying those authors may focus on slightly different topics within the field of agile software development. From studying author collaboration, other researchers, students or those researchers themselves may also find new names for collaboration or follow-up.

We decided not to analyze the collaboration between the different affiliations for three main reasons. Most importantly, the information about affiliations was not available (in the raw data from Scopus) for all papers. Secondly, the names of the affiliations may be lengthy and thus difficult to differentiate without information about the location. Thirdly, it is the researchers doing the work and our intention is not to study e.g., funding related issues. For example, a person interested in finding authors writing about specific topics, could do a topic analysis or find papers with specific keywords from a database, and then analyze the related authors and their collaboration. We studied the collaboration of the authors among the topics presented in Sect. 3.4 and list the ten authors having the most collaboration within those topics combined, see Table 11. Academic

**Table 10.** Collaboration of top collaborators in the papers (2002–2018)

| Author | Fraser S. | Maurer F. | Abrahamsson P. | Marchesi M. | Wang X. | Concas G. | Martin A. | Sharp H. | Holcombe M. | Eckstein J. | Succi G. | Hussman D. | Dingsøyr T. | Poppendieck M. | Wild W. | Total |
|---|---|---|---|---|---|---|---|---|---|---|---|---|---|---|---|---|
| Fraser S. | + | − | + | − | − | − | + | − | + | + | + | + | − | + | + | 9 |
| Maurer F. | − | + | + | − | + | − | − | − | − | − | − | − | − | − | − | 3 |
| Abrahamsson P. | + | + | + | − | + | − | − | − | − | + | − | − | − | − | + | 6 |
| Marchesi M. | − | − | − | + | − | + | − | − | − | − | + | − | − | − | − | 3 |
| Wang X. | − | + | + | − | + | − | − | − | − | − | − | − | − | − | − | 3 |
| Concas G. | − | − | − | + | − | + | − | − | − | − | − | − | − | − | − | 2 |
| Martin A. | + | − | − | − | − | − | + | − | + | + | + | + | − | + | − | 7 |
| Sharp H. | − | − | − | − | − | − | − | + | − | − | − | − | − | − | − | 1 |
| Holcombe M. | + | − | − | − | − | − | + | − | + | − | + | − | − | − | − | 4 |
| Eckstein J. | + | − | + | − | − | − | + | − | − | + | − | + | − | + | + | 7 |
| Succi G. | + | − | − | + | − | − | + | − | + | − | + | − | − | − | − | 5 |
| Hussman D. | + | − | − | − | − | − | + | − | − | + | − | + | − | + | − | 5 |
| Dingsoyr T. | − | − | − | − | − | − | − | − | − | − | − | − | + | − | − | 1 |
| Poppendieck M. | + | − | − | − | − | − | + | − | − | + | − | + | − | + | − | 5 |
| Wild W. | + | − | + | − | − | − | − | − | − | + | − | − | − | − | + | 4 |
| Total | 9 | 3 | 6 | 3 | 3 | 2 | 7 | 1 | 4 | 7 | 5 | 5 | 1 | 5 | 4 | |

**Fig. 6.** Authors collaborating with Fraser S. (54).

**Fig. 7.** Authors collaborating with Abrahamsson P. (36).

**Fig. 8.** Authors collaborating with Maurer F. (36).

research is not just about citations but about finding interesting results that can be shared with stakeholders, either with researchers or with practitioners in the industry, or with both. It it interesting to see that researchers working on more fresh, "emerging topics" are collaborating actively, too.

# 4    Threats to Validity

Every research study is prone to a variety of validity threats. We used the guidelines presented by Wohlin [25] to analyse the threats to validity. *Internal validity* reflects the extent to which a causal conclusion based on a study is warranted [25]. In our study, the data collection and analysis is presented comprehensively in Sect. 2 along with a link to access the raw data (https://bit.ly/2LiqQ3S) and used scripts. In this way, we were aiming to ensure repeatability and reproducibility of our study.

*Construct validity* is concerned with issues to what extent the object of study truly represents the theory behind the study [25]. Scopus claims to be to be *"the largest abstract and citation database of peer-reviewed literature"*[6]. Our data set is extracted from the Scopus database and we rely on that data as it is provided to all users of that service. However, we noticed that that the papers of year 2011 were not properly indexed and that forced us to fetch those missing papers manually (see Table 1). We present the previous finding as a limitation and explain that data retrieved from a database like Scopus may not be 100% accurate considering e.g., citation counts or author names. Regarding the citations counts, we used only the figures available from Scopus. The author names may be problematic in a bibliometrics analysis like this, as names may be spelled in a different way in different papers and special characters may need to be processed for analysis tools (for example, a Finnish name *"Päivi"* can be written in English as *"Paivi"*, or there may be cases where the name of an author may cause confusion, e.g., in the case of *"Nguyen-Duc A."* or *"Duc A.N."*). Such problems may be extremely difficult to observe in cases where the data set is very large.

**Table 11.** Top collaborators in the papers covering topics presented in Sect. 3.4

| Author | Within Hot Topcis |
| --- | --- |
| Marchesi M. | 17 |
| Wang X. | 17 |
| Concas G. | 14 |
| Taibi D. | 10 |
| Abrahamsson P. | 9 |
| Kuvaja P. | 9 |
| Rodriguez P. | 9 |
| Dingsøyr T. | 8 |
| Ahmad M.O. | 8 |
| Bosch J. | 8 |
| Martini A. | 8 |

(a)Hot Topics

| Author | Within Hot Topcis |
| --- | --- |
| Fraser S. | 20 |
| Holcombe M. | 13 |
| Crispin L. | 11 |
| Gregory J. | 11 |
| Lundh E. | 11 |
| Rising L. | 10 |
| Beck K. | 9 |
| Maurer F. | 9 |
| Williams L. | 9 |

(b)Cold Topics

[6] https://www.elsevier.com/solutions/scopus.

*Conclusion validity* of a study deals with whether correct conclusions are reached through rigorous and repeatable treatments [25]. The results of this study were elaborated with quantitative measures and statistics based on the extracted data. Based on such approach, any replications of this study will not have major deviations from our results. *External validity* is concerned with the extent the results of this secondary study for generalization [25]. This study was based on the analysis of the XP conference publications and cannot be generalized to the whole software engineering field. However, our approach was to identify the top cited papers, the emerging hot topics, the citation landscape and the most active and collaborative authors of the XP conference papers in SE area.

## 5   Conclusions and Future Work

This paper identifies and classifies: the highly cited papers, topic trends, top individuals, authors collaboration and institutes who have significantly published in the XP conference since 2002 until 2018. The trend of the papers shows that the XP conference has received interest from both the academic community and industry. The papers highlight that much of research is stirred by practices emerging in industry. Overall, 62% of the XP conference papers received at least one citation, which is a sign of good visibility relevance of the published papers. However, about 38% of the XP papers so far have received no citations at all. This raises questions such as: what are the reason(s) of non-cited XP conference papers? Does this have anything to do with paper or venues quality? Or, is it about the topics of the papers, the indexed keywords, or the keywords provided by the author(s)? The data, which we make publicly available, can be used to conduct various analysis (i.e., characteristics of highly cited papers) on XP conference papers.

The analysis shows that XP community interest has been moving away from "Process Simulation", "Education" and "Coaching & Experimenting" related topics to more practice and process oriented topics. According to the trend analysis, the hottest research topics, i.e., the topics gaining the most interest are "Coordination", "Technical Debt", "Teamwork", "Startups" and "Agile Practices". The identified trends are helpful for both researchers and practitioners to see topics that have more impact and to align their future research activities.

The study found an active core intellectual pool of authors along with their highly cited work. The newbie researchers can start their journey from these papers and follow listed active researchers to stay up to date about latest trends in the Agile world. Additionally, the active publishing institutes in the XP conference can be helpful for doctoral students to approach experts on the specific topic for further research and doctoral studies. We hope that this paper encourages further discussions in the SE community towards further analysis and formal characterization of the highly-cited software engineering papers in general and specifically in XP conference community. The important thing about citation count is that it is an *"objective measure of the utility or impact of the scientific work"* [6].

Our future work directions include replication of this analysis for other SE publication venues in order to conduct comparison between research venues and provide more depth to our analysis. In addition, we intend to mine typical features for highly cited papers and to assess the extent to which the inner quality, external features and the reputation of both the authors and journals of the papers contribute to generation of highly cited papers in the future. Furthermore, we consider studying the indexed keywords within a publication venue, in more detail, e.g., by years, to see whether we could find trends from those, too.

# References

1. Ahmad, O.M., Raulamo-Jurvanen, P.: Preliminary citation and topic analysis of international conference on agile software development papers (2002–2018). In: FedCSIS 2019, September 2019
2. Aksnes, D.W.: Characteristics of highly cited papers. Res. Eval. **12**(3), 159–170 (2003). https://doi.org/10.3152/147154403781776645
3. Chuang, S.W., Luor, T., Lu, H.P.: Assessment of institutions, scholars, and contributions on agile software development (2001–2012). J. Syst. Softw. **93**, 84–101 (2014). https://doi.org/10.1016/j.jss.2014.03.006
4. Dingsøyr, T., Nerur, S., Balijepally, V., Moe, N.B.: A decade of agile methodologies: towards explaining agile software development. J. Syst. Software. Spec. Issue Agil. Dev. **85**(6), 1213–1221 (2012). https://doi.org/10.1016/j.jss.2012.02.033
5. Farhoodi, R., Garousi, V., Pfahl, D., Sillito, J.: Development of scientific software: a systematic mapping, bibliometrics study and a paper repository. Int. J. Softw. Eng. Knowl. Eng. **23**(4), 463–506 (2013). https://doi.org/10.1142/S0218194013500137
6. Garfield, E.: Is citation analysis a legitimate evaluation tool? Scientometrics **1**(4), 359–375 (1979). https://doi.org/10.1007/BF02019306
7. Garfield, E.: Citation indexes for science. A new dimension in documentation through association of ideas. Int. J. Epidemiol. **35**(5), 1123–1127 (2006). https://doi.org/10.1093/ije/dyl189
8. Garousi, V., Fernandes, J.M.: Highly-cited papers in software engineering: the top-100. Inf. Softw. Technol. **71**, 108–128 (2016). https://doi.org/10.1016/j.infsof.2015.11.003
9. Garousi, V., Fernandes, J.M.: Quantity versus impact of software engineering papers: a quantitative study. Scientometrics **112**(2), 963–1006 (2017). https://doi.org/10.1007/s11192-017-2419-6
10. Garousi, V., Mäntylä, M.V.: Citations, research topics and active countries in software engineering: a bibliometrics study. Comput. Sci. Rev. **19**, 56–77 (2016). https://doi.org/10.1016/j.cosrev.2015.12.002
11. Garousi, V., Varma, T.: A bibliometric assessment of Canadian software engineering scholars and institutions (1996–2006). Comput. Inf. Sci. **2**(2), 19–29 (2010)
12. Glass, R.L., Vessey, I., Ramesh, V.: Research in software engineering: an analysis of the literature. Inf. Softw. Technol. **44**(8), 491–506 (2002). https://doi.org/10.1016/S0950-5849(02)00049-6
13. Griffiths, T.L., Steyvers, M.: Finding scientific topics. Proc. Natl. Acad. Sci. **101**(1(suppl)), 5228–5235 (2004). https://doi.org/10.1073/pnas.0307752101
14. Hoonlor, A., Szymanski, B.K., Zaki, M.J.: Trends in computer science research. Commun. ACM **56**(10), 74–83 (2013). https://doi.org/10.1145/2500892

15. Karanatsiou, D., Li, Y., Arvanitou, E.M., Misirlis, N., Wong, W.E.: A bibliometric assessment of software engineering scholars and institutions (2010–2017). J. Syst. Softw. **147**, 246–261 (2019). https://doi.org/10.1016/j.jss.2018.10.029
16. Kitchenham, B.: Whats up with software metrics? A preliminary mapping study. J. Syst. Softw. **83**(1), 37–51 (2010). https://doi.org/10.1016/j.jss.2009.06.041
17. Letchford, A., Moat, H.S., Preis, T.: The advantage of short paper titles. Roy. Soc. Open Sci. **2**(8), 1–6 (2015). https://doi.org/10.1098/rsos.150266
18. Noorden, R.V., Maher, B., Nuzzo, R.: The top 100 papers. Nature **514**(7524), 550–553 (2014). https://doi.org/10.1038/514550a
19. OECD: Oecd frascati manual, 6th edn., annex 7, paras. 20–22. Oxford dictionaries (2013). https://stats.oecd.org/glossary/detail.asp?ID=198. Accessed 4 Sept 2019
20. Ponweiser, M.: Latent Dirichlet allocation in R. Master's thesis, Institute for Statistics and Mathematics, University of Economics and Business, Vienna, Austria (2012)
21. Raulamo-Jurvanen, P., Mäntylä, M.V., Garousi, V.: Citation and topic analysis of the ESEM papers. In: 2015 ACM/IEEE International Symposium on Empirical Software Engineering and Measurement (ESEM), pp. 1–4, October 2015. https://doi.org/10.1109/ESEM.2015.7321193
22. Wohlin, C.: An analysis of the most cited articles in software engineering journals 1999. Inf. Softw. Technol. **47**(15), 957–964 (2005). https://doi.org/10.1016/j.infsof.2005.09.002
23. Wohlin, C.: An analysis of the most cited articles in software engineering journals - 2000. Inf. Softw. Technol. **49**(1), 2–11 (2007). https://doi.org/10.1016/j.infsof.2006.08.004
24. Wohlin, C.: An analysis of the most cited articles in software engineering journals 2001. Inf. Softw. Technol. **50**(1), 3–9 (2008). https://doi.org/10.1016/j.infsof.2007.10.002
25. Wohlin, C., Runeson, P., Höst, M., Ohlsson, M.C., Regnell, B., Wesslén, A.: Experimentation in Software Engineering: An Introduction. International Series in Software Engineering, vol. 6. Springer, Heidelberg (2000). https://doi.org/10.1007/978-1-4615-4625-2

# Playing the Sprint Retrospective:
# A Replication Study

Yen Ying Ng[1][(✉)], Jędrzej Skrodzki[2], and Maciej Wawryk[2]

[1] Department of English Studies, Nicolaus Copernicus University,
Toruń, Poland
nyysang@gmail.com
[2] Faculty of Electronics, Telecommunications and Informatics,
Gdańsk University of Technology, Gdańsk, Poland
jedrzej.skrodzki@gmail.com, wawryk2@gmail.com

**Abstract.** The Sprint Retrospective is a vehicle for continuous process improvement. Even though it is a well established agile practice, running effective retrospective meetings is challenging. There have been a lot of identified problems that commonly occur during these meetings. To address them, Przybyłek & Kotecka [20] successfully revitalized retrospective meetings by adopting collaborative games, which represent a powerful tool in improving interactions among team members. In this paper, we report on a replication of their study in Bluebay Poland and IHS Markit Gdańsk. The received feedback confirms the original findings and indicates that game-based retrospectives improve team members' creativity, involvement, and communication as well as produce better results than the standard retrospectives. This paper is an extended version of our previous work [25].

**Keywords:** Retrospective · Collaborative games · Agile · Scrum

## 1 Introduction

Agile methods emerged as a response to traditional ways of software development and acknowledged that in today's competitive environment, which creates demand for high quality services at lower costs and with shorter cycle times, customers are not able to definitively express their needs up front [16, 17, 22]. In agile software development requirements and solutions evolve through the collaboration of all stakeholders. The Agile Manifesto [8] promotes principles and values such as face-to-face conversation within a development team, motivated individuals, self-organizing teams, and retrospectives at regular intervals. Besides, agile team members are expected to be proactive and creative in solving complex software development problems [3, 7, 11, 15, 21, 22, 26]. Nevertheless, agile methods do not define techniques to support these attitudes. Responding to this challenge, Przybyłek and his team [19–22, 26] suggested to equip agile teams with collaborative games.

Collaborative games are structured techniques that help a team think together. They are inspired by game play, but designed for the purpose of solving practical problems [20], for instance they are quite widely used as a requirements gathering technique [14,

© Springer Nature Switzerland AG 2020
A. Przybyłek and M. E. Morales-Trujillo (Eds.): LASD 2019/MIDI 2019, LNBIP 376, pp. 133–141, 2020.
https://doi.org/10.1007/978-3-030-37534-8_7

22]. By involving visual activities like moving sticky notes and drawing pictures, they provide multiple dimensions of communication, which results in deeper, richer and more meaningful exchanges of information [9, 21]. Furthermore, several research indicates that fun is a powerful tool in unleashing creativity and facilitating collaboration [6, 9, 24].

Przybyłek & Kotecka [20] showed that the promised benefits of collaborative games were materialized when running a game-based retrospective in 3 teams in Intel Technology Poland. The Sprint Retrospective is a postmortem meeting at the end of a Sprint in which the team inspects and adapts its way of working [10, 23]. It aims to recognize the successes and failures of the last Sprint and to define steps to improve the process in the future. The importance of retrospectives for the agile community is reflected in one of the principles of the Agile Manifesto [8]: "At regular intervals, the team reflects on how to become more effective, then tunes and adjusts its behavior accordingly". While retrospectives can positively impact teamwork, productivity, and work satisfaction, findings presented in the literature [4, 5, 12] suggest that running successful retrospectives is challenging.

In this paper, we report on a replication of the study carried out in Intel by Przybyłek & Kotecka [20]. The feedback received from 3 Scrum teams confirms the findings from the original work and indicates that collaborative games improve participants' creativity, motivation, communication, knowledge sharing, make participants more willing to attend Scrum meetings, and produce better results than the standard retrospective.

The rest of this paper is organized as follows. Section 2 provides an overview of the previous studies. Section 3 explains the employed research methodology. Sections 4 and 5 report the research project and its results. Finally, the last section concludes the paper.

## 2    Related Work

There has been lots of interest in adopting collaborative games to support agile teams. Trujillo et al. [24] proposed a game-based workshop used as an alternative for the Inception phase of a project. The workshop combines classical and game-based techniques to increase stakeholders' involvement and improve collaboration between stakeholders and the team.

Przybyłek & Olszewski [19] proposed an extension to Open Kanban, which comprises of 12 collaborative games divided into four categories in accordance with four Open Kanban principles. The extension was proved to help inexperience team members better understand the principles of Kanban and promote teamwork.

Przybyłek & Zakrzewski [22] elaborated a framework for extending Scrum with 9 collaborative games. This framework was proved to improve agile requirements engineering.

Besides, a web portal which provides 8 collaborative games to be used in agile software development was implemented by Przybyłek & Kowalski [21].

Przybyłek & Kotecka [20] adopted 5 collaborative games to support running an effective and enjoyable retrospective meetings. Our study is a continuation of their work, since we evaluate these games in other companies and teams.

# 3   Research Method

Our study was carried out as Action Research [1]. In Action Research, the researcher plays the role of a facilitator to coordinate a group of practitioners, so as to solve a real-world problem while simultaneously expanding scientific knowledge [22]. The researcher contributes his knowledge of action research while the practitioners provide their practical knowledge and context [1]. A precondition for Action Research is to have a problem owner willing to collaborate to identify a problem, engage in an effort to solve it, analyze the results, and determine future actions [22].

There are two independent problem owners in this research: (1) Bluebay Poland, which is a software development house; and (2) the Product Development & Delivery department of the Gdańsk-based office of IHS Markit. IHS Markit is a global information provider specializing in conducting economic, financial and subject analyses on financial and capital markets as well as supporting decision-making processes for both business and institutional clients across 165 countries. Both organizations were interested in auditing their work practices related to the Sprint Retrospective and improving identified deficiencies. As for Bluebay Poland, two Scrum teams participated in the study. Team 1 developed a web store for Aclari Diamonds, which is a jewellery company, while Team 2 developed print management software for POSperita, which is a printer & advertising agency. When it comes to IHS Markit Gdańsk, one team engaged in our research. The team was responsible for developing shared components and libraries of IT platform used by IHS Markit and its clients. The participated teams are presented in Table 1. All teams worked in two-week sprints.

**Table 1.** Participating teams (role, experience in years); SM denotes Scrum Master.

| Team 1 - Bluebay Poland | Team 2 - Bluebay Poland | Team 3 - IHS Markit Gdańsk |
| --- | --- | --- |
| Team Leader & SM, 10 | Team Leader & SM, 10 | Team Leader & SM, 8 |
| Developer, 5 | Developer, 8 | Front-end developer, 1 |
| Developer, 3 | Developer, 6 | Front-end developer, 1 |
| Tester, 2 | Developer, 5 | Front-end developer, 3 |
|  | Tester, 5 | Full-stack developer, 3 |
|  |  | Back-end developer, 6 |
|  |  | Tester, 3 |
|  |  | UX Designer, 7 |
|  |  | UI Designer, 6 |

## 4  Diagnosing and Planning

Teams 1 and 2 held regular Sprint Retrospective meetings. As for team 3, several members considered the Sprint Retrospective as useless, so it was run only every few sprints. Moreover, only three members of team 3 actively contributed to the discussion during retrospective meetings, while others seemed to be boring. Overall, we discovered that the participated teams encountered similar issues related to the Sprint Retrospective as those presented in the original study [20] and these issues hindered the teams in realizing their retrospective's full potential. Therefore, we decided to implement all the games introduced in the original study. In addition, we decided to implement one new game, i.e. 360° Appreciation.

360° Appreciation [2] is a game to promote a conducive working environment that strengthens people relationship and boosts team morale. It allows team members to give open positive feedback as well as appreciating the time and effort contributed by the team members. In other words, it focuses only on the developers' strength instead of their weaknesses. The game is easy to be conducted in any environment. What is more, no additional equipments such as blackboards, posters and sticky notes are required. In order to run this activity, the facilitator asks every participant to write down their appreciations about one another on a piece of paper. After that, the team forms a circle with one team member sitting in the middle. The other participants will then read their appreciation feedback to the one in the center. The same process is repeated until everybody in the team has received appreciations.

## 5  Action Taking and Evaluating

Each game was run twice in each team. An explanation of the rules of the game was given before the team plays the game for the first time. After each game session, we distributed a questionnaire to collect feedback from the participants. The responses were made on a five-point Likert scale. Finally, the results were analyzed and discussed with the respondents.

## 6  Bluebay Poland

Besides 5L's and 360° appreciation, all games were evaluated positively with respect to all categories. This is due to the fact that playing 5L's consumed too much time, while the obtained results were worse when compared to Starfish, Sailboat or Mood++. As for 360° appreciation, although low scores were obtained for questions 3–6, it is still successful overall, because it was not designed to promote these issues. This game was considered helpful in relieving the tension or getting to know new team members. Since this game does not provide any feedback on the issues during the Sprint, it should be carried out together with another collaborative game during one retrospective session. As for Sailboat, it was especially appreciated for allowing participants to identify risks in a project. The detail results obtained from both teams are presented in Fig. 1. Note that in Bluebay Poland we did not implement Mad-Sad-Glad, which was depreciated in the original study and revised by Mood++.

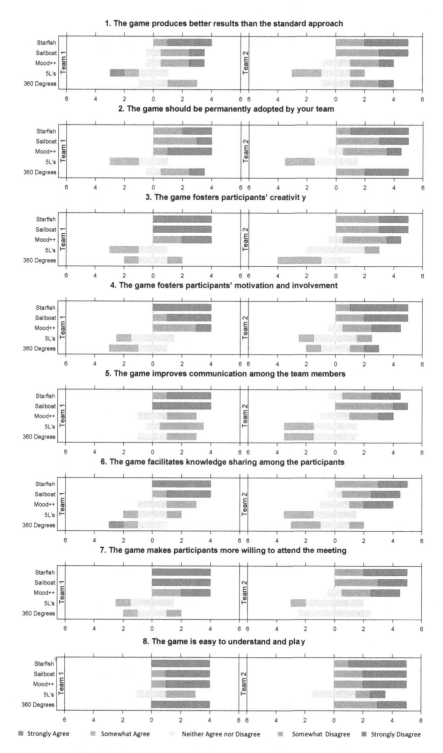

**Fig. 1.** Aggregated results for the teams in Bluebay Poland.

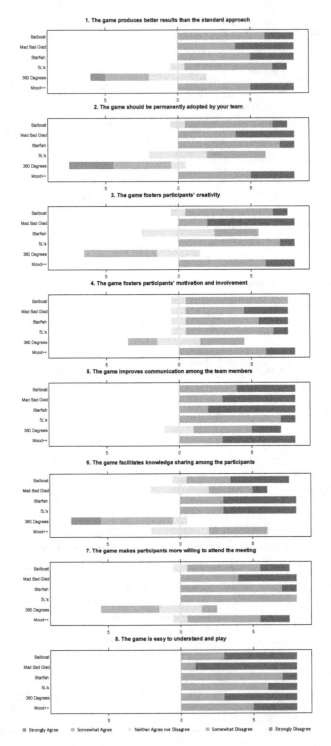

**Fig. 2.** Aggregated results for the team in IHS Markit Gdańsk.

## 6.1  IHS Markit Gdańsk

All games except 360° appreciation were evaluated positively with respect to all categories. The detail results scores are presented in Fig. 2. The 360° appreciation game was considered useful only in the context of improving communication. Other conclusions on 360° appreciation were consistent with the findings from Bluebay Poland. As for Sailboat, it was praised for its game board which unleashes imagination, creativity and introduces well defined, unambiguous areas. The team even named the painted sailboat with the team's name. On the other hand, the team claimed that Starfish and 5L's introduce ambiguous categories and provide unattractive game boards. When it comes to Mad-Sad-Glad and Mood++, they were praised for covering different aspects than had been usually discussed during a retrospective. Indeed, both games focus on feelings and emotions instead of organizational or technical issues. At the same time, this explains why both games performed worse than Sailboat, Starfish and 5L's with regard to knowledge sharing. To summarize, the social and entertaining aspects of the proposed games, except 360° appreciation, improved motivation in retrospective meetings.

## 7  Conclusions

This paper reports on Action Research projects carried out in Bluebay Poland and IHS Markit Gdańsk. In accordance with the best practices developed by Przybyłek & Kotecka [20], we freshened retrospective meetings by introducing collaborative games. The feedback gathered from three Scrum teams confirms the positive influence of collaborative games in the Sprint Retrospective. Game-based retrospectives provided structure and guided teams through the meeting. They enforced balanced participation and led to a variety of measurable societal outcomes. The most successful games, i.e. Sailboat, Mad-Sad-Glad, Mood++, and Starfish improved team members' creativity, motivation, communication, knowledge sharing and make them more willing to attend retrospective meetings. The results obtained form both companies are very consistent except 5L's, which received high scores only from the team in IHS Markit Gdańsk. Moreover, the participated teams intended to continue playing collaborative games after the research finished.

As future work, we intend to conduct a control experiment with settings similar to [18] whether game-based retrospectives are more effective than standard retrospectives. Moreover, we would like to spread the use of collaborative games in other companies. After collecting more data from more teams, we plan to build a recommender system [13] that will help scrum teams to choose a retrospective game suitable for a given context.

# References

1. Baskerville, R., Myers, M.D.: Special issue on action research in information systems: making IS research relevant to practice—foreword. MIS Q. **28**(3), 329–335 (2004)
2. Caroli, P., Caetano, T.: Fun Retrospectives - activities and ideas for making agile retrospectives more engaging. Leanpub (2016)
3. Crawford, B., León de la Barra, C., Soto, R., Monfroy, E.: Agile software engineering as creative work. In: 5th International Workshop on Co-operative and Human Aspects of Software Engineering, Zürich, Switzerland (2012)
4. Drægert, A., Petersen, D.: ScrumBut in professional software development. MSc thesis, Department of Computer Science, Aalborg University (2016)
5. Eloranta, V., Koskimies, K., Mikkonen, T.: Exploring ScrumBut—an empirical study of Scrum anti-patterns. Inf. Softw. Technol. **74**, 194–203 (2016)
6. Ghanbari, H., Similä, J., Markkula, J.: Utilizing online serious games to facilitate distributed requirements elicitation. J. Syst. Softw. **109**, 32–49 (2015)
7. Highsmith, J., Cockburn, A.: Agile software development: the business of innovation. Computer **34**(9), 120–122 (2001)
8. Highsmith, J., Fowler, M.: The agile manifesto. Softw. Dev. Mag. **9**, 29–30 (2001)
9. Hohmann, L.: Innovation Games: Creating Breakthrough Products Through Collaborative Play. Addison-Wesley Professional (2006)
10. Ilyés, E.: Create your own agile methodology for your research and development team. In: 2019 Federated Conference on Computer Science and Information Systems (FedCSIS 2019), Leipzig, Germany (2019). https://doi.org/10.15439/2019f209
11. Jarzębowicz, A., Ślesiński, W.: Assessing effectiveness of recommendations to requirements-related problems through interviews with experts. In: 2018 Federated Conference on Computer Science and Information Systems (FedCSIS 2018), Poznan, Poland (2018)
12. Jeffries, R.: Fractional Scrum, or "Scrum-But". AgileAtlas (2013)
13. Karpus, A., Raczyńska, M., Przybyłek, A.: Things you might not know about the k-Nearest neighbors algorithm. In: 11th International Joint Conference on Knowledge Discovery, Knowledge Engineering and Knowledge Management, Vienna (2019)
14. Marciniak, P., Jarzębowicz, A.: An industrial survey on business analysis problems and solutions. In: Madeyski, L., Śmiałek, M., Hnatkowska, B., Huzar, Z. (eds.) Software Engineering: Challenges and Solutions. AISC, vol. 504, pp. 163–176. Springer, Cham (2017). https://doi.org/10.1007/978-3-319-43606-7_12
15. Miler, J., Gaida, P.: On the agile mindset of an effective team – an industrial opinion survey. In: 2019 Federated Conference on Computer Science and Information Systems (FedCSIS 2019), Leipzig, Germany (2019)
16. Przybyłek, A.: The integration of functional decomposition with UML notation in business process modelling. Adv. Inf. Syst. Dev. **1**, 85–99 (2007). https://doi.org/10.1007/978-0-387-70761-7_8
17. Przybyłek, A.: A business-oriented approach to requirements elicitation. In: 9th International Conference on Evaluation of Novel Approaches to Software Engineering, Lisbon, Portugal (2014). https://doi.org/10.5220/0004887701520163
18. Przybyłek, A.: An empirical study on the impact of AspectJ on software evolvability. Empirical Softw. Eng. **23**(4), 2018–2050 (2018). https://doi.org/10.1007/s10664-017-9580-7
19. Przybyłek, A., Olszewski, M.: Adopting collaborative games into open Kanban. In: 2016 Federated Conference on Computer Science and Information Systems (FedCSIS 2016), Gdansk, Poland (2016). https://doi.org/10.15439/2016f509

20. Przybyłek, A., Kotecka, D.: Making agile retrospectives more awesome. In: 2017 Federated Conference on Computer Science and Information Systems (FedCSIS 2017), Prague, Czech Republic (2017). https://doi.org/10.15439/2017f423
21. Przybyłek, A., Kowalski, W.: Utilizing online collaborative games to facilitate agile software development. In: 2018 Federated Conference on Computer Science and Information Systems (FedCSIS 2018), Poznan, Poland (2018). https://doi.org/10.15439/2018f347
22. Przybyłek, A., Zakrzewski, M.: Adopting collaborative games into agile requirements engineering. In: 13th International Conference on Evaluation of Novel Approaches to Software Engineering (ENASE 2018), Funchal, Madeira, Portugal (2018). https://doi.org/10.5220/0006681900540064
23. Sutherland, J., Schwaber, K.: The Scrum Guide—The Definitive Guide to Scrum: The Rules of the Game. Org and Scrum Inc., Scrum (2016)
24. Trujillo, M.M., Oktaba, H., González, J.C.: Improving software projects inception phase using games: ActiveAction workshop. In: 9th International Conference on Evaluation of Novel Approaches to Software Engineering (ENASE 2014), Lisbon, Portugal (2014)
25. Wawryk, M., Ng, Y.Y.: Playing the sprint retrospective. In: 2019 Federated Conference on Computer Science and Information Systems (FedCSIS 2019), Leipzig, Germany (2019). https://doi.org/10.15439/2019f284
26. Zakrzewski, M., Kotecka, D., Ng, Y.Y., Przybyłek, A.: Adopting collaborative games into agile software development. In: Damiani, E., Spanoudakis, G., Maciaszek, Leszek A. (eds.) ENASE 2018. CCIS, vol. 1023, pp. 119–136. Springer, Cham (2019). https://doi.org/10.1007/978-3-030-22559-9_6

# Comparison User Engagement of Gamified and Non-gamified Augmented Reality Assembly Training

Diep Nguyen[✉] and Gerrit Meixner

UniTyLab, Heilbronn University, Max-Planck-Strasse 39, 74081 Heilbronn, Germany
{diep.nguyen,gerrit.meixner}@hs-heilbronn.de

**Abstract.** Augmented Reality (AR) is expanding its application field through many areas, including marketing, education, and medicine. Furthermore, industrial training and instructional support, especially in the context of maintenance and assembly, are also among the key field of application. Also, evidence has shown that good user experience and engagement leads to better performance, an engaged employee delivered a better result than those who not. Gamification is one of the various methods to enhance user experience and engagement. In this work, we present a training approach to guide novice users through an assembly task of changing batter for a robot arm. The training is developed as an augmented reality training with and without a gamification design. Furthermore, we evaluated the designs with 22 objects to validate if user engagement and performance of one design is better than the other. The result indicates a better outcome on the gamified application, however, the difference is not statistically significant.

**Keywords:** Augmented reality · Gamification · Gamified training · Gamified assembly task · Augmented reality training

## 1 Introduction

With a global market size estimated at 198 billion dollars by 2025 [1], Augmented Reality (AR) is expanding its application field through many areas, including marketing, education, and medicine. Furthermore, industrial training and instructional support, especially in the context of maintenance and assembly, are also among the key field of application [2]. AR applications aim to provide personnel different levels of in situ guidance either from on-site support or remote experts. This technology enables users to manipulate in real-time the virtual objects which are superimposed upon the physical world. AR training and support reduces staff cognitive load, improve performance while minimizing mistakes, therefore, efficiency is increasing. In the new era of Industry 4.0 where

---

This paper is an extended version of work published in Federated Conference on Computer Science and Information Systems 2019 [5].

© Springer Nature Switzerland AG 2020
A. Przybyłek and M. E. Morales-Trujillo (Eds.): LASD 2019/MIDI 2019, LNBIP 376, pp. 142–152, 2020.
https://doi.org/10.1007/978-3-030-37534-8_8

products and processes are highly complex and diverse, AR is particularly one of the most essential technologies [3].

"It's the total experience that matters" is how the usability engineering pioneer Don Norman said about the importance of user experience. Evidence has shown that good user experience and engagement leads to better performance, an engaged employee delivered a better result than those who not [4]. Among various methods to enhance user experience and engagement is the idea of turning the prosaic tasks into more fun and exciting version by borrowing tools and knowledge from the game industry into other domains, so-called gamification. While the academic world is still debating on the consensus of definition and scope, hereby we agree with the most widely accepted definition from Sebastian Deterding [15]:

*"Gamification is the use of game design elements in non-game contexts."*

In this work, we combine the two techniques to create a gamified AR training for an assembly task. Our main hypothesis is that users will significantly prefer the gamification version of the training to the non-gamification one. Moreover, we expect a significantly better performance in the gamification training over the non-gamification.

The paper is structured as follows: Sect. 2: we provide the related work. Section 3: we describe the design of the application as well as gamification design. Section 4: we present the experiment design. The result of the study is presented in Sect. 5, followed by a short discussion in Sect. 6. Lastly, Sect. 7 concludes the paper.

## 2    Related Work

Although the term "gamification" is relatively new, since around 2003, its applications have already widespread across many industrial as well as scholarly fields. Recently in the Gamification 2020 report, Gartner predicted that gamification in combination with emerging technologies will create a significant impact on several fields including the design of employee performance and customer engagement platform [13]. In this context, there are numerous examples of studies for either AR training or gamified training, yet there was hardly any work on the combination of those.

A recent survey of Seaborn et al. [19] provides a good overview of gamification from a Human-Computer-Interaction perspective in both theoretical and practical lights. The work showed that gamification is primarily practiced in the domain of education, e-learning especially. In the theoretical foundations, there was a dynamic movement towards carving the boundaries between gamification and other similar concepts. The applied research, meanwhile, painted a positive-leaning but mixed picture about the effectiveness of gamified systems. Despite usual expectation, similar gamified designs under different settings returned clashing result over user experience along with performance. The reason was believed to be highly context-specific requirements. Furthermore, learning about the effects of gamification on the human is a complicated subject. The overall effort toward this direction is still nascent.

While the gamified system was well accepted in business contexts, it is not necessarily the case in production training, left alone Augmented Reality training. Lee [18] showed that AR for education and training innovation was leaning towards the "serious game" pole while gamification was left outside of the picture. According to Lee, AR games were particularly interested in by both "educators and corporate venues." A role-playing game for teaching history [16], for example, proved the benefit of enabling students for problem-solving, increasing collaboration and exploration via the virtual identities.

However, whether we like it or not, production training is different from traditional classroom training. When transforming the operational work into a game, a serious game, there will always be a risk of taking the focus away from the task at hand. This is when gamification comes to play as integrating gamification can provide the fun aspect while still keeping the workers' full attention on the operative job [17].

Probably the most well-known gamification in production is a series of works from Korn et al. [17,20–22]. The center of his works is to evaluate users' acceptance of gamification in modern production environments. Different designs, "Circles & Bars" and "Pyramid," were proposed [17]. Both designs were used to visualize work steps as well as their sequences. Color-coded from dark green to yellow, orange and read is employed to indicate user specific time progression. Later on, they were projected into users' working space as an assistive application for impaired individuals. The result indicated a good acceptance level for gamification designs and the "Pyramid" approach was favorable in general. While the study showed a promising outcome, it focused on user acceptance and did not measure the quantitative factor of gamification on task completion time and error rates.

## 3   Implementation

In this section, we present the implementation of the application under study. A process of replacing the battery for a robot arm was implemented based on the instruction manual of the Mitsubishi Industrial Robot RV-2F Series. Two prototypes were made, one with the gamification design and the other without. The designs were named Gamification AR (GAR) and Non-Gamification AR (NGAR) according to their characteristics.

The application ran on the Microsoft HoloLens (Fig. 1). Microsoft HoloLens is a standalone mixed reality device which showcases a field of view of 30 degrees by17.5 degrees. Due to Microsoft HoloLens small field of view, here we provide the user interfaces captured from Unity Editor to showcase the whole scene setup. Figs. 3 and Figure 2 illustrate the GAR and NGAR design respectively.

**Fig. 1.** HoloLens - the mixed reality head-mounted display (HMD) from Microsoft. [23]

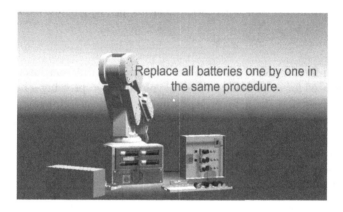

**Fig. 2.** The NGAR design with no gamification elements. Only text instruction was provided. [5]

## 3.1   The Application

The process for changing the battery was identically built for both prototypes. There were 21 actions made up 10 steps. Disassembling the cover of the battery compartment, for example, included two steps of removing the screws and removing the cover. While removing each of the screws was counted as an action.

For navigating the process, we augmented the instruction text for each step as a head-up display which was always facing the user at the top right corner of the user view. An instruction manager was used to control the flow of text visualization. The requirement from the instruction manual specified that the steps of the process had to be performed in a fixed order that's why only one instruction was displayed at a time. The next instruction triggered when the user carried the current step correctly.

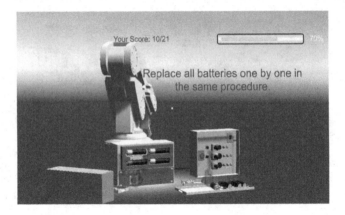

**Fig. 3.** The GAR design with gamification elements: points, progress bar and signposting. [5]

Two main interaction types were used to simulate different interactions. Air tap [23] was used for interacting with static objects (e.g. pressing a button) while we utilized drag and drop for assembling actions (e.g. removing the screw). Similar to the real working space, disassembled objects were designed to be placed at a specific location. For instance, the screws needed to be placed inside a designated tray instead of dropped on the floor.

To simulate a sense of reality, sounds such as robot arm were running or turned off were used.

## 3.2  Gamification Design

The game design elements were implemented only for the GAR version. It allows to isolate and analyze the effect of gamified system on the user. This could be reflected by comparing the outcome of the two experiments.

As a result of Korn's investigation [17], gamification in the production environment has its own specific requirements. To avoid resistance from users or the potential of taking away their main focuses, we followed the identified requirements in designing gamified application for production settings. First, "keep the visualization of gamification simple." This focuses mainly on avoiding animation, moving elements and using complex graphical structures. The second and third requirements come together as "avoid explicit interaction with gamification elements" and "support implicit interaction with gamification elements." For that matter, in our designs we did not ask for any user's effort to direct input or reach out to the gamified items.

**Point System.** The point system was built based on users' actions. There was a maximum of 21 points according to 21 actions. Points were rewarded to the user when the action was done. As the first attempt to study the effect of gamification design on user engagement, we did not implement a complex point system with losing points or rewarding extra points at this stage.

**Progress Bar.** While the points were based on actions, progress bar visualized the steps. As stated as one of the requirements, the user interface was intentionally kept simple with only one color. Additional text was in place for indicating the percentage.

**Signposting.** Signposting aims to direct the user in the right direction. While users without background knowledge could be confused with the mechanical part names (e.g. Controller box), signposting highlighted the part corresponding to the currently displayed instruction. It provided the "just-in-time" hints for the trainees, especially the totally beginner one.

**Sound System.** Audio cues are employed to exemplify achievement. A coins collect sound effect plays simultaneously to acknowledge that users receive a point. It also indicates that users have just finished a step.

# 4    Experiment Design

The experiment was conducted to investigate how gamification in AR training impacts user engagement and performance. The studies for both conditions (GAR and NGAR) took place in the same room at our research laboratory. To avoid the learning effect, we employed the between-group design in which each participant randomly exposed to only one design, either GAR or NGAR.

Due to the fact that Microsoft HoloLens requires specific hand gestures for interaction, the participants were asked if they have experience with this device. In the case of none, the participant used the default HoloLens "Learn gesture" application. This was especially important because the main task could not be carried on without this step. Before the experiment, regardless of the HoloLens experience, we repeated the main information about the interactive gestures to all participants.

Once the participants were confident interacting with the device, the main experiment task proceeded. When the user hit the "Start" button at the first scene of the application, the timer for measuring task completion time was started until the last step completed.

As we focused on the user engagement we used a post-study questionnaire with the refined User Engagement Scale (UES) [24]. UES is a five-point rating scale: strongly disagree, disagree, neither disagree nor agree, agree and strongly agree, respectively from 1 to 5 point. Given the task was not complicated, the level of fatigue after that was expected not to be high so that we decided to use the UES long form (UES - LF). The UES - LF consists of 30 items covering 4 factors:

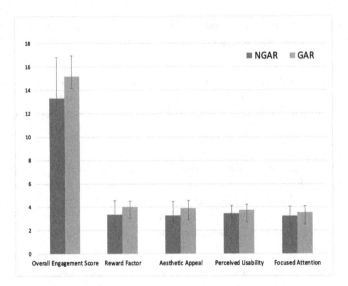

**Fig. 4.** User engagement score as a bar chart with indicated standard deviations. [5]

1. FA: Focused Attention
2. PU: Perceived Usability
3. AE: Aesthetic Appeal
4. RW: Reward Factor

As constructed in the guide to use of UES, all items were randomized and the indicators (e.g. AE.1) were not visible to the users.

## 5    Results

Most of the participants reported having little or none experience with AR technology, in particular, Microsoft HoloLens, before this experiment. So, a potential novelty effect when initially establishing interaction with new technology might influence the research result. The test population was 22 participants with 11 regarding each condition. Participants ages vary from 18 to 34 years old, 15 male and 7 female subjects. Although some unease and uncertainty were expressed at the beginning, all participants were more certain after the learning gesture phase.

Figure 4 displays that the GAR design was rated better in all sub categories. In general, it was clearly preferred to the NGAR approach. The overall Engagement score was 15.2 (SD = 1.8) in GAR and 13.3 (SD = 3.5) in NGAR. However, this did not make up a statistically significant difference between the two groups. Table 1 provides the results in more detail, looking at the average score, standard deviation and also the result of a t-test for both the overall engagement score and its factor.

**Table 1.** Comparision of user engagement score

| Factor | Mean score (SD) | | p value |
|---|---|---|---|
| Design | GAR | NGAR | GAR vs. NGAR |
| Focused attention | 3.5 (0.6) | 3.2 (0.8) | 0.418 not significant |
| Perceived usability | 3.7 (0.5) | 3.4 (0.7) | 0.281 not significant |
| Aesthetic appeal | 3.9 (0.7) | 3.3 (1.2) | 0.162 not significant |
| Reward factor | 4.0 (0.5) | 3.4 (1.2) | 0.128 not significant |
| Overall score | 15.2 (1.8) | 13.3 (3.5) | 0.153 not significant |

The standard deviation in the overall user engagement score was much lower in the GAR design (SD = 1.8), versus SD = 3.5 in NGAR, which shows that the GAR subjects more homogenously perceived the result throughout the group. This tendency, lower standard deviation, remained true for all four subfactors in the GAR design as shown in Fig. 4. On the other side, the opinions of NGAR subjects seem to be more diverse.

Looking at the training performance, the difference regarding average task completion time (in seconds) between the two study conditions is statistically significant. The t-test resulted in $p < 0.032$. The average time was 306.9 (SD = 123.2) and 439.5 (SD = 134.4) for GAR and NGAR groups respectively. This positive outcome probably directly influenced by the signposting design element.

## 6  Discussion

Besides the required surveys, participants often complained about the cumbersome of the hardware. Even though Microsoft HoloLens is one of the mixed reality device market leaders, it is still heavy for constantly wearing. A missing of ergonomic design makes it difficult for the device to stably seating on user's heads, especially those with small heads. To interact with the device, it is mandatory to learn the hand gestures. These fix hand gestures are not intuitive, as reported by participants, leads to the result that users often forget them along the way.

As a preliminary result, this work demonstrates the potential of gamified AR training for assembly tasks in improving user engagement and performance. Nevertheless, there is a need for further investigation focusing on both short-term and long-term training effectiveness. A consideration over skills and knowledge acquisition should be taken into account. To serve this goal more complex tasks should be implemented with a higher level of gamification, different training levels and challenges design for individual specific demands for example.

As we focused on the improvement of user engagement in gamified AR training, we did not take in to account the isolated effect of how each game design elements affects the user. As mentioned in the Related Work, gamification design is highly context-specific so that the next important step will be a qualitative study on how the users perceive different design elements and their impacts.

Points, Badge and Leader Board are the most common elements of gamification, one of the reason is due to their ease to implement. The use of these external rewards recently raises an ethical question in academia. When a user is exposed to external rewards for a long time, disappointment and frustration may appear once these elements are absent. Turning the research direction to investigate the use of implicit motivation is believed to provide an enduring effect on user engagement. However, how to design a meaningful and relevant user experience requires great effort and long-term design studies.

# 7    Conclusion

As the Literature review reveals a shortage of using gamification in the modern industrial environment, our goal is to fill the gap. In this project, we developed an assembly training system using gamified Augmented Reality. Firstly, we created two versions of the same training, with and without game design elements. The training guides novice users through a process of changing a robot arm battery. Then, we reported a study over 22 participants with none to limited knowledge of this assembly task. The study's goal is to confirm our hypothesis if the gamified training creates better user engagement and performance over the non-gamified version.

As a result, the gamified version returned a better score on user engagement and performance over the non-gamified version. However, the difference in user engagement score is not statistically significant. Even though, the outcome of the gamified group indicates a more homogeneous effect on the users. This suggests potential in using gamification in industrial training. To obtain a more in-depth result, the study should be extended with more complex training on multiple platforms (HMD, mobile) and a bigger population.

# References

1. Augmented reality (AR) market size worldwide in 2017, 2018 and 2025 (in billion U.S. dollars), Statista. https://www.statista.com/statistics/897587/world-augmented-reality-market-value/. Accessed Oct 2019
2. Lamberti, F., et al.: Challenges, opportunities, and future trends of emerging techniques for augmented reality-based maintenance. IEEE Trans. Emerg. Top. Comput. 2(4), 411–421 (2014)
3. Meixner, G., Petersen, N., Koessling, H.: User interaction evolution in the Smart-FactoryKL. In: Proceedings of the 24th BCS Interaction Specialist Group Conference, pp. 211–220 (2010)

4. The Best Employee Engagement Statistics You Should Know, Dynamic Signal. https://dynamicsignal.com/2018/01/08/the-best-employee-engagement-statistics-you-should-know/. Accessed Oct 2019
5. Nguyen, D., Meixner, G.: Gamified augmented reality training for an assembly task: a study about user engagement. In: 2019 Federated Conference on Computer Science and Information Systems, vol. 18, pp. 901–904 (2019). https://doi.org/10.15439/2019F136
6. Azuma, T.R.: A survey of augmented reality. Presence: Teleoperators Virtual Environ. **6**(4), 355–385 (1997)
7. Billinghurst, M., Kato, H., Poupyrev, I.: The magic book moving seamlessly between reality and virtuality. IEEE Comput. Graph. Appl. **21**(3), 2–4 (2001)
8. Ong, S.K., Yuan, M.L., Nee, A.Y.C.: Augmented reality applications in manufacturing: a survey. Int. J. Prod. Res. **46**, 2707–2742 (2008)
9. Friedrich, W.: ARVIKA: augmented reality for development, production and service. In: The 1st International Symposium on Mixed and Augmented Reality (ISMAR), pp. 3–4 (2002)
10. For AR/VR 2.0 to live, AR/VR 1.0 must die, Digi-Capital. https://www.digi-capital.com/news/2019/01/for-ar-vr-2-0-to-live-ar-vr-1-0-must-die/. Accessed May 2019
11. Transform Business Outcomes With Immersive Technology, Smarter with Gartner. https://www.gartner.com/smarterwithgartner/transform-business-outcomes-with-immersive-technology/. Accessed May 2019
12. Dale, S.: Gamification: making work fun, or making fun of work? Bus. Inf. Rev. **31**(2), 82–90 (2014)
13. Gamification 2020: What Is the Future of Gamification? https://www.gartner.com/en/documents/2226015. Accessed May 2019
14. McGonigal, J.: Reality is Broken: Why Games Make Us Better and How They Can Change the World. Penguin, New York (2011)
15. Deterding, S., Dixon, D., Khaled, R., Nacke, L.: From game design elements to gamefulness: defining gamification. In: Proceedings of the 15th International Academic MindTrek Conference: Envisioning Future Media Environments, MindTrek 2011, vol. 11, pp. 9–15 (2011)
16. Schrier, K.L.: Revolutionizing history education: using augmented reality games to teach histories. Institute of Technology. Department of Comparative Media Studies, Massachusetts (2005)
17. Korn, O., Funk, M., Schmidt, A.: Design approaches for the gamification of production environments. In: Proceedings of the 8th International Conference on PErvasive Technologies Related to Assistive Environments, pp. 1–7. ACM, New York (2015)
18. Lee, K.: Augmented reality in education and training. TechTrends **56**, 13–21 (2012). https://doi.org/10.1007/s11528-012-0559-3
19. Seaborn, K., Fels, D.I.: Gamification in theory and action: a survey. Int. J. Hum Comput Stud. **74**, 14–31 (2015)
20. Oliver, K.: Industrial playgrounds. How gamification helps to enrich work for elderly or impaired persons in production. In: Proceedings of the 4th ACM SIGCHI Symposium on Engineering Interactive Computing Systems, New York, pp. 313–316 (2012)
21. Korn, O., Funk, M., Abele, S., Schmidt, A., Hrz, T.: Context-aware assistive systems at the workplace. Analyzing the effects of projection and gamification. In: PETRA 14 Proceedings of the 7th International Conference on PErvasive Technologies Related to Assistive Environments. ACM, New York (2014)

22. Korn, O., Funk, M., Schmidt, A.: Towards a gamification of industrial production. A comparative study in sheltered work environments. In: Proceedings of the 7th ACM SIGCHI Symposium on Engineering Interactive Computing Systems. ACM, New York (2015)
23. Introduction to the HoloLens. https://msdn.microsoft.com/en-us/magazine/mt788624.aspx. Accessed May 2019
24. O'Brien, H.L., Cairns, P., Hall, M.: A practical approach to measuring user engagement with the refined user engagement scale (UES) and new UES short form. Int. J. Hum Comput Stud. **112**, 28–39 (2018)

# Author Index

Ahmad, Muhammad Ovais 108

Cygańska, Sara 63

Gaida, Paulina 41

Hanslo, Ridewaan 82

Kottke, Mario 1

Łukasiewicz, Katarzyna 63

Marner, Kristina 19
Meixner, Gerrit 142
Miler, Jakub 41
Mnkandla, Ernest 82

Ng, Yen Ying 133
Nguyen, Diep 142

Poth, Alexander 1

Raulamo-Jurvanen, Päivi 108
Riel, Andreas 1

Skrodzki, Jędrzej 133

Theobald, Sven 19

Vahed, Anwar 82

Wagner, Stefan 19
Wawryk, Maciej 133

Printed in the United States
By Bookmasters